Library

READING ROMANS

READING THE NEW TESTAMENT SERIES

Reading Colossians, Ephesians, and 2 Thessalonians
by Bonnie Thurston

Reading Corinthians
by Charles H. Talbert

Reading John
by Charles H. Talbert

Reading Luke
by Charles H. Talbert

Reading Matthew
by David Garland

Luke Timothy Johnson

READING ROMANS

A LITERARY AND THEOLOGICAL COMMENTARY

A Crossroad Book
The Crossroad Publishing Company
New York

1997
The Crossroad Publishing Company
370 Lexington Avenue, New York, NY 10017

References to the Christian Old Testament use the
chapter-and-verse numbers of the Septuagint (LXX), upon which
the author's translation is based. Unless otherwise noted, New Testament
texts and commentary refer to the Revised Standard Version (RSV).

Library of Congress Cataloging-in-Publication Data

Johnson, Luke Timothy.
    Reading Romans : a literary and theological commentary / Luke
Timothy Johnson.
        p.   cm. -- (Reading the New Testament series)
    ISBN 0-8245-1624-9 (pbk.)
    1. Bible. N.T. Romans--Commentaries. I. Title. II. Series.
BS2665.3.J64   1996
227'.107 – dc20   96-32460
                                                              CIP

To Professor Hendrick Boers
Esteemed Colleague

CONTENTS

EDITOR'S PREFACE

"Reading the New Testament" is a commentary series that aims to present cutting-edge research in popular form that is accessible to upper-level undergraduates, seminarians, seminary-educated pastors, and educated laypeople, as well as to graduate students and professors. The volumes in this series do not follow the word-by-word, phrase-by-phrase, verse-by-verse method of traditional commentaries. Rather they are concerned to understand large thought units and their relationship to an author's thought as a whole. The focus is on a close reading of the final form of the text. The aim is to make one feel at home in the biblical text itself. The approach of these volumes involves a concern both for *how* an author communicates and *what* the religious point of the text is. Care is taken to relate both the *how* and the *what* of the text to its milieu: Christian (New Testament and non-canonical), Jewish (scriptural and postbiblical), and Greco-Roman. This enables both the communication strategies and the religious message of the text to be clarified over against a range of historical and cultural possibilities. Moreover, a section of commentary on a large thought unit will often contain a brief excursus on some topic raised by the material in the unit, sometimes sketching Old Testament, postbiblical Jewish, Greco-Roman, New Testament, and noncanonical Christian views on the subject. Throughout, the basic concern is to treat the New Testament texts as religious documents whose religious message needs to be set forth with compelling clarity. All other concerns are subordinated to this. It is the hope of all participants in this project that our efforts at exposition will enable the New Testament to be understood better and communicated more competently.

Charles H. Talbert, General Editor

PREFACE

In the spirit of this commentary series, I have tried to give a single, strong reading of Romans from beginning to end. The voice you hear in conversation with Paul is my own. I hope that by using my own voice I have also enabled Paul's to be heard as freshly as possible. To attempt this sort of synthetic interpretation demands a certain willingness to take risks. It also means that many points that could be debated endlessly must finally be decided one way or another and then let go.

When Charles Talbert asked me to write this book, he said it might be a good thing to have a Roman Catholic like myself read a composition that has been the classic text for Reformation theology. There are some emphases in my reading that I do think are recognizably "Catholic": the tendency to argue for a "both/and" solution to many problems rather than an "either/or"; the focus on the reality of the gift of grace and its transforming power in human freedom; the conviction that chapters 5 and 8 are as central to Paul's argument as are chapters 3 and 7. Other emphases are my own. I came to the conviction when teaching my first Greek Exegesis class in Romans at Yale Divinity School, now almost twenty years ago, that "the faith of Christ" was key to Paul's argument in Romans. The opinion that "salvation" in Romans should be read as a social reality is of more recent vintage.

As in other volumes in this series, the references to scholarly literature are meant to be useful rather than to be a display of learning. These references, as also those to ancient writings, are almost infinitely expandable. I do want to acknowledge the debt I owe to the work done in particular by my teachers, Nils Dahl, Wayne Meeks, and Abraham Malherbe, and by my peers Richard Hays, Stanley Stowers, and Steven Kraftchick.

With regard to the biblical text, I have followed the Greek text used by Paul, which is found in the Septuagint (LXX) version of the Christian Old

Testament. Readers who are startled by text discrepancies will find the familiar text references in the Revised Standard Version (RSV) Study Bible.

This book is dedicated to Hendrick Boers, who for many years has engaged Paul's thought with fierce independence and integrity, giving his students and colleagues at Emory University a model of how ancient texts can be engaged both with the best tools of intelligence and the noblest aspirations of the heart. I join many others in thanking him for his insistence that the study of the New Testament is worthwhile only when it is a pursuit of meaning, and of truth.

Luke Timothy Johnson
Candler School of Theology
Emory University

INTRODUCTION

P aul's letter to the Romans has had an obvious and powerful impact on
the history of Christianity. From the time the New Testament was first
collected, Romans held a distinctive importance for the shaping of Christian identity and self-understanding (see J. D. Godsey, "The Interpretation
of Romans in the History of the Christian Faith," *Interpretation* 34 [1980]:
3-16). Romans was as dear to the arch-heretic Marcion, who wanted to base
all Christianity on Pauline theology, as it was to the arch-heresiologist
Irenaeus, who used Romans to refute Marcion's dualistic, anti-Jewish, and
anti-cosmic version of Christianity. Patristic authors such as Origen, Cyril of
Alexandria, and Ambrose of Milan not only wrote extensive commentaries
on Romans but used it extensively in their trinitarian and christological trea-
tises. It was upon the reading of Rom 13:11-14 that Augustine redirected
his life (*Confessions* 8.12), and Augustine's highly personal appropriation
of Romans was to prove decisive for the formation of theology in the Christian West. For Martin Luther, Romans was, together with Galatians, the
supreme expression of the gospel and the catalyst for the reformation of the
church. The letter's continuing capacity to reform and reshape consciousness was shown in the early twentieth century, when Karl Barth's *Commentary on Romans* (1918) declared a stunning no to any identification of
God's rule with human progress and affirmed through a passionately direct
engagement with Romans the sovereignty of God over all human effort,
will, and even thought. From Marcion in the second century, then, to Ernst
Käsemann in the twentieth century (see his *Perspectives on Paul,* trans. M.
Kohl [Philadelphia: Fortress, 1971]), the heart of Christianity has been
located in Paul's theology, and the heart of Paul's theology has been found
in Romans (see R. Jewett, "Major Developments in the Theological Interpretation of Romans since Barth," *Interpretation* 34 [1980]: 17-31).

This long history of theological interpretation is both a benefit and a bar-

1

rier to contemporary readers of Romans. The benefit is obvious in the wealth of insight previous interpreters have had into every nuance of Paul's text. The barrier is that Paul's own meaning has inevitably been overlayed by a succession of theological appropriations. Theologians have tended to assume that Paul was interested in, and speaking about, the same matters that interested them. They forgot that Paul was not simply another sharer in the Christian language but an original shaper of it. It was all too easy for Augustine to find in Paul's language about grace and sin his own understanding of these terms, as though the almost four centuries between Paul and Augustine—four centuries of church appropriation!—had made no difference. And when Martin Luther, in turn, read Romans 7 in terms of a continuing struggle within humans between the demands of the law and human sensuality, he like Augustine assumed that Paul should be read entirely in terms of the personal quest for salvation. Likewise, when John Calvin read Romans 9-11 in terms of God's eternal predestination of souls to heaven or hell, he assumed that this topic, so critical to his own theology, was Paul's topic as well (see *Institutes of the Christian Religion* III, 21-22). The history of theological interpretation has obscured Paul's meaning with layer after layer of subsequent significance discovered in or imposed on Paul's composition. Present-day readers find it difficult to cut through these layers in order to encounter what Paul himself wrote.

The goal of the present commentary is to enable the present-day reader to engage Paul's composition as directly and freshly as possible. For this to happen, the reader should be willing to suspend notions of what Paul "must have been saying" and to exercise a certain amount of historical imagination. Paul was writing not for posterity but for specific readers of his own generation, who inhabited a distinctive Mediterranean culture, formed their thoughts and values according to a complex symbolic world made up in equal parts of Greco-Roman and Jewish components, and had formed communities based on a set of experiences and convictions concerning a recently executed man named Jesus. In all these ways they were necessarily different from Christian readers of today, for whom Romans is read as part of the Bible. Getting out of our world and into the world of Paul's readers requires energy and commitment.

We seek to understand Paul's original meaning insofar as we can recover it. This does not suggest a claim to have access to "Paul's intention," for what he intended is unavailable to us except as it is inscribed in the composition itself. Rather, we try to place ourselves in the position of Paul's implied readers, those Christians of first-century Roman churches who spoke and read their Scriptures in Greek. Because we are the beneficiaries of centuries of research, however, we can also aspire to be Paul's "ideal readers," whose alertness, intelligence, learning, and imagination would enable them to catch nuances, allusions, and cross-references that Paul's "real readers" might never have caught or even heard.

The commentary will help present-day readers construct the meaning of Romans *through the process of reading*, coming as close as we can to the way the first readers experienced it. This means, practically, that after some opening remarks intended to situate present-day readers as close to first-century readers as possible, Romans will be read *in sequence* as a developing argument.

Our reading will try to maintain the "otherness" of Romans. We will not assume possession of its meaning. Instead we will seek to find it. By so doing, we do not abandon the task of theology, but better prepare for it. Only by allowing Romans to be "other" can a responsible theological engagement with it be possible. Trying to hear Romans as it was first heard enables present-day readers to experience it as a challenging word to their own lives.

The process of reading Romans in sequence will be improved if we consider first some of the critical issues facing any reading of this letter. These have to do with the original circumstances and purpose of the letter, its character as moral instruction or theological argument, and its literary structure and texture. Discussion of these issues serves to locate the present interpretation within contemporary scholarly debates, as well as to alert us to important dimensions of the composition we will encounter in our reading.

The Occasion and Purpose of the Letter

Considerable attention has been given to this issue in recent years, forming what has come to be called "The Romans Debate" (see K. P. Donfried, ed., *The Romans Debate* [Minneapolis: Augsburg, 1977]). That there should be such a debate is itself instructive, since Romans tells us as much concerning the circumstances of its composition as any New Testament writing— more indeed than most. Yet it is still possible for readers to disagree on this most basic point. The debate concerns the degree to which Romans should be read as responding to problems in the Roman community or as generated by a turning point in Paul's mission.

We can begin by reviewing the data concerning which there is no disagreement. Paul did not himself found the church at Rome. According to Acts 28:15, Paul's arrival in the city as a prisoner was greeted by "the brothers" already living there. Paul himself declares that he had longed to meet the Roman Christians but had not yet, at the time of this writing, had the opportunity (Rom 1:10–13). This letter, in fact, announces his intention finally to remedy that situation by traveling to Rome (15:22–24) in the expectation that the Roman church would support him financially in his mission to Spain (15:24). Before visiting Rome, however, Paul plans to complete his "service for Jerusalem" by delivering to that church the collection of money to which he had devoted a substantial portion of his energy in recent years (see Gal 2:10; 1 Cor 16:1-4; 2 Cor 8-9). It appears that Paul regards this collection as an appropriate climax to his missionary work in the East (15:22), and although he fears that his gift may not find acceptance (15:31) and begs the prayers of the Roman Christians (15:30), he is confident that he will be visiting them shortly, and he looks forward to opening up a new mission field in the West (15:24, 32).

Some of these planned movements overlap the account in the Acts of the Apostles. According to Acts 20:2, Paul spent three months in Greece after the riot in Ephesus. During that time, he received emissaries from various locations, and then, after Passover, began his final journey to Jerusalem (Acts 20:6), a trip he was eager to complete by Pentecost (20:16). Although Acts makes no mention of a collection in connection with this journey, the overall circumstances appear to agree substantially with those suggested by Paul's personal remarks in Romans (see K. E. Nickle, *The Collection: A Study in Paul's Strategy* [London: SCM, 1966]).

It is quite likely, then, that Paul wrote this letter during the winter months of 57-58, and from the city of Corinth. In Rom 16:23, he sends greetings to the Romans from "Erastus, the city treasurer," and Erastus is connected to Corinth by 2 Tim 4:20. Paul appears, in short, to be writing Romans at what is, for him, a major turning point in his career. Events turn out otherwise. He is arrested in Jerusalem (Acts 21:27) and spends at least four years in the Roman legal system before we lose sight of him at the end of Acts (28:30).

We cannot be certain of the social makeup of the Roman church (or churches) at the time Paul wrote this letter. Acts would lead us to suppose that Rome had a number of Jewish believers. According to Acts 18:2-3, for example, Paul meets Aquila and Priscilla in Corinth. They were Jewish believers who had been expelled from Rome by the decree of the emperor Claudius, an event that can be dated with some confidence to the year 49. In a short mention of the expulsion, the Roman historian Suetonius says that it was instigated by a commotion caused by a certain "Chrestus"—probably a muddled reference to the proclamation of Jesus among Jews (*Life of Claudius* 25.4). Acts shows Paul under house arrest in Rome, repeatedly preaching to the Jewish leaders in that city with some small success (Acts 28:24). Finally, the letter itself suggests that some of Paul's readers were Jewish. In 2:17, he directly addresses one "who calls [him]self a Jew," refers to Abraham as "our forefather according to the flesh" (4:1), and speaks of those in the community who are stricter than others in the observance of diet and special days (14:2, 5, 20-21).

On the other hand, Romans as a whole gives the impression that Paul's readers are predominantly Gentile in origin. He describes his mission as one of bringing about "the obedience of faith for the sake of his name among all the nations [or: Gentiles], including yourselves" (1:5-6; see also 16:26). He says that he had wanted to "reap some harvest among you as among the rest of the Gentiles" (1:13). And in 11:13, Paul explicitly says, "Now I am speaking to you Gentiles." Most scholars have concluded from this evidence that Paul addressed Christians of a mixed background. Were Jews and Gentiles together in a single community? Were there separate house-churches for persons of different backgrounds? The letter does not give sufficient information to decide the matter more closely.

An ethnically and culturally mixed population in the Roman church or churches seems to some scholars to be the most important clue for deciphering Romans. They view the letter as similar in function to others written by Paul, such as 1 Thessalonians or 1 Corinthians, that were generated by problems arising in specific communities and requiring correction. In this case, the disagreements over food and festivals touched on in chapter 14 are taken to be the cause of real and severe conflict between Jewish and Gentile Christians in Rome. Paul therefore writes as a pastor to heal these rifts. The rest of Romans is read through the lens provided by the practical issues in chapter 14, and Paul's entire point is summarized by this practical exhortation: "Welcome one another, therefore, as Christ has welcomed you, for the glory of God" (15:7). Paul's earlier argument, turning now to the Jewish believer and now to the Gentile believer, has the goal of convincing them of their reciprocal and mutual role in God's mysterious plan of salvation. This reading of Romans has much to recommend it (see, e.g., P. Minear, *The Obedience of Faith* [London: SCM, 1971]).

Other scholars, however, conclude that Romans was motivated less by a local crisis than by Paul's present circumstances and future plans (see, e.g., R. Jewett, "Romans as an Ambassadorial Letter," *Interpretation* 36 [1982]: 5-10; G. Bornkamm, "The Letter to the Romans as Paul's Last Will and Testament," in *The Romans Debate*, 17-31). They note that Paul does not anywhere adopt the tone of rebuke, or even of direct instruction of his readers. He is extraordinarily circumspect concerning his authority to speak to them at all. After stating that he had hoped to "impart some spiritual gift to strengthen you" (1:11), he quickly qualifies any implication of authority by adding, "that is, that we may be mutually encouraged by each other's faith, both yours and mine" (1:12). They observe that much of Paul's moral exhortation in chapters 12-13 has a general character, not linked to specifically Jew-Gentile tensions. Most of all, they take seriously Paul's own conclusion that "I myself am satisfied about you, my brethren, that you yourselves are full of goodness, filled with knowledge, and able to instruct one another"

(15:14). It is true that Paul goes on to say that he has "written on some points very boldly by way of reminder" (15:15), but these comments do not suggest a community in crisis or in danger of dissolving. The hardest passage to reconcile with this understanding of things is 16:17–18, concerning those who cause "dissensions and difficulties." But it should be noted that such people are described as "in opposition to the doctrine you have been taught," not of taking sides in a debate over observance. And even in this passage, Paul insists concerning the Romans themselves that "your obedience is known to all." In the view of these scholars, Paul is not writing to resolve an internal crisis.

I agree with the position of those who think that Paul's composition of Romans was generated less by a crisis in the Roman church than by Paul's own plans. To make that position convincing, we must turn to his explication of those plans and the role he wants Rome to play in them. Before doing that, however, I want to acknowledge that a position on one side or another here need not be exclusive. The data are mixed, enabling the debate to continue. While arguing, therefore, that Paul's purpose was not primarily to correct faults in the community, I would not want to deny that there could have been such problems of which Paul was aware, or that in this case his goals and the needs of the community might happily have coincided (see the reasonable conclusions of A. J. M. Wedderburn, *The Reasons for Romans* [Minneapolis: Fortress, 1991]).

I understand the basic purpose for the writing of Romans to have been intensely practical. In a word, Paul seeks the financial backing of the Roman church for his proposed mission to Spain. He hints at this financial expectation already in the thanksgiving: earlier on, he had "desired some harvest" among the Romans as among other Gentile churches (1:13). The most reasonable way to understand this is that Paul had previously hoped to include them in his great collection for the church in Jerusalem. But his work in the East had prevented him from coming (15:19–22). Now, he hints, he is giving the Romans a second chance. He is offering them the opportunity to be his new base of operations in the West. We know from other evidence that basing himself in an important metropolitan community was, in fact, Paul's practice. He was originally sponsored by the Antiochean church (Acts 13:1–3), and, in Europe, his community at Philippi had provided him with financial backing (see Phil 4:15; 2 Cor 11:9). He now tells the Roman Christians that he hopes to "be sped on my journey there [viz., Spain] once I have enjoyed your company for a little" (15:24). The Greek term for "speed on a journey" (*propempein*) is used technically for the outfitting of an expedition (see 3 John 6). Paul adds in 15:32 that he expects to be "refreshed" (*synanapauesthai*) among them. This term also strongly suggests financial support (see Phlm 7; 1 Cor 16:18).

Such a straightforwardly pragmatic purpose helps us make sense of chapter 16, which otherwise may appear as an odd appendix. Indeed, some scholars have doubted whether it was originally part of Romans and have thought that perhaps it was a separate letter of commendation for Phoebe, addressed to the church at Ephesus (see E. J. Goodspeed, "Phoebe's Letter of Introduction," *Harvard Theological Review* 44 [1951]: 55–57). The suggestion is intriguing. A careful analysis of Romans' textual history, however, shows that chapter 16 had been part of this letter from the beginning, a conclusion that other thematic links might also have supported (see H. A. Gamble, *The Textual History of the Letter to the Romans: A Study in Textual and Literary Criticism* [Grand Rapids: Eerdmans, 1977]).

Chapter 16 as a whole and as part of Romans serves Paul's purposes admirably. The first two verses form, as noted, a short letter of commendation for Phoebe (see S. Stowers, *Letter-Writing in Greco-Roman Antiquity* [Philadelphia: Westminster, 1986] 153–65). Paul identifies her as deacon of the church at Cenchreae (a port of the city of Corinth), and declares that "she has been a helper of many and of myself as well" (16:2). The term that the RSV translates as "helper" is also used for "patron" (see, e.g., Aristotle, *Politics* 1275A), which in this case would surely mean someone who provided Paul with financial support (see Paul's remarks on other leaders in 1 Cor 16:15–18). Furthermore, Paul asks the Romans to "assist her in whatever she may require of you." The Greek diction again suggests financial affairs, and coming immediately after 15:32, which expresses Paul's expectation of "refreshment" from the Romans church, makes Phoebe's mission clear. She has served as a patron of Paul's work in the East, and he is now sending her to Rome in order to organize and prepare for Paul's expedition to Spain. Paul recommends her to the Roman church as his business agent.

The list of names in 16:3–16, indicating people who send greetings or who are greeted, will be considered in detail in the commentary. For now, it should be noted not only that the list is remarkably extensive for one who had never visited the Roman church, but that it serves Paul's practical purposes, by providing, in effect, a network of people who can testify to his worthiness of support, as well as his enmeshment in the larger missionary effort of the churches. As Paul recommends Phoebe, so can these people recommend Paul.

The question irresistibly arises: If Paul's purpose in writing was simply to raise funds, why did he write so elaborately and at such great length? Why could he not have written 1:1–15 and 15:14–16:27 and be done with it? The answer to this most pertinent question lies in the symbolism of apostleship in early Christianity, and the peculiar character of Paul's own status as an apostle. First, the symbolism: the early church considered the case of apostles to be like that of prophets. They were sent out with a commission to represent another. To accept the messenger or agent, therefore, was to accept the one who sent the messenger or agent (see Luke 10:16). To accept or reject such an emissary, furthermore, was to accept or reject the emissary's message as well (see 2 John 10). It follows that to *support* an apostle would mean as well to support the message the apostle proclaimed, that messenger's version of the good news. To persuade the Romans to support his apostleship in the West, therefore, Paul needs to persuade them as well of the trustworthiness of his "gospel."

There is also the peculiar character of his apostleship. Paul had insisted to the Corinthian church that he did not need letters of recommendation from churches (2 Cor 3:2). The reason was that he had founded those communities and expected them to be his recommendation "written on their hearts" (2 Cor 3:3). Part of what is involved here is Paul's conviction that he had been appointed as an apostle not by a local community but directly by the Lord (1 Cor 9:1; 15:8; Gal 1:15). Since no humans could recommend him—and, indeed, since many humans questioned his credentials—Paul required such commendation from the work God did in his communities.

But now Paul finds himself in a position of needing recommendation to a church that does not know him face to face. Sending greetings from fellow workers helps. But Paul needs above all to recommend himself by recommending his *gospel*. Romans completely transcends its immediate purpose as a fund-raising letter by providing Paul's most complete and ordered exposition of what he understood his ministry to be about, and therefore what he thought God was up to in the world by using him as an instrument. At this moment of transition, having responded to local fights in Galatia concerning circumcision, and having responded to local disputes in Corinth over issues of social practice, and above all having thought through the symbolism of his gift of money to Jerusalem, by which he hoped to reconcile Jews and Gentiles in the church, Paul worked all these concerns into a single magisterial argument to recommend his ministry to the church in Rome by recommending a good news in whose service he was expending his life.

Theology or Moral Instruction?

As I noted above, much interpretation of Romans through Christian history proceeded on the assumption that it was simply a theological writing, that what the commentators conceived of as theology was also Paul's conception, and that no gap existed between Paul's language and their own. Since Christian theology thought of salvation, for example, primarily in terms of an individual's participation in the life of God, it was taken for granted that Paul also thought of it that way. Likewise, Paul's language about God and

Christ and Spirit was read in the light of later trinitarian and christological development in a way that allowed alien philosophical concepts to be read into and out of Paul's writing without remainder. In this way, Romans could be read as a theological treatise, a collection of *theologoumena*. It took a long time to recognize that there was something not only anachronistic but also wrong-headed about such an approach. Paul's treatment of Christ and Adam in chapter 5 can legitimately be seen as the basis for Irenaeus's great conception of divine pedagogy extending from the first human to a restored humanity, but that conception is not Paul's (see *Against Heresies* 5.15–25). Similarly, Paul's statements on desire or coveting in chapter 7 clearly serve as the basis for Augustine's understanding of concupiscence, but it would be a mistake to think that what Paul meant by *epithymia* is the same as what Augustine meant by *concupiscentia*. Nor can Luther's appeal to "righteousness by faith *alone*" as a liberation from an oppressive law, be regarded as Paul's own understanding.

In an understandable reaction to this tradition of theological reading (or perhaps, in Harold Bloom's terms, "strong misreading"), it has recently been argued that Paul had *no* theological interest of the sort that the Christian tradition constantly found in Romans. The most forceful expression of this position is S. K. Stowers, *A Rereading of Romans: Justice, Jews, and Gentiles* (New Haven: Yale University Press, 1994). He argues that Romans should be seen primarily as a form of *moral exhortation* specifically directed at Gentile believers. Paul's concern was not "theology" but the shaping of a certain kind of community ethos. This is an important and badly needed corrective. Paul was surely not a speculative or systematic theologian, inventing the Christian religion in opposition to the religion of Judaism, and Romans is not his *Summa Theologica*. Paul can, furthermore, be read intelligibly as a moral philosopher of the first-century Hellenistic world, whose interest is in creating communities of character. Stowers's argument is particularly valuable for reminding us that we cannot take a full third of Romans (chapters 12–16) and dismiss it as irrelevant to Paul's purposes. We must, rather, if we are to make sense of Romans as a whole, assume a connection between that part of Paul's argument that appears more "theological" and his instructions intended to shape the Roman church's moral attitudes and actions, a connection made absolutely clear by Paul himself in 15:1–13.

Like much reactive or revisionist scholarship, Stowers's work is more convincing in its deconstruction than in its construction. The corrective can itself become a distortion when it seems to imply that there is no theological dimension to Romans. If Romans is not a systematic theological treatise, neither is it simply a moral essay. Such a diminishment can be convincing only by ignoring the specific language of the composition itself. Romans is demonstrably theological in important ways. The most obvious is that Paul's subject concerns God. His discourse begins with the human experience of God in the world, that is, with religious experience. For Paul, terms such as faith, sin, grace, and glory are not *moral* qualities capable of being developed autonomously by individuals, but refer rather to *relational* states between persons, specifically between the personal God and humans. These relational states, furthermore, are based for Paul in real experiences and have genuine behavioral consequences. Part of the work of the interpreter of Romans is the uncovering of some of the first-order language of religious experience and conviction that underlies Paul's argument.

Romans is not simply the immediate expression of religious experience. Although it uses the language of prayer, it moves beyond prayer into critical thought. Although it celebrates the gift of grace, it pushes beyond that celebration to cerebration: How does the character of the gift reveal something of the character of the giver? If theology in the proper sense is the effort of human intelligence to move from the experience of God's work in the world to some small understanding of the character of the God who is at work, then Romans must be called quintessentially theological. As Paul reflects on what the meaning of his mission might be for the salvation of humanity, he is literally trying to catch up with what God is doing. In this sense, Romans is quite rightly designated as Paul's missionary theology (see N. A. Dahl, "The Missionary Theology in the Epistle to the Romans," in *Studies in Paul* [Minneapolis: Augsburg, 1977] 70–94).

If Christian theology, furthermore, involves the reinterpretation of Torah in the light of how God has worked through the death and resurrection of Jesus, then Romans is surely Christian theology, for in its every line the symbols of the Law and Prophets and Writings are given new values because of the good news from God in Christ. Finally, if Christian theology means making explicit what was implicit in the story of Jesus, on this count also, we will find, Romans is decidedly theological. In conclusion, as it would be a mistake to read Romans as though it were a doctrinal treatise, because it is far too rooted in experience to be considered an exercise in speculative reason, so also it would be a mistake to read Romans as a simple moral treatise, because Paul's mind pushes past the traces of God's activity in the experience of his work and the life of his churches, to the boldest sort of conclusions concerning who God might really be.

Genre and Rhetoric

A final set of critical considerations draws us closer to the texture of Romans as a composition, and how its form works to shape reader expectations and responses. I will briefly discuss here five aspects of the rhetoric of Romans: the implications of its being in the form of a letter; the importance of its having the argument of the diatribe; the manner in which it engages the symbolic world of Torah; the significance for Romans of the traditions of the church and the story of Jesus; and the proper understanding of Paul as the author of Romans.

1. *Romans is a real letter.* By this, I mean that it is not simply an essay with a greeting and farewell appended. It was written to real people with a real purpose. Indeed, I have already suggested that at the most obvious level its rhetoric was aimed at convincing the Roman church to support Paul's apostleship and missionary excursion to Spain. Such rhetoric would be particularly effective because of the conventions attached to letter writing in the Hellenistic world. A letter was considered to make the writer present to the readers (see A. J. Malherbe, "Ancient Epistolary Theory," *Ohio Journal of Religious Studies* 5 [1977]: 3–77). In a very real sense, then, especially if the letter was read aloud to the assembly, the Romans already had Paul among them, presenting his case and making his appeal.

In its form, Romans has the features of the typical Pauline letter (see W. G. Doty, *Letters in Primitive Christianity* [Philadelphia: Fortress Press, 1973]). The greeting (1:1–7) is followed by a thanksgiving period (1:8–15), which is both real prayer and a preparation for some of the letter's themes. The body of the letter extends from 1:16 to at least 15:13. From 15:14 to 16:16, Paul begins to discuss his plans, recommends Phoebe, and sends greetings. There follow then a final appeal (16:17–20), more greetings (16:21–23) and a final prayer (16:25–27). This commentary will try to demonstrate how each part of the letter serves the rhetorical aims of the composition as a whole.

2. *Romans is a scholastic diatribe.* Although Paul's letters resemble one another formally, they also can be located within the various letter types described by ancient rhetorical handbooks, such as those of Pseudo-Libanius. It is in the body of the letter that we find the distinguishing characteristics. Paul's letter to the Philippians, for example, fits the form of a "friendly letter," while 2 Timothy is best characterized as a "parenetic letter." As with all literary conventions, detecting the sub-genre of a letter helps the reader grasp the specific literary shape and intention of the composition. For a letter as long and complex as Romans, unfortunately, it is impossible to find a single such "type" that adequately covers everything Romans is doing. I have already shown how chapter 16 functions as a "letter of commendation" and have suggested that Romans as a whole might be seen in that light.

That the body of Romans most resembles the form of Greco-Roman discourse called the diatribe has been known for some time (see R. Bultmann, *Der Stil der paulinischen Predigt und die Kynisch-stoische Diatribe* [FRLANT; Göttingen: Vandenhoeck & Ruprecht, 1910]). The diatribe is a vivid, dialogical form of discourse, one of whose most identifiable features is the presence of an imaginary interlocutor who can be addressed and who can in turn raise questions. The reader is drawn into the fictive conversation. Other Pauline letters (especially 1 Corinthians) contain elements of what is sometimes called the diatribal style, but it is above all Romans that contains the fullest display of the features associated with this form of discourse, the best known examples of which are the *Discourses* of the philosopher Epictetus. The diatribe uses all these tropes of oral discourse: apostrophe (see Rom 2:1, 3, 17; 9:20), rhetorical questions (2:3-4, 21-23; 7:1; 8:31-35; 9:19-21, 30; 10:14-15; 11:34-35), questions that are answered by abrupt responses such as "by no means" (3:2-9; 6:1-2, 15; 7:7, 13; 11:1, 11), hyperbole (8:37-39; 9:3), sorites, or a chain of interconnected clauses (5:3-5; 8:30; 9:14-15), lists of vices (1:29-31), virtues (12:6-8), and hardships (8:35), examples from the past (4:1-25; 5:12-21), and the citation of written texts as authorities (e.g., 9:1-11:36).

Recent research on the diatribe has emphasized that it is not simply a collection of stylistic features but is above all a form of argument that finds its natural social location in the classroom rather than, as previously was thought, in the forum (see S. K. Stowers, *The Diatribe and Paul's Letter to the Romans* [SBLDS 57; Chico, Calif.: Scholars Press, 1981]). The diatribe provides the literary representation of the lively give-and-take of teacher and student in the classroom. As such a scholastic diatribe, therefore, Romans presents Paul in his role as teacher more than as preacher.

Such analysis also suggests that we look in Romans for a specific sort of rhetorical argument, similar to those developed by such examples of the diatribe as Philo's *That Every Good Man Is Free*. In such arguments we would expect (not always in the same order) certain consistent features: the statement of a thesis (e.g., "that every good person is free"), its demonstration by antithesis (e.g., "that every wicked person is enslaved"), by example (e.g., "the freedom demonstrated by the good person Moses"), and by such devices as comparison and contrast (e.g., "the freedom of Israel compared to the slavery of Sparta"). We would also expect to find responses to possible objections to the thesis, usually raised by the imaginary interlocutor (e.g., "How could Israel be free if it was in bondage to Egypt?"). We don't always find all these elements in every example of the diatribe, but Romans exhibits them all in full display.

Recognizing the various aspects of the diatribe is perhaps the most important key to understanding the argument in Romans. Paul states his thesis in 1:16-17. This is followed immediately by the antithesis (1:18-

3:20). The thesis is then restated more fully in 3:21–31. It is demonstrated by means of example in 4:1–25, by the evidence of experience in 5:1–11, and by *synkrisis* (the rhetorical device of comparison) in 5:12–21. Paul then takes up a series of objections to his thesis (anticipated already in 3:1–8), running from 6:1 to 11:36. The specifically *deliberative* aspects of his argument ("I appeal to you therefore, brethren") are spelled out in 12:1–15:13, as Paul applies the truth about God's righteousness to life in the Christian community.

3. *Romans is a form of midrash.* If the diatribe points to Paul's Hellenistic heritage, his use of Scripture (= Torah) points to his Jewish identity. It was a common feature of the Greco-Roman diatribe to cite authoritative texts for purposes of illustration or example. Epictetus, for example, makes frequent allusions to Homer's *Iliad* and *Odyssey* (the "Scriptures" of the Hellenistic world). Paul's way of citing authorities reveals his background in the interpretation of sacred texts within Judaism. Midrash is the broad term used to describe the interpretation of Torah in the light of changing circumstances (see G. G. Porton, "Midrash," in *The Anchor Bible Dictionary* [New York: Doubleday, 1992] 4:818–22). In rabbinic circles, *halakic* midrash was the searching through legal materials for precedents to present-day practice, while *haggadic* midrash was the appropriation of nonlegal texts for every imaginable circumstance from prayer to entertainment. The term can also be used of the sort of interpretation of the texts of Torah that was carried out among the sectarians at Qumran; their method of lining up ancient texts and the experiences of their own community has come to be called *pesher* midrash.

It was the world of Torah—the texts, stories, and symbols that are found in Law, Prophets, and Writings—that was inhabited by all the first Christians, who, even if not born Jewish, inevitably were drawn into the orbit of Judaism. The form in which they read Torah, however, was not in the Hebrew (or Masoretic Text = MT), but in the Greek translation of the Hebrew that had been carried out some 250 years before the time of Paul, called the Septuagint (= LXX). They interpreted this text with the same freedom that their fellow Jews did the Hebrew text. The difference between them was the hermeneutical starting point. For Paul's fellow Pharisees, Torah was interpreted from the perspective of a fierce commitment to the observance of its commands, both moral and ritual, without distinction. For the Dead Sea sectarians, Torah was to be read in the light of the community's own experience, especially as it revolved around the life and teachings of the Teacher of Righteousness. For Paul and other first-generation Christians, it was above all the experience of Jesus as crucified and raised messiah that provided the interpretive key to the Scripture.

Paul makes use of texts from every part of Torah. From the Law (for Jews, *Torah* in the proper sense) he uses above all narrative materials, particularly those dealing with Adam (5:12–21), Abraham (4:1–25), and the patriarchs (9:6–13), with only a few references to Moses and the exodus tradition (9:1–5, 14–18; 10:5–8). He also uses the writings (*kĕtûbîm*) thoroughly. It is noteworthy that he appears to make use of the Wisdom of Solomon (found only in the LXX) for his attack on idolatry in 1:18–31. An allusion to Job in 11:35 is an important clue to Paul's whole argument. And he makes obvious and extensive use of the Psalms, to illustrate the sinful character of humans (3:13–18), and the free gift of righteousness (4:7–8) even to the Gentiles (15:9–12), as well as the suffering already undergone by Christ (15:3) and currently being experienced by Christians (8:36).

Paul clearly understood all the texts of Torah to have a certain prophetic force: "whatever was written in former days was written for our instruction" (15:4). Nowhere does this principle apply more directly than in the prophets themselves (*nĕbîʾîm*). Paul understood the good news itself to have been "promised beforehand through the prophets in the holy writings" (1:2), and "witnessed to by the law and prophets" (3:21); the mystery of God, he says, is made known to all nations through the prophetic writings (16:26). He brings a rich selection of prophetic texts to bear in his argument, most noticeably in chapters 9–11.

In addition to the explicit citation of texts, Paul frequently alludes to Torah in ways that are significant for the development of his presentation. Richard Hays has alerted us to the "echoes" of Old Testament texts that are present in Romans (*Echoes of Scripture in the Letters of Paul* [New Haven: Yale University Press, 1989]). Close examination shows that Isaiah was particularly important for Paul, especially the section of Isaiah that contains what scholars have come to call the "servant songs." Echoes of Isaiah 49–65 run throughout Romans, making it probable in the highest degree that Paul's use of this material comes from careful study and deliberate appropriation. The precise meaning of Rom 10:16, I will argue, depends on how this use of Isaiah is evaluated.

4. *Romans is a Christian writing.* Speaking of Paul's use of midrash—his citations of, allusions to, and echoes of Scripture texts—points us to a complex aspect of the writing of Romans. Contemporary scholars speak of *intertextuality* as the intricate ways in which all written texts interact with other texts that have preceded them, helping to shape the symbolic world such compositions engage and themselves reshape. Some forms of intertextuality are observable in the forming of Torah itself, as newer texts pick up threads of older ones and weave them into new combinations (see M. Fishbane, "Inner Biblical Exegesis: Types and Strategies of Interpretation in

Ancient Israel," in *Midrash and Literature,* ed. G. Hartman and S. Burdick [New Haven: Yale University Press, 1986] 19-37). In the broadest sense, intertextuality can refer not only to specific written texts but also the variety of cultural scripts that might legitimately be posited as influences on a particular composition (see V. K. Robbins, "The Reverse Contextualization of Psalm 22 in the Markan Crucifixion: A Socio-Rhetorical Analysis," in *The Four Gospels 1992*, ed. F. Van Segbroeck et al. [BETL 100; Leuven: Leuven University Press, 1992] 1161-83). In the case of Romans, the influence of the Christian movement preceding Paul and, above all, the story of Jesus should not be discounted.

Paul's sense of a shared Christian identity manifests itself throughout the letter, from the traditional shaping of the "good news" in his greeting (1:1-4) to the list of fellow workers he includes in his closing salutations (16:3-16, 21-23). Paul frequently signals the presence of shared understanding by the simple assertion "we know" (2:2; 3:19; 5:3; 6:9; 7:14; 8:22, 28). When he asks the question, "Do you not know?" he implies that his readers *should* know (see 6:16; 11:2). Paul shares with his readers not only general perceptions concerning the symbolic world of Torah, but the specific structures and symbols of the messianic movement. For example, he assumes a shared understanding of the rite of baptism as an identification with the death and resurrection of Christ (6:5-11), that the Holy Spirit provides the power for life and righteousness within the community (8:1-27) as well as the gifts of ministry among believers (12:3-8), that the commandment of love of neighbor surpasses and summarizes all others (13:8-10), and that the present age is one lived in expectation of Jesus' return in judgment (2:16; 13:11-14) and eventual triumph over Satan (16:19).

Even more specifically, Paul in Romans (as in other letters) makes use of the story of Jesus in ways that are subtle and indirect but nevertheless important as a kind of narrative substructure of his theology (see R. B. Hays, *The Faith of Jesus* [SBLDS 56; Chico, Calif.: Scholars Press, 1983]). Two interrelated aspects of Paul's understanding of Jesus are critical for his argument. The first concerns the proper way to translate *pistis Christou*, especially in Rom 3:21-26. Does Paul's expression mean a "faith that believers have in Christ"? Or, as I will argue, does it mean "the faith of Christ in God" that revealed itself in his obedient death (see Rom 5:12-21)? At issue is the entire theological argument of Romans (see R. B. Hays, "*Pistis* and Pauline Christology: What is at Stake?" *SBL Seminar Papers 1991*, ed. D. J. Lull [Atlanta: Scholars Press, 1991] 714-29). God makes humans righteous, says Paul, by faith. But *whose* faith makes righteous? The second aspect of the story of Jesus is the way Paul applies the pattern of life for others that was demonstrated by the death of Jesus as a moral exemplar for life in the community (see especially 14:9, 15; 15:1–3). Paul in all likelihood wrote Romans before any of the Gospel narratives reached finished written form. But the story of Jesus nevertheless had a central significance for his argument concerning God's way of making humans righteous.

5. *Romans is a Pauline writing.* This discussion has, I hope, suggested that the designation of Romans as "Paul's letter" may be more complex than it at first appears. Certainly few even of the most radical critics have challenged the authenticity of Romans (but see W. C. Van Manen, "Romans," *Encyclopedia Biblica* [London: Adam & Charles Black, 1914] 4127–45). Indeed, this is one of the few letters in the corpus (with Ephesians, 1 Timothy, 2 Timothy, Titus) that do not have Paul's name joined to several cosponsors (see, e.g., 1 Cor 1:1; 1 Thess 1:1; Phil 1:1). In the case of Romans, the abrupt declaration in 16:22 that "I, Tertius, the writer of this letter, greet you," may safely be taken as the interjection of a scribe rather than a coauthor!

Nevertheless, Romans does not emerge from Paul's mind in isolation from all the influences I have enumerated. The rhetorical constraints of the letter form and of the diatribe, the symbols of Torah, the traditions of the nascent messianic movement, and the story of Jesus' death and resurrection: these all help to shape Paul's mind and message as well as the medium of communication. In fact, both the diatribe and midrash were in that world essentially social activities, carried out in schools. It is not in the least unlikely that Romans had more than one mind at work in its construction and that some of its more intricate turns might have been plotted ahead of time by Paul with his school—that is, his associates and fellow workers. The "Pauline school" is not something that sprang into existence after Paul's death; on the evidence, it was at work in the production of his letters already during his lifetime.

Despite such considerations of intertextuality and social activity, there is no doubt that a single imagination "authored" this letter, in the sense of generating its vision and directing its argument. Romans is simply too magisterial a work to have emerged from a committee. Romans is, as countless minds have perceived before, simply the most powerful argument concerning God in the New Testament. Its nearest rivals for depth and dialectic (the Gospel of John, the Letter to the Hebrews, Ephesians), simply confirm the fact that nothing in the earliest Christian movement (and little else since) matches Romans for theological profundity, argumentative tensile strength, and, above all, energy. Only Paul's experience was, in those first years, sufficiently paradoxical (persecutor turned apostle, Pharisee become missionary to Gentiles) to have provoked the problem of God's righteousness in this fashion. Only Paul's intelligence in the first generation of Christians was powerful and brave enough to push beyond that problem to the very edge of its mysterious heart, enabling him to assert in one breath the universality of God's will to save humans and the particularity of God's way of bringing that about.

The argument of Romans is, at root, simple. God is one and God is fair. Only a gifted and complex mind could, in the tangle of human experience (much of it pointing directly the other way), discover and disclose that breathtakingly simple proposition.

Romans so successfully transcends its immediate practical purpose that it challenges all attempts to reduce literary and religious significance to the circumstances of composition. Just as Paul saw intimations of the good news concerning Jesus in the ancient writings of the prophets, so does his perception of the intimation of God's mercy in Israel's temporary rejection, and his perception of faith as a principle of response to God for all humans, make his writing prophetic for every age. They are not far wrong who see in Romans something touched by more than the brave intelligence of a seasoned missionary interpreting the meaning of his ministry, who see in Romans something of the activity of the Spirit, "who intercedes for the saints according to the will of God" (8:27), and who in this great Pauline effort see "the revelation of the mystery which was kept secret for long ages but is now disclosed" (16:25-26).

THE GOOD NEWS OF GOD'S RIGHTEOUSNESS

Romans 1:1-17

The opening section of Romans consists of the greeting (1:1-7), the thanksgiving (1:8-14), and the thesis statement that begins the body of the letter (1:16-17). The first two elements are standard in the Pauline letter. The thesis statement is unique to Romans and identifies the distinctive character of this letter as a scholastic diatribe that will carry through a sustained argument from beginning to end. The greeting and thanksgiving, we shall see, also anticipate elements in his argument and provide hints of what Paul hopes to accomplish by writing.

As we begin "Reading Romans," we will simultaneously try to carry out two sorts of responses to the text. In one, we place ourselves at the level of the implied readers whom Paul supposed to be members of the Roman church. In this posture, we "discover" the meaning of the text only as it unfolds. Because so much of Romans is an argument, we are required not simply to discourse about the text but to follow through the explicit language of the text very carefully.

We do well to remember that in Paul's day, letters written for a group would have been read aloud in the midst of the assembly. The text would lack the sort of chapter-and-verse divisions added by later editors, as well as any but the most meager punctuation indicators. The original reciter would have been required to supply some sense as he read, just as the listeners would "construct" the meaning as they heard it unfold through the act of oral delivery (see especially S. K. Stowers, *A Rereading of Romans: Justice, Jews, and Gentiles* [New Haven: Yale University Press, 1994] 1-41). We most approximate the implied readers when we hear the text read aloud bit by bit rather than when we apprehend it visually as a whole.

At the same time, we are trying to be "ideal readers" of Romans, which means, in practical terms, that at least *this* reader has worked through the text many times before and has some ideas about where the argument is going. Part of my job as commentator on the text is to alert you, the present-day reader, to the later implications of parts of the text now unfolding, suggesting structural and stylistic interconnections, trying to give you a richer appreciation of what you are reading while not depriving you of the excitement of discovery that can come from a genuine "reading" in sequence. Such a twofold reading of the text helps compensate present-day readers for some of the ways in which our competencies for understanding Paul fall short of those of the first hearers of these words.

The Greeting (1:1-7)

In Hellenistic letters, the greeting formula was simple: from sender to recipients, greetings (*chairein*; see, e.g., 1 Macc 10:22; Acts 15:23; Jas 1:1). Paul characteristically expands the greeting for rhetorical effect by expanding one of the three elements. The element he chooses to elaborate provides readers a clue to his concerns in the letter. In Galatians, Paul expands the first element, dealing with his authority, and the third, dealing with the grace of Christ, because those two points are in dispute among his readers (Gal 1:1-5). In contrast, 1 Cor 1:1-3 expands the element dealing with the recipients, revealing Paul's concern about the church of God at Corinth.

In Romans, we see that the third element, the statement of greeting itself, is unadorned, except that Paul has as usual replaced the secular "greetings" (*chairein*) with the more religiously weighted, "grace and peace from God our father and the Lord Jesus Christ" (1:7; compare 1 Cor 1:3; Phil 1:2). This single alteration, however, has several implications. It indicates, first, how Paul's correspondence is explicitly religious literature: the greeting itself takes the form of a prayer and places the rest of the composition under the authority and blessing of God. We notice, second, the powerful understanding of the resurrection of Jesus that Paul can assume without any explanation among his readers. He can wish for them grace and peace not only from the living God but also from "Jesus Messiah." Jesus is therefore not simply an executed criminal of the past. He is a present and powerful "Lord." Third, even though the expression "grace and peace" is formulaic, it has a particular force in Romans, where the argument concerns how humans are to be in right relationship with God. Paul will insist that such a relationship is established by means of a gift (that is, "grace," *charis*), from God in Christ (see 3:24; 4:4, 16; 5:15, 17, 20, 21; 6:1, 14, 15; 11:5-6). The term "peace" (*eirēnē*) also takes on deeper resonance in this letter, even though it is a standard greeting between Jews (see, e.g., LXX Judg 6:23; 1 Sam 1:17; 20:42; 2 Kgs 5:19). In the LXX, the word *eirēnē* is used to translate the Hebrew *šālôm*, which defines the proper covenantal relationship between God and humans (see LXX Exod 18:23; Lev 26:6; Num 25:12). In this letter, Paul will describe sinners as not seeking the ways of peace (3:17), even though peace is the reward for those who do good (2:10). Most of all, peace is that which humans now have with God (5:1) through the gift ("grace") given by Christ (5:2), and can therefore characterize their life together in community (14:17). As "ideal readers" we are able to detect nuances in Paul's language that first-time readers could not—even though hearing such language from their own experience of prayer would certainly have set off its own resonances, and echoes of it could easily be heard as the subsequent parts of Paul's argument were read.

The second element of the greeting, concerning the recipients, is remarkably undeveloped in the case of Romans. Or perhaps not so remarkably, given the fact that Paul did not know his readers directly. He focuses most explicitly on the ethnic background of his readers. They are among the Gentiles (or "nations," the same word in Greek) to whom God has sent Paul to preach (1:5). Depending on how the Greek is parsed, it is possible that Paul may also be referring to a Jewish component in the church, by the expression "beloved of God." This term is explicitly reserved for the Jews in 11:28. Perhaps this early, Paul signals the mixed population he is addressing. He also emphasizes that all his readers are *called*. In 1:6, he says that those who are Gentiles are "called of Jesus Christ." The expression is cryptic. It could mean "called by Jesus Christ," or "called to belong to Jesus Christ" (see RSV). In either case, the expression denotes a strong identification between them and Jesus. In 1:7, those Paul refers to as "beloved of God" are also "called to be holy," a designation that recalls 1 Cor 1:2, and anticipates Paul's dramatic declarations concerning the call of God in 4:17; 8:30; and 9:7–26.

Paul most expands that part of the greeting dealing with the sender. In a letter that has as one of its purposes the introduction of Paul to the Roman church, an elaboration of Paul's apostolic qualifications should not surprise. Paul typically interweaves his own ministry with his understanding of the message that motivates his mission, making the Greek syntax complex. Paul begins with himself and his calling (1:1), then elaborates on the good news (1:2–4), and then returns to his own mission (1:5). The elements can be separated for purposes of analysis, but the way Paul intertwines them is essential for the impression he seeks to make.

His first self-designation is as a slave (*doulos*) of Jesus Christ, a role he applies to himself elsewhere (2 Cor 4:5; Gal 1:10; Phil 1:1). It suggests a particularly close form of allegiance to Jesus the Lord. Although slaves could attain to positions of authority in that culture and the title could suggest a certain authority for the one speaking in the name of his Lord (see, e.g., Jas 1:1, and D. B. Martin, *Slavery as Salvation: The Metaphor of Slavery in Pauline Christianity* [New Haven: Yale University Press, 1996]), the sense of personal commitment and submission dominates here, especially when the text is read in the light of

Paul's language in 6:16–20. Paul's first self-recommendation to the church at Rome, therefore, is that he is "marked for service" to Jesus.

Paul next says that he is "called to be an apostle," which describes the specific mission given him by Jesus. Paul understood his encounter with the risen Lord to be a call to represent him as his emissary (see 1 Cor 9:1; 15:7–11; Gal 1:15). The designation *apostolos* denotes a particular kind of agency: the one who is sent out with a commission truly represents the one sending (see K. H. Rengstorf, *"apostolos," TDNT* 1:407–47). In effect, to accept or reject the emissary is to accept or reject the commissioner (see Luke 10:16).

It is necessary, then, for Paul to make clear who he considers himself to be representing as an apostle. He declares that he is "set apart for the gospel of God." The expression is noteworthy first of all because Paul will directly speak of Jesus as being "set apart" as Son of God by virtue of the resurrection. This verbal link between his own designation as apostle and the commissioning authority of the resurrected Lord cannot be accidental (see also 1 Cor 9:1). But what are we to make of the expression *euangelion tou theou,* which Paul elsewhere uses equivalently to the *euangelion tou Christou?* The word *euangelion* means a message of good news. But what is its relation to "God" or "Christ" in the respective expressions? The phrase gives us a chance to discuss a peculiarity of Greek grammar that is only interesting here, but becomes critical later.

The Greek language is inflected, which means that relationships between words are signaled less by word order than by internal changes in words. The standard relationship indicators for nouns are called cases. One of the most frequently used is the genitive case, which makes one noun something of an adjective with regard to another. The genitive is an extraordinarily flexible case and can indicate a variety of adjectival relations. The most familiar to us is the possessive, but there are many others as well. A classic problem in translating Greek is deciding whether a genitive is objective or subjective. When the genitive is objective, then the word in the genitive is the object of the other noun; in this case, the phrase *euangelion tou theou* would mean "good news about God." When the genitive is subjective, the relationship is reversed; in our case, the phrase *euangelion tou theou* would be read, "good news from God." Another example would be the phrase "love of God," which could mean either God's love toward humans, or humans' love toward God. In the phrase we are considering now, the decision is not so crucial; indeed, it is likely that the expression contains elements of both subjective and objective senses: this is a message from God about God, as we shall see in Paul's thesis statement (1:16–17). The definition of genitives will become more important, however, when we come to the expression "faith of Christ."

Paul now goes on to develop more fully what he means by this good news from and about God. It was a message, we may be surprised to hear, that was "promised beforehand through his prophets in the holy scriptures." The implications of this assertion are considerable. Paul suggests not only that everything in Torah has its goal in Christ, but that because Torah already contained the "word about the Christ," his fellow Jews should have recognized Jesus as the messiah (see 10:4-18). The promise has its fulfillment in the story of Jesus, and Paul proclaims "good news concerning his son" (1:3).

Paul's thumbnail characterization of Jesus in the greeting is thoroughly traditional. Jesus is "descended from David according to the flesh." Although apart from 2 Tim 2:8 Paul does not use this precise expression, he is careful to assert in 9:5 that the messiah is of Jewish descent "according to the flesh," and in Gal 4:4 he notes that "when God sent forth his son he was born of a woman, born under the law." The specific element of Davidic descent is emphasized in other early Christian writings (see Matt 1:1-20; Mark 11:10; Luke 1:27-32; John 7:42; Acts 2:25-34; 13:22-36; Rev 3:7; 5:5; 22:16). Saying that Jesus was "designated/set apart as Son of God in power according to the Spirit of holiness" (1:4) is also somewhat unusual for Paul, for whom it is more characteristic to speak of "God's Son" as one sent into the world (see Rom 8:3; 2 Cor 1:19; Gal 4:4). The connection between Jesus' resurrection and his divine sonship is found more prominently in non-Pauline writings (see, e.g., Luke 20:41; Acts 13:33; Heb 1:5). Couching his description of Jesus in terms less peculiar to him but more broadly attested in the early messianic movement may be deliberate, a *captatio benevolentiae* to assure his readers that this apostle affirms the traditional understanding of the good news (see J. D. G. Dunn, *Romans 1-8* [Word Bible Commentary 38; Waco, Tex.: Word Books, 1988] 4-26).

After his sketch of the good news, Paul turns to the purpose for which he received "grace and apostleship," namely, to bring about "the obedience of faith" among the Gentiles (1:5). He touches here on a distinctive aspect of his own sense of call, that God chose him to spread the message among non-Jews (see Gal 1:16; 2:2; Eph 3:1; Col 1:27; 1 Thess 2:16). In 15:16, he will return to this specific mission, when he asks the Romans to support his plans to work in the West. It is only in this letter that we get some sense of what Paul thought God had in mind by choosing him—the least likely of candidates—to be the one to proclaim a Jewish messiah to peoples who had never known a Jew and had certainly never heard of a messiah. For Paul, his mission is rooted in the "impartiality" of God, a fairness and righteousness that demands of itself a way of making access to God available to all the world's people, even if that means as well shaking the foundations of his recorded commitment to the Jews as his special children (see chapters 9-11).

For the first time in this greeting, Paul uses the term that will come to stand as that means of access for all nations, namely, "faith." In this initial use, faith occurs in combination with and modifies "obedience" (it is one of those tricky genitive constructions I mentioned above). One could translate the phrase as "faithful obedience." But Paul's argument in chapters 3–5 will show that what he means by "faith" is in fact a kind of "obedience." It is better, therefore, to translate the phrase epexegetically as "for that obedience which is faith." That the expression is not casually chosen is indicated by its recurrence at the very end of the letter, where Paul refers to the mystery "made known to all the nations [Gentiles] according to the command of the eternal God, to bring about the obedience of faith" (16:26).

The Thanksgiving (1:8–15)

The thanksgiving is a distinctive feature of the Pauline letter not found in ordinary Hellenistic epistolary practice. Most often, as here, it begins with a statement of thanks to God which leads into the reasons for being grateful. This provides Paul with an opportunity to praise his readers and is thus another form of *captatio*. On two occasions (Ephesians and 2 Corinthians), Paul uses instead the Jewish blessing formula ("Blessed be God"), which in Romans occurs only in shorter prayerful expostulations (1:25; 9:5). He is capable of omitting the thanksgiving altogether when his emotion (Gal 1:6) or desire to deal with business (Titus 1:5) presses on him.

The thanksgiving periods have been closely analyzed with respect to both their form and their functions (see P. Schubert, *The Form and Function of the Pauline Thanksgiving* [Berlin: Töpelmann, 1939]; and P. T. O'Brien, *Introductory Thanksgivings in the Letters of Paul* [Leiden: Brill, 1977]). Such analysis makes clear that, while the thanksgivings are certainly real prayer—and a further indication of the religious character of Paul's correspondence—they are also rhetorically purposeful, enabling Paul to begin his process of persuasion by touching on concerns that he will later develop thematically.

Two aspects of the Romans thanksgiving are noteworthy. The first is that in contrast, say, to 1 Cor 1:4–9, Paul makes no suggestion that the Roman church is in any way deficient or in need of correction. He thanks God for their faith "which is proclaimed in all the world" (1:8; compare 1 Thess 1:7). He thus recognizes the fact that this foundation in the capital city of the empire already has a stature and reputation worthy of its location. When he speaks of wishing to impart to them some spiritual gift, therefore, he quickly amends that to a desire "that we may be mutually encouraged by each other's faith, both yours and mine" (1:12). Although *faith* is to be a major element in the letter, Paul does not begin with the implication that his readers are deficient in it. Rather, the gift he seeks to impart is that of deeper insight into what they already practice.

Second, Paul alludes to his earlier desire to visit the Romans "in order to reap some harvest among you as among the rest of the Gentiles" (1:13). He uses here the word "fruit" (*karpos*), which is precisely the same term he uses in 15:28 with reference to his collection for the saints in Jerusalem: "When therefore I have completed this and have delivered to them this fruit, I shall go on by way of you to Spain." There can be little doubt that Paul has this same collection in mind, or that he had earlier wanted to include the Romans in his circuit of Gentile churches taking part in the collection. In 15:22, Paul indicates that it has been his preaching in the East that prevented him from coming to Rome. But now, he hopes to come, "for I am eager to preach the good news to you also who are in Rome." Paul's language here works to prepare his readers for his later appeal for hospitality and financial support, for he has joined the preaching of the gospel to an expectation of a "harvest" from among them.

The same process of preparing his readers can be detected in Paul's language about his own ministry for God, "whom," he says, "I serve with my spirit in the gospel of his son" (1:9). The English word "serve" translates the Greek *latreuein*, which means "to worship" (see Acts 7:7, 42; 24:14). Paul will use similar "liturgical" language again in 15:16 with reference to his mission: "to be a minister of Christ Jesus to the Gentiles in the priestly service of the gospel of God, so that the offering of the Gentiles may be acceptable." Likewise, in 1:14, he says that he is "under obligation (*opheiletēs*) to both Greeks and Barbarians, both to the wise and the foolish." Paul will use exactly that term (*opheiletēs*) in 15:27, with reference to the obligation of Gentile churches to materially support—through the collection—the Jerusalem church, from which they had received spiritual blessings. These delicate linguistic brush strokes are typical of the way Paul prepares readers for the appeal he later makes to them. He will ask them to join in the "service of worship" of God which is the "offering of the Gentiles" through their support of his Spanish mission. The contrast between Greek and barbarian, foolish and wise, is a shorthand way of indicating "all people," but it also sets up the thematic contrast between the Greek and the Jew that Paul will next make thematic in his thesis statement.

The Thesis (1:16–17)

Romans is distinctive among Paul's letters for having a thesis that will be argued throughout the letter (see K. Grayston, "'Not Ashamed of the Gospel': Rom 1:16a and the Structure of the Epistle," *Studia Evangelica* 2 [1964]: 569-73). The language of the statement is appropriately dense; it will require the rest of the letter to explicate what it contains in compressed form. For the moment, it is important mainly to identify the elements in the statement and their relationship to each other.

Paul begins by stating, "For I am not ashamed of the good news." The connective "for" (*gar*) indicates that the entire argument to follow provides the basis for Paul's expressed eagerness to "preach the good news to you also who are in Rome" (1:15). This is the message he is recommending in order to recommend himself as an apostle. "I am not ashamed" is actually *litotes*, a form of emphasis by understatement. As we shall see, the good news is in truth the ground on which Paul stands to *boast* (3:27; 5:2-3), in contrast to any human accomplishment (compare 1 Cor 1:31; 2 Cor 10:17; Gal 6:13-14).

Present-day readers who find any talk of boasting offensive (and who sometimes find Paul off-putting because of the amount of it he seems to do) should remember the cultural context of the letter. The Mediterranean world was one in which honor and shame were pivotal values that required recognition (see B. J. Malina, *The New Testament World: Insights from Cultural Anthropology* [Louisville: John Knox Press, 1981]). The issue was not whether or not one would boast, but whether there were appropriate grounds for boasting. Thus, Paul will shortly complain that humans did not give God the "glory" that God deserved. Preaching a crucified messiah was not obviously an honorable role (see Heb 12:1-3). Paul is deeply aware of the shock to Hellenistic sensibilities provided by the cross (see 1 Cor 1:18-25; and M. Hengel, *Crucifixion in the Ancient World and the Folly of the Cross*, trans. J. Bowden [Philadelphia: Fortress, 1977]). He therefore begins with the deliberate assertion that *his* boast is in this paradoxical message of strength in weakness.

It is the dimension of strength or power that Paul next addresses. The "good news from God" is not simply verbal. It is what we would call a performative utterance, one that has the capacity to change and transform lives. Paul calls this a "power" (*dynamis*). We all know that a verbal message can have transforming effect, as when someone declares to us, "I love you." But the power Paul attributes to this message from God is deeper and more pervasive than any words exchanged between humans. The claim to have experienced *power* is one of the most characteristic and distinctive made by the first Christians, who saw themselves possessed by the personal and transforming presence of God through the resurrection of Jesus (see L. T. Johnson, *The Writings of the New Testament: An Interpretation* [Philadelphia: Fortress, 1986] 91-97). The power in this message, Paul says, is to "effect salvation" (*eis sōtērian*). His formulation is close to that in 1 Cor 1:18-21 and 2 Cor 1:15.

The theme of salvation is central to Romans. Paul here asserts that it is the entire goal of the message he proclaims (see 5:9–10; 8:24; 9:27; 10:1, 9–10, 13; 11:11, 14, 26; 13:11). The pertinent question is, What does he mean by salvation? Here is a case where later Christian understanding—derived from a variety of sources in addition to all the canonical witnesses—should not be allowed to obscure Paul's own. There is no sign in Romans itself that Paul conceived of "salvation" as something that pertained mainly to individuals or to their respective eternal destinies ("heaven or hell"). I am not suggesting that such a perception would be utterly incompatible with Paul. Indeed, he has clear statements concerning a future life shared with God and Christ (2 Cor 5:1–10; Phil 1:21–26; 1 Thess 4:17). The issue is only whether this is what he means in Romans by *sōtēria*. Careful analysis of his usage in this letter suggests that Paul thinks of salvation here in social rather than individual terms, and that it is something that occurs in this life. In effect, as we shall see especially in Romans 9–11, "salvation" in Romans means something close to "belonging to God's people" (see L. T. Johnson, "The Social Dimensions of *sōtēria* in Paul and Luke-Acts," in *SBL Seminar Papers 1993*, ed. E. H. Lovering [Atlanta: Scholars Press, 1993] 520–36]).

That Paul conceives of salvation in social terms is suggested also by his following statement, that it is for "the Jew first and also the Greek," since these are designations not of individuals but of peoples or ethnic groups. The use of "the Greek" here and in 1:14 is perhaps a bit startling, since we have grown accustomed to think of the distinction as one between Jew and *Gentile* (as in Romans 9–11 and 15), but in fact the Jew–Greek distinction is common in Paul (see 2:9, 10; 3:9; 10:12; 1 Cor 1:22, 24; 12:13; Gal 3:28; Col 3:11). Still, as his later argument will show, Paul does have in mind the extension of salvation (or inclusion within God's people) for all nations. But in addition to the note of universality, this phrase suggests a rootedness in historical particularity: it is to the Jew *first*, and then the Greek. The tension between universality and particularity lies at the heart of the problem Romans addresses, or, better, at the heart of the mystery of God's will that Romans seeks to discern.

The next phrase in the thesis provides the qualifier for inclusion in the saved people: "to every one who has faith." The several dimensions of what Paul means by faith will be discussed in the course of this commentary. For now we need only note that it is a specifically human response to the action and power of God.

The reason the good news itself is a "power for salvation" is that it reveals or manifests or makes known something about God, or, better, makes God known under some aspect. We note that Paul defines the good news not in terms of information about Jesus but in terms of power shown by God. The message of good news not only is from God but is about God. What has happened (within the past twenty-five years!) in the death and resurrection of Jesus reveals the very character of God.

The aspect of God that Paul will argue here is that of righteousness or justice. The Greek noun *dikaiosynē* is polyvalent. In the context of Greek political and ethical theory, justice denoted the proper relationship between members of the city-state and the virtue on the part of the individual that worked for such proper relationships (see G. Schrenk, *"dikaiosynē," TDNT* 2:192-210). Paul's readers, therefore, could correctly hear him as discoursing about God's virtue or attribute of being "just." That it was appropriate for God so to be designated is well attested by the LXX (see, e.g., LXX Pss 7:11; 10:8; 118:137; Jer 12:1; Tob 3:2; 2 Esdras 9:15). Indeed, God's "fairness" is an important part of Paul's argument, spelled out in terms of God's being "without favoritism" in judging humans (see 2:11; 3:22; 11:33-36).

Readers of the LXX could pick up another nuance in Paul's expression "the righteousness of God," which is God's will to "do justice" on the earth by intervening actively in human affairs to establish right relationships where they do not yet exist because of human sin or folly. The translators of the LXX used the word *dikaiosynē* to translate such Hebrew words as *ṣĕdāqâ* and *mišpāṭ* that have those connotations. Thus the Psalmist says of God, "You have done justice in Israel" (Ps 98:4), meaning not simply that God has judged "fairly," but that God has intervened on the side of the poor and lowly against the rich and wicked. Again, the Psalmist says, "in your righteousness give me life" (Ps 118:40). Paul brings these two aspects of *dikaiosynē* together in 3:26 when he says, "he himself is righteous and he makes righteous." In Romans, then, God's righteousness is both an aspect of God's being and a work to which God is committed (see E. Käsemann, "The Righteousness of God in Paul," in *New Testament Questions of Today* [Philadelphia: Fortress, 1969] 168-82).

In 1:16, Paul said that salvation was for all "who believed/had faith." Now, in 1:17, he further qualifies the revelation of God's righteousness through the good news. Unfortunately, he uses an extraordinarily cryptic phrase to do so. The RSV (Revised Standard Version) renders the Greek phrase *ek pisteōs eis pistin* as "through faith for faith." A more literal translation is "out of faith for faith." But what does it mean? Several possibilities can be identified, but it will require the rest of Paul's argument to explicate the phrase adequately. It could be taken as adverbial, "thoroughly faithwise," or "beginning and ending in faith." Read this way, it expresses Paul's conviction that the good news is about faith throughout—it never becomes something else. The problem with this reading is that it reflects what might be called a particularly Protestant fear that "faith" might become "works" (as some erroneously suppose happens in the Letter of James 2:21-24). But that problem is not at issue here; in fact, Paul is eager to show how faith "becomes" a way of life expressed in deeds, without ever ceasing to be faith.

Besides, it is likely that Paul intends a more precise differentiation by the distinction of prepositions, "out of" (*ek*) and "to/for" (*eis*). One possibility is that he is pointing to the dynamic of gift and response. The revelation of God's righteousness begins "out of" God's faithfulness to humans and is adequately answered by their obedient acceptance of that gift. This dialectic of offer and response, we shall see, fits the balanced restatement of the thesis in 3:22 (see K. Barth, *The Epistle to the Romans,* 6th ed., trans. E. C. Hoskyns [London: Oxford University Press, 1933] 41–42).

Building on this gift/response pattern, there is still a third possibility. Paul may be suggesting that God's righteousness is being revealed "out of the faith of Jesus" and "leads to the faith of Christians." I will try to show later that "the faith of the messiah" Jesus is an essential part of God's free gift to humans (see 3:25–26; 5:12–21). It is Jesus' faithful response to God that enables others to respond in the same faithful and obedient way (see 5:18–19).

The thesis statement is concluded by Paul's first citation from Scripture. The text is from the LXX version of Habakkuk 2:4. It is introduced to provide scriptural warrant for the phrase "from faith to faith," because it contains the Greek phrase *ek pisteōs* ("out of faith"). A literal translation of the Hebrew of Habakkuk is, "the righteous shall live by his faith," meaning the person who has faith. The LXX itself, however, has "the righteous one will live out of my faith," meaning God's fidelity. Paul uses the Greek text, but his understanding seems to be closer to the Hebrew. What does the quotation signify in its present context? The RSV translates, "He who through faith is righteous shall live," making the phrase "out of faith" an adjective describing the righteous person. It is also possible to translate *ek pisteōs* adverbially, describing the means by which life is gained: "the righteous person shall live out of (= on the basis of) faith." Whichever rendering seems better, it is clear that Paul's use of the citation here (as in Gal 3:11) establishes a thematic connection between life, righteousness, and faith.

It remains to ask who Paul might have had in mind by "the righteous one." It could be read as a general statement about righteous people. But it is intriguing that he should use the definite article and that Jesus was known in some early Christian circles as *ho dikaios* ("the righteous one"; see Luke 23:47; Acts 3:14; 1 John 2:1), a title that seems to be echoed in Paul's own reference to him in 5:19. If Paul argues that the faith of Jesus is in fact the means by which God makes relationships right between himself and humans, and if it is true that Jesus is the righteous one who "lives" truly with the life of God by virtue of the resurrection, then the Habakkuk citation may not unfairly be taken as a reference to Jesus (see D. A. Campbell,

"Romans 1:17–a *Crux Interpretum* for the *Pistis Christou* Debate," *Journal of Biblical Literature* 113 [1994]: 265–85).

Much of Paul's thesis statement would have sounded familiar to any Jewish readers (or hearers). The connection between human righteousness, faith, and life, after all, is contained in the text of Torah Paul cites and is found in other Jewish literature (see, e.g., 1QpHab 8:1–3, and *b. Mak.* 24a). But there are other elements that would have sounded new. Paul attaches life, faith, and righteousness to a "message of good news from God" that is a "power of salvation" not only to Jews but also to Gentiles. Both the potential inclusiveness of salvation and its being attached to a message about a crucified messiah would at the very least have made some Jewish listeners uneasy. But only the rest of Paul's argument will reveal just how radical and world-transforming his thesis truly is.

FAITHLESS HUMANITY AND THE POWER OF SIN

Romans 1:18–3:20

Immediately after stating his thesis, Paul begins its exposition by means of an *antithesis* in 1:18–3:20. Notice how the opening words of 1:18, "for the wrath of God is being revealed from heaven against all ungodliness," deliberately echoes that in 1:17, "for the righteousness of God is being revealed." The function of the antithesis in a diatribal argument is to demonstrate the thesis by its contrary. Thus, if I want to argue that "every good person is free," then by antithesis I will try to show that "every wicked person is enslaved." In the present case, we look for the antithesis to show the opposite of the power of God for salvation, and it does, by describing the power of sin that enslaves humans.

The question of how to read this section is one of the most difficult in the interpretation of Romans. Two interrelated issues should be touched on before we trace Paul's argument in detail. The first is whether this section represents Paul's own views or is a rhetorical straw position he sets up for demolition. Some scholars find Paul's statements concerning God's judgment according to human deeds (2:5-10) to be incompatible with his own position on righteousness "by faith not works" (for two recent divergent views, see K. R. Snodgrass, "Justification by Grace—to the Doers: An Analysis of the Place of Romans 2 in the Theology of Paul," *New Testament Studies* 32 [1986]: 72-93; and C. L. Porter, "Romans 1:18-32: Its Role in the Developing Argument," *New Testament Studies* 40 [1994]: 210-28). But this is to read Paul through some rather narrow and later theological lenses. There is every reason to think that 2:5-10 represents not only Paul's own view but in fact one of his fundamental premises (compare 1 Cor 7:19, and see H. Boers, "'We who are by Inheritance Jews; not from the Gentiles, Sinners,'" *Journal of Biblical Literature* 111 [1992]: 273-81).

The second issue concerns the truth claims implied by Paul's discourse, which in a sense is another "straw-position" question. Is the portrayal of wretched humanity under God's wrath essentially a *logical* exercise—that is, if the power of God is revealed through the gospel, then is the state of humans apart from the gospel logically wretched? Or is this Paul's perception of the empirical realities of his world, now viewed from the side of his conversion to Christ? Did Paul really perceive the entire Gentile world as one so given over to idolatry that no one could escape the vices described in 1:29–31? Did he regard all philosophers who condemned others' vices as guilty of the same ones (2:1)? Did he think all Jews unworthy of their calling (3:1–24)?

It is perhaps best to conclude that, although Paul would in all likelihood grant the empirical reality of morally upright Jews and Gentiles (which is assumed by 2:14–15, 25), he was nevertheless convinced, in light of the new power that he and his fellow believers had experienced, that the dominant power at work in the world apart from that "good news" was one that enslaved and degraded humans, with the capacity to make even moral behavior relationally skewed. This section of Romans, then, lays out for the reader some of what Paul sees as the basic "rules of the game" concerning relations between God and humans, as well as the way humans have managed to distort the game by their idolatrous turning away from the source of their being.

In terms of the diatribal argument, 1:18–3:20 provides the shadow that makes the light of the good news appear even brighter. Paul will state in 5:8 that God recommended his love toward humans by the fact that while they were still sinners, Christ died for them. Paul's purpose here is less to show a universal condition of humanity than to describe for the people of his own world how the rejection of God leads to destruction and despair. The thesis argues that God's righteousness comes by gift; here he shows how every form of grasping misses the mark.

Attack on Idolatry (1:18–32)

From the time of the prophets, Israel had cultivated a tradition of polemic against idolatry (e.g., Isa 44:9–20), which specifically connected the rejection of the true God with societal disorder. Paul is heir to that tradition. His most obvious influence, however, is the Wisdom of Solomon, written ca. 250 B.C.E., a writing included in the LXX but not in the Hebrew canon. Wisdom contains a sustained attack on Egyptian idolators (chapters 13–19), but expresses some sympathy toward those whose "delight in the beauty" of created things might lead them astray (13:3). Paul is much harsher. For him, "there is no excuse" (1:20; 2:1). The reason is his far deeper grasp of the nature of idolatry as a rebellion of the heart rather than a mistake of the mind. For Paul, idolatry is a disease of human freedom, not failed science. He speaks of humans "suppressing the truth," which suggests a conscious and willful choice.

Before entering into Paul's analysis of idolatry, we should pause for a moment over his use of the term "wrath of God," for it is precisely the sort of expression that would have been instantaneously grasped by Paul's first hearers but seem puzzling and off-putting to present-day readers. The "wrath of God" (*orgē tou theou*) is not a psychological category but a symbol (widely used in Torah) for the retribution that comes to humans as a result of their willful turning away from God; indeed, it is a concept that derives precisely from the prophetic warnings against idolatry (see Isa 51:7; Jer 6:11; 25:25; Hos 13:11; Zeph 1:15). Although it plays a thematic role in Romans (2:5, 8; 3:5; 4:15; 5:9; 9:22; 12:19), it is used elsewhere by Paul as well for the eschatological ("final") threat that looms over those who oppose God. God's wrath is therefore the symbol for the destruction that humans bring on themselves by rebelling against the truth. For those alienated from the ground of their own being, even God's mercy appears as "anger." It is a retribution that results, not at the whim of an angry despot but as the necessary consequence of a self-distorted existence.

Back to Paul's exposition: he begins with the assumption shared by Wis 13:1, that God can be known by humans from the shape of creation: "what can be known about God is plain to them because God has shown it to them" (1:19). Paul is not engaging here in a post-Enlightenment argument for the existence of God "from design." His starting point is completely different. After the Enlightenment, the existence of God seemed like something that was not in the least obvious and required demonstration. For Paul, as for most humans who have lived in the world, the religious sense of the reality of God *is* obvious, simply from the fact of existence itself. The existence of God is not the goal of reason; the existence of God is the premise for right reason. God is not what is left over after everything else has been accounted for; God is what enables anything else to be accounted for.

For Paul, "what can be known about God" is not grasped simply from "creation out there," as in the existence of the cosmos. It is grasped with immediate intuition from the human experience of contingency and dependence. It is *my* world that is experienced as at once empty and full, needy and rich, that is, both contingent and gifted. For Paul, this reality is so obvious that its denial requires a "suppression of the truth" (1:18) that in the fashioning of every human creature "his eternal power and deity has been clearly perceived" (1:20). Therefore, Paul declares, "they are without excuse; for although they knew God they did not honor him as God or give thanks to him" (1:20–21). This is an absolutely critical distinction between knowing and *acknowledging*. To acknowledge God as my creator means to recognize that God has a claim on me that no creature can make, indeed, the ultimate and immediate claim on my very existence. The only proper response, says Paul, is to "give him glory" (in the RSV, "honor him"). In the biblical tradition, to "glorify God" means to recognize or acknowledge the reality of God's presence and power (see LXX Ps 21:23; 85:9; Isa 43:23). Whether or not humans "glorify God" is a major motif running through Romans. In addition to recognizing God's claim, humans should "give thanks to God" for the gift of their creation. Idolatry begins with the refusal of this recognition and of this thanksgiving.

For Paul, then, idolatry begins not in the mind but in the will. It is fundamentally an act of *disobedience*, of failing to "hear responsively" the claim of the creator on one's life. It is from this basic lie about reality, this "suppression of the truth" that idolatry begins its distorting effects. First to go is the capacity to perceive reality truly: "they became futile in their thinking and their senseless minds were darkened" (1:21). What happens is that they begin to perceive the world in the distorted mirror they themselves have constructed: "claiming to be wise they became fools" (1:22).

Paul seems here to be using the tradition of Gen 1:26 that the first humans were created in the "image (*eikōn*) and likeness (*homoiōma*) of God," for he says "they exchanged the glory of the immortal God in the likeness (*homoiōma*) of the image (*eikōn*) of a mortal man" (1:23). We remember that in 1 Cor 11:7 Paul declared the man to be "the image and glory of God" (see M. Hooker, "Adam in Romans 1," *New Testament Studies* 6 [1959–60]: 297–306). Now, that likeness to God, which enabled humans to perceive reality itself in accordance with God's mind, revealed in the shape of creation, has been darkened. Humans who have rejected the creator in order to have the world to themselves end up seeing only a mirror "image" of themselves, a hominized universe. And from this first lie falsehood becomes ever more systemic. The suppression of the one essential truth about humanity falsifies every other relation and every other activity.

Perhaps an extended analogy will help make what I see as Paul's point. The reality of God's presence and power is as inescapable as if someone who is giving a toast at a crowded party should suddenly and noisily collapse and die. Everyone in the room knows what has happened. There is suddenly a dead body in the room. But knowing there is a dead body in the room is the sort of knowledge that calls for acknowledgment; a dead body makes a claim on us. We should call the doctor or the police or the coroner. We should notify relatives. We should grieve and look to our own mortality. The one thing we cannot truthfully do is "suppress the truth" and continue the party as though nothing had happened. If we continue to eat and drink and gossip and dance *while there is a dead body in the room*, we falsify everything we are doing, and we become colluders in that falsification.

Thus does idolatry become systemic as we conspire in the suppression of what each one of us somehow knows to be true.

Paul marks the stages of distortion and degradation resulting from the first great lie by the threefold repetition of the phrase "God handed them over" (1:24, 26, 28). It is clear, however, that God is simply letting happen what their own choices have set in motion. It is because they "exchanged the truth about God for a lie" (1:25) that they "receive in their own persons the due penalty for their error" (1:27). It is in this section that Paul moves from the lusts that lead to "the dishonoring of their own bodies" (1:24) to what he calls the "dishonorable passions" which drive men and women alike to engage in sexual acts with persons of their own gender, acts that Paul calls "exchanging natural (*physikē chrēsis*) relations for unnatural (*para physin*)" (1:26-27).

This is one of the few passages in the Bible that mentions homosexuality (in the New Testament, see only 1 Cor 6:9-11), and it does so in an obviously negative fashion. The passage has, furthermore, played a key role in shaping Christian discourse about homosexuality. Some amount of special attention should be given to it, precisely because the issue of homosexuality is one that all Christians today must engage in a responsible fashion. At the exegetical level, the passage contains little ambiguity. As a Jew, Paul shared his people's ancestral detestation of homosexuality in any form (see Lev 18:22-23), regarding it as a "perversion" (Lev 18:23). As a moral teacher in the cosmopolitan cities of the Greco-Roman world, on the other hand, he could not but have been acquainted with this widespread sexual practice (see E. Cantarella, *Bisexuality in the Ancient World* [New Haven: Yale University Press, 1992]). For purposes of his polemic, homosexuality therefore serves as the perfect example of a specifically *Gentile* vice (universally rejected by Jews; see *The Sentences of Pseudo-Phocylides* 190-92). It could serve, furthermore, as the classic example of how the denial of the "natural" relation of the world to its creator could end in "unnatural" relations among humans. For Paul, finally, there seems to be no question that homosexuality should be considered a vice that is freely chosen because of "a perverted view of the world."

The critical question for present-day Christians is not exegetical but hermeneutical—that is, what to think and do about such passages as these in light of later experience and perception. Is it the case that homosexuality is a vice that is freely chosen? Or is it, as some studies and many people claim, the "natural" mode of sexual expression for a small portion of the world's population? Is homosexuality then, as it seems to Paul, entirely a matter of *porneia* (sexual sin incompatible with the rule of God, 1 Cor 6:9-11), or is it compatible with a chaste and covenantal relationship? These are hard questions, to be sure, and not likely to be answered on the

basis of Scripture texts alone but by a long and difficult process of discernment within the church (see L. T. Johnson, "Debate and Discernment,
Scripture and the Spirit," *Commonweal* 121 [1994]: 11–13).

Two further points can be made briefly about the treatment here in
Romans. First, homosexuality is not the topic but only the illustration. Paul's
topic is the rebellion of humans against God the creator. Whatever the
church decides about this example does not affect the validity of Paul's
argument concerning the distortion of human freedom cut off from its true
roots. Second, it is important to note that Paul does not make homosexuality the ultimate perversion. He moves in 1:29 from sexual immorality to
forms of vice that are far more destructive of persons and human society.

Paul brings his attack on idolatry to a fine rhetorical flourish by using the
common feature of Hellenistic moral teaching called the vice list (see J. T.
Fitzgerald, "Virtue/Vice Lists," *The Anchor Bible Dictionary* [New York:
Doubleday, 1992] 6:857–59). The proper way to read such lists is not to
dwell so much on their individual elements as to assess their overall impact.
Such lists of vices were based on the premise that wicked people tended to
practice all vices, just as good people practiced all the virtues. Philo
Judaeus produced possibly the world's longest vice list—some 140 elements
(*Sacrifices of Cain and Abel* 32)! Although the literary convention of the
vice list cautions us against excessive attention to specific items, one cannot
help in this case noting that the list contains few vices associated with
human weakness, such as drunkenness or lust. The list focuses instead on
the malign and antisocial vices that are often associated with "strong"
people: "insolent, haughty, boastful . . . heartless, ruthless" (1:30). The cold-
hearted vices that seek to do harm to others or build up the self at others'
expense are far worse than vices of weakness that mainly bring distress to
the self. In a fine rhetorical reversal of his starting point (those who knew
God did not give him glory), Paul says of these people, "Although they know
God's decree that those who do such things deserve to die, they not only do
them, but approve of those who practice them" (1:32). This is indeed willful rebellion and disobedience.

The Fairness of God (2:1–16)

We meet another stylistic feature of the diatribe in 2:1, when Paul addresses
an imaginary interlocutor, "You have no excuse, O Man, when you judge
another." The shift to the dialogical style may seem a bit abrupt. Equally surprising is the apparent shift in thought, for Paul connects this warning to
the previous attack on idolatry, "Therefore you are without excuse." What
"Man" (*anthrōpos* = "human being" in Greek) is this, and how is judging a

neighbor continuous with the vice list? It is likely that Paul has in mind here the Hellenistic moral teacher, the sage who purports to identify and condemn the vices of others. Such diagnosis and condemnation were a stock feature of moral teaching carried out by philosophers such as Dio Chrysostom (see *Oration* 32.14–30) and Epictetus (*Discourses* 3.23.30).

But what does Paul mean when he says that "you the judge are doing the very same things"? There are two possibilities. One is the commonplace complaint that those who preached to others did not themselves practice. Satirists such as Lucian of Samosata mocked the disparity between "daytime virtue and nighttime vice," with his brilliant thumbnail sketches of philosophers who were models of sobriety by day but given to drink and lechery at night (see *Timon* 54). This option, however, would be inconsistent with the statement in 1:32 about "approving those who do such things," for the philosophers who practiced vice in private never stopped condemning it in public.

Another possibility seems more likely, which is that judging another (in the sense of condemning them) is itself an act of "insolence, haughtiness, boastfulness" (1:30). The one who stands in judgment on the morality of another asserts a superior status and is in effect engaging in a moral one-upmanship or self-aggrandizement. This seems to make the best sense of Paul's saying, "in passing judgment upon him you condemn yourself," above all because in chapter 14, Paul will return to the problem of judging the neighbor and will once more prohibit it on the ground that no one is in the position to judge "the servant of another," namely, God.

The judgment of God is, in any case, the major point that Paul asserts in this section. That God judges the world is axiomatic for the tradition of Torah (see LXX Deut 32:36; Isa 30:18; 33:22; 63:7; Ps 7:11; 49:6; 67:5; Sir 32:12). Indeed, the concept of God's "righteousness" finds its home in just this forensic context of God's judgment of the world (see LXX Ps 9:4, 8; 66:4; 71:2). God is judge because God is creator. Because God has "maker's knowledge" of all the world and above all of that secret place which is the human heart (see Jer 17:9–10), God alone can judge the world with justice and "judge the secrets of people" (Rom 2:16). For Paul, the reality of God's judgeship is as obvious and vivid as God's creating the world out of nothingness at every moment: "Do you suppose . . . you will escape the judgment of God?" (2:3).

The concept of God as judge is difficult for some people. Perhaps influenced by memories of parental disapproval, they find it too harsh and negative to be associated with a loving God. Properly understood, however, God's judgeship is one of the most profoundly liberating of all theological concepts. Deep in the human heart, after all, is the fear of not ever being truly known, and if not truly known, then also not truly being real. How comforting it is (and yes, also how frightening) to know that the one who creates us also knows us utterly. And this is simply what God's judgment means: God's knowing humans through and through. Paul in fact emphasizes the "richness of [God's] kindness and forbearance and patience" with humans (2:4). God does not rush to condemnation. Again, we see in 2:5 that Paul speaks not of God's anger toward humans but rather of "the wrath you are storing up *for yourself* on the day of judgment," because of a "hard and impenitent heart" (2:5). Paul presents no harsh "hanging judge." Indeed, the final word of God to humans, as we shall see, is one of mercy (11:32; 15:9); God is a loving and loyal creator who hopes that all creatures will come to the truth. But God's mercy is meaningless if God does not know humans in all their frailty, and God cannot save if God does not judge sin.

Paul's central point here is that God's judgment is absolutely fair, since it is based on no considerations apart from what humans themselves do: "He will render to each person according to that person's works" (2:6). The term "works" here means what it does most of the time in Paul's letters, namely, "deeds." Paul's statement places him squarely among ancient moral teachers who insisted that it was not holding the right opinions or saying the right things that counted morally, but rather doing the right things (see Seneca, *Moral Epistles* 20.1; Plutarch, *On Stoic Self-Contradictions* 1 [*Mor.* 1033B]). Thus, God will reward with eternal life those who "seek for glory and honor and immortality" in well doing (2:7), just as there will be wrath and fury "for those who are factious and do not obey the truth but obey wickedness" (2:8). Note, please, the emphasis on obedience and disobedience, here, and on "the truth," which continues the line of thought begun in 1:18.

Paul makes the point of God's fairness explicitly in 2:9–11: "everyone" who does either good or evil will be rewarded or punished accordingly, "for God shows no partiality" (RSV). The term "partiality" translates *prosōpolēmpsia*. It is a term unknown in Greek before the New Testament, where it is found in several cognates (see Jas 2:1, 9; Acts 10:34; Eph 6:9; Col 3:25). It is a neologism based on the LXX phrase *prosōpon labein* (literally, to "receive a face"), which translates the Hebrew *nāśā' pānîm* in Lev 19:15: "You shall do no injustice in judgment; you shall not be partial to the poor or defer to the great, but in righteousness you shall judge your neighbor." Notice that "impartiality" is the fundamental expression of "righteousness" in the context of judging. In the human courts of Israel, it meant, in effect, not to be swayed by appearances, either of the poor or of the rich, but to judge entirely on the merits of the case. The "impartial" judge was righteous because he could not be bribed or corrupted. This human ideal is projected as an intrinsic quality of God as judge: "there is no partiality with God," since he deals with humans entirely on the basis of the deeds that they have done. Paul has here enunciated a fundamental premise that will run throughout the letter (see J. Bassler, *Divine Impartiality: Paul and a Theological Axiom* [SBLDS 59; Chico, Calif.: Scholars Press, 1981]).

All this is fine in the abstract, but Paul gives it a distinctive—and to his Jewish readers perhaps a disturbing—application to specific social realities. God's fairness in punishing the wicked applies "to the Jew first and then the Greek," as does his rewarding of the good deeds, "to the Jew first and also the Greek." Paul has extended the range of God's impartiality to all peoples. The effect of this, as he will next make clear, is to relativize the status of being a Jew. What's the sense of being one of "the chosen" if it does not ultimately matter? Paul is going to suggest that being a member of this people is one of those "appearances" to which God pays no attention in his judgment of human deeds.

Paul continues to play on the Jew/Greek distinction in 2:12–16, making the relative character of the specific revelation to the Jews even more obvious, by placing Jew and Gentile on the same footing before God. Jews who have been given the law, which tells them what they are to do, are not benefited unless they actually do what the law commands: "It is not the hearers of the law who are righteous before God, but the doers of the law who will be declared righteous" (2:13). Paul has hereby stripped away any claim to special standing Jews might have had on the basis of their ethnic heritage or even the possession of Torah. Paul speaks of Torah here in its function of providing behavioral norms, but knowing these norms does not replace observing them. In fact, the Gentiles—most of whom had never heard of Torah—are no worse off. They too have a guide to proper behavior in the "law written in their hearts," which is made known to them by their conscience bearing witness to the rightness or wrongness of their deeds (2:15). Philo also could speak of the patriarchs, who lived long before Torah was revealed on Sinai, as being *nomoi empsychoi* ("ensouled laws") because of the virtues they demonstrated in their lives (see, e.g., *On Abraham* 1.5).

It is clear, then, that Paul recognizes the possibility of Gentiles living morally upright lives, even in the context of a sinful world. Otherwise, he would have no basis for positing a Gentile with an "approving conscience." (For an opposing view, see J. W. Martens, "Romans 2:14–16: A Stoic Reading," *New Testament Studies* 40 [1994]: 55–67). In the *Discourses* of Epictetus, we also find the concept of an internal "governing principle" that acts as an inner guide to right behavior, even when that determination may be contrary to society's norms or expectations (see, e.g., 1.15.4; 1.26.15; 2.18). For Paul, this inner guide is of fundamental importance; in 1 Cor 8:9–10, the individual's conscience (*syneidēsis*) determines the very moral character of an action, and he returns to the same principle in Rom 14:22–23.

Two further aspects of 2:1–16 are worth noting. Both show Paul's language shifting from that of moral behavior to religious response. First, Paul introduces in 2:12 the concept of *sin*: "all who have sinned without the law will perish without the law, and all who have sinned under the law will be judged by the law." Although the cognates *hamartanein/hamartia* in wider Greek usage could mean simply to "miss the mark" or "make an error," Paul follows the LXX's understanding of "sin" as an offense against God, an act of disobedience, a breaking of covenantal obligation (see W. Grundmann, "*hamartanō*," *TDNT* 1:267–316). In short, sin is considered to be the rupture of a *personal* relationship, not simply a moral failure (see, e.g., Exod 10:16; 23:33; Deut 1:41; 9:16; and, above all, Ps 50:4, "against you alone I have sinned"). It is perhaps not accidental that language about sin enters just as Paul begins to use language about *law*, for it is when a law is given forbidding something that the deed in question becomes disobedience against a lawgiver. This makes it all the more interesting that Paul can speak of the "sin" of Gentiles without the law. The voice of conscience is taken to be equivalent to a "law written in the heart," that is, a norm placed there by *God* the creator, the rejection of which is also disobedience. Paul will very shortly make some important distinctions, but for now we note as significant that sin and law are religious and not simply moral categories.

Second, we observe that Paul brings in the figure of Jesus as judge in 2:16: "on that day when, according to my gospel, God judges the secrets of men by Christ Jesus." By so doing, he once more aligns himself with a broad conviction in earliest Christianity, that Jesus would be the eschatological judge of the living and the dead (see, e.g., Jas 5:8–9; Heb 9:28; 12:23–24; Rev 20:11–13; Acts 17:31; Matt 25:31–46; John 5:28–29). Paul will return to the theme of God and Jesus as judge in 14:3, 9–11.

The Advantage of the Jew (2:17–3:8)

The Jews among Paul's hearers would have thoroughly enjoyed the lambasting of Gentile idolatry and philosophy, but in the last few verses, may have worried that the edge of criticism would soon be turned in their direction. Certainly that had been the pattern of the classical prophets, who had followed the denunciation of "the nations" with a withering attack on Israel itself (see, e.g., Amos 1:3–3:15). Paul shows himself heir to that prophetic tradition. In 2:17, he engages another imaginary interlocutor, this time one who styles himself as a Jew (2:17). Stowers makes a good case that Paul presents him as a stereotyped figure in Greco-Roman moral teaching, the *alazōn* ("braggart"), or, as Stowers characterizes him, "the pretentious person" (*A Rereading of Romans: Justice, Jews, and Gentiles* [New Haven: Yale University Press, 1994] 101–2; 145–50). Masters of the diatribe such as

Epictetus would skewer the pretensions of the would-be philosopher who was all talk and no performance (see Epictetus, *Discourses* 2.21.11-12; 2.19.19; 3.7.17; 3.24.40-43). In this case, Paul allows the Jewish interlocutor to recite a number of reasons to boast—with which Paul himself agrees!—before puncturing his pomposity with a series of rhetorical questions that drive home his point about God's impartiality to both Jew and Greek.

The list of claims in 2:17-20 amounts to the first of Paul's three encomiastic acknowledgments of the privileges of the Jews (see also 3:1-4; 9:4-5). In the present case, the list of claims is put in the mouth of "one who calls himself a Jew": (1) he relies on the law; (2) he boasts in God; (3) he knows God's will; (4) he tests what should be done; (5) he is instructed in the law; (6) he is a guide to the blind; (7) he is a light to those in darkness; (8) he is a corrector of the foolish; (9) he is a teacher of children; (10) he has in the law the very form of knowledge and truth. Paul does not dispute these claims, and, living within the symbolic world of Torah, he hardly could: such affirmations are found throughout Scripture (see, e.g., LXX Psalm 118). We notice how all these claims cluster around one basic one, and that is the possession of Torah itself! It is Torah that gives knowledge and enables Jews to instruct the world in what God wants. And on the basis of Torah, Jews could "boast in God," for God gave Torah only to them. In contrast to the foolish Gentiles, who perceive the world in perverted ways, and in contrast to the sincere pagans, who must rely on the subtle promptings of conscience, the Jews have "the very form of knowledge and truth" to guide them and others into righteousness.

Paul turns on this apparently obvious and benign boast with a startling series of rhetorical questions that make clear how knowledge without performance is useless and perhaps even dangerous. Knowledge of the truth makes the failure to practice the truth even more reprehensible. The Jew who has been given God's clear instruction not to commit adultery, yet does so, rebels against God in a more obvious and shocking fashion than the poor Gentile who is confused about "natural and unnatural relations" (2:21-22a). Paul even turns the Jews' contempt for idolators on them: "you who abhor idols, do you rob temples?" (2:22)—a nice way of distinguishing religious orthodoxy and moral rectitude.

His final charge could be punctuated either as a question or as a statement: "you who boast in the law dishonor God by breaking the law" (2:23). Paul rhetorically joins the note of "boasting" from 2:17 to the "dishonoring" of God that was associated with *idolatry* in 1:21. He cites Isa 52:5 in support of his assertion: "the name of God is blasphemed among the nations because of you" (2:24). We will observe again how carefully Paul has read this section of Isaiah. The charge contained in the citation, however, could not be more serious. Torah had been given to the Jews so that the nations might be attracted to the one true God. It was Israel who was first told, "I have set you to be a light for the Gentiles, that you may bring salvation to the uttermost parts of the earth" (Isa 49:6). It does not matter if Jews know Torah or boast in it. But if they do not keep it, they bring dishonor to the God who revealed it (see H. Moxnes, "Honor and Righteousness in Romans," *Journal for the Study of the New Testament* 32 [1988]: 61–77). The Gentiles who observe that Jewish behavior is no better than their own can legitimately conclude that the Jewish God is not superior to their own, and indeed is more ludicrous for having such exalted claims made in his behalf. To "blaspheme God's name" is, in effect, the opposite of "giving God glory." The damage done by Jews who do not keep Torah, Paul suggests, is not simply to themselves or to each other but to the honor of God!

The symbol of circumcision provides Paul the chance to make his point about the importance of practice rather than profession. As a physical act, circumcision is the cutting of the male foreskin. As a ritual act, it was the sign of inclusion in God's people. As a symbol, it signified a commitment to keeping Torah (see Gen 17:10, 26; 21:4; Exod 4:25; 12:44; Lev 12:3; Deut 10:16; Josh 5:2; Luke 1:59; Acts 7:8; 15:1; 16:3; 1 Cor 7:18; Gal 5:2–3; 6:12–13). Paul will recognize circumcision as the sign of Abraham's being "father of the Jews" in 4:11. But now he claims that the Jew who breaks the law in effect loses his circumcision (2:25). Paul here redefines membership in God's people in terms of religious commitment and not in terms of physical descent or ethnic ethos: "For neither circumcision counts for anything nor uncircumcision, but keeping the commandments of God" (1 Cor 7:19). It follows from this that Gentiles who *keep* the law (even unwittingly) are inwardly true Jews (2:26). Paul locates membership in the people not in external ritual but in the orientation of the heart and the actions that flow from that orientation: "He is a Jew who is one inwardly, and real circumcision is a matter of the heart, spiritual and not literal" (2:29).

Paul's assertion would not have seemed utterly strange to Philo Judaeus, who emphasized the universal moral realities signified by ritual commandments (see, e.g., *Sacrifices of Cain and Abel* 1–11). Philo would never have called for a stop to circumcision, however, and he in fact severely criticized his fellow Jews whose liberalism led them to abandon circumcision (*Migration of Abraham* 89–93). Nor is there any indication that Paul thought that Jews should not be circumcised. His point is not that circumcision is bad, but that it is useful only if it corresponds to a faithful response to God in obedience (2:25). Then a person's "praise is not from humans but from God." On the other hand, if circumcision is not the outward sign of a genuinely inner obedience to God, then it is only a show, a form of empty and arrogant boasting.

Once having established the absolute equality of Jew and Gentile before

God–for judgment will be based on nothing other than what they have done–Paul must turn to the most obvious and pressing question for a Jew like himself: "What advantage has the Jew? Or what is the value of circumcision?" (3:1). This question, in fact, begins a series of questions in 3:1-8. Paul does not in this section enter into a sustained answer to any of them, but uses this rapid-fire set of questions and answers as a way of anticipating his fuller response to them after the demonstration of his thesis. Thus, Paul's immediate and reflexive answer to the question concerning the advantage of the Jew is "much in every way." But he contents himself for the moment with declaring that they "have been entrusted with the oracles of God," by which he means all that is contained in the writings of Torah. This is the same "advantage" that Paul has been asserting implicitly since 2:12. In 9:4-5, he will go on to spell out in greater detail what gifts come with Torah: not only the "words of God" are there recorded but also all the powerful acts that come under the rubric of the "word of God" in the prophetic tradition.

Paul's second question also points forward to chapters 9-11: "What if some of them were unfaithful? Does their faithlessness nullify the faithfulness of God?" (2:3). This question cuts to the heart of monotheistic faith: Is God reliable and trustworthy, or not? If there is evil in the world (faithlessness), does this show that God is powerless or that God is evil? The issue is scarcely abstract for Paul or concerned only with the infidelities of his people in the distant past. The experience pressing on him is what he perceives as the present apostasy of his own people because of their failure to recognize Jesus as messiah (9:33-10:4). What does this signify for God's ability to control history, or–even harder–his character as a reliable God? In 9:6, Paul will deny that "God's word has failed" and will try to demonstrate that position. In the present context, he contents himself with the diatribal response "by no means," a sharp rejoinder based on LXX Ps 15:2, "let God be true though every human be false," and an explicit citation from LXX Ps 50:6, "that you may be justified in your words and prevail when you are judged." These are words the psalmist addresses to God after acknowledging, "I have sinned against you alone." In other words, it is unthinkable that God should either be powerless or perverse. We must look for the fault on the side of humans.

That response, however, opens the door to still another difficulty. If human failure works to show God's righteousness–if God is all-powerful and good, and uses human sin to achieve good ends–then isn't God unjust in another way if he still punishes sinners? As Paul asks, "If through my falsehood God's truthfulness abounds to his glory, why am I still being condemned as a sinner?" (3:7). Please note here how Paul shifts to the first person singular. We will meet this again in chapter 7 and will need to discuss what to make of this style of writing. In the present case, it is obvious that Paul is using the first person simply as a rhetorical device. He could as easily say "anybody." The question asks whether God might be playing something of a sick game with human freedom. It is a problem in theodicy that has both fascinated and frustrated thinkers in the three great monotheistic traditions of Judaism, Christianity, and Islam: How can God's omnipotence and human freedom not cancel each other out? Paul will return to the question in 9:14-23.

He puts still another twist to the question by pushing it to a logical reduction: "Why not do evil that good may come?" (3:8). Paul recognizes that this is a charge that some people are slanderously making against him—that he is somehow encouraging people to become sinners in order to increase God's mercy. Some hint of that charge might be detected in Gal 2:17, when Paul asks, "If, in our effort to be justified in Christ, we ourselves were found to be sinners, is Christ then an agent of sin?" The problem was that, for Jews, Jesus really *was* a sinner, certified as such by the fact that his death was one cursed by Torah (Deut 21:23; Gal 3:13). To associate oneself with *this* "Christ" looked dangerously like associating oneself with sin. Paul deals with one side of this question in 6:1 ("Are we to continue in sin so that grace may abound?") and 6:15 ("Are we to sin because we are not under the law but under grace?"). His answer is emphatically in the negative. The deeper issue of how God works with human sinfulness in order to bring about mercy, Paul confesses at the end of his long argument in chapters 9-11 to be simply a "mystery" (11:25-36).

Humanity under Sin (3:9-20)

Paul's next question is extraordinarily difficult to interpret, not only because its text and punctuation are uncertain but also because Paul's use of language is obscure (see N. A. Dahl, "Romans 3:9: Text and Meaning," in *Paul and Paulinism*, ed. M. D. Hooker and S. G. Wilson [London: SPCK, 1982] 184-204). The introductory question "What then" is common in diatribes and serves to suggest that the next statement will respond to what has gone before (see 3:1; 4:1; 6:1, 15; 7:7; 8:31; 9:14, 30; 11:7). The next word is the most problematic, since Paul's use is unusual. The most obvious way to translate it is as "Are we excelled/surpassed?" But whom does Paul mean by "we"? The immediate grammatical antecedent would be himself, since he had just made reference to the slander made against him (3:8). But this is unlikely, since Paul places himself within the "thesis" of God's gracious gift (5:1-12), and not within the "antithesis" here being developed. The "we," then, must refer to the Jews, since they are the subject established in 3:1.

The natural way to read the question now would be, "Are we Jews excelled/surpassed?"—presumably by the Gentiles, who would now have the advantage. Paul's response, however, is not clear either, since it could be read as "not at all" or "not entirely." The RSV translation tilts the issue against the logic of the grammar, by posing the question this way, "What then, are we Jews any better off?" and then translating the response as, "No, not at all." This translation actually reverses the ordinary meaning of *proechesthai* and relies heavily on a certain understanding of the flow of the argument (see S. Stowers, "Paul's Dialogue with a Fellow Jew in Romans 3:1-9," *Catholic Biblical Quarterly* 46 [1984]: 707-22).

A final resolution appears impossible. Fortunately, Paul's following words do throw some light on his intended meaning, for he places Jews and Greeks once more on equal footing, "we have already charged that all humans, both Jews and Greeks, are under sin" (3:9). Whether 3:9a appears to "give advantage" either to Jew or Greek, therefore, is irrelevant, for 3:9b places them both firmly in the same place. What the entire sequence of 3:1-9 seems to suggest, then, is that although the Jews have been gifted with Torah, this gift has not given them any edge with regard to pleasing God, for it has not kept them from falling into the same pattern of faithlessness and rebellion as the Gentiles.

In 3:10-18, Paul adduces a *catena* ("chain") of Scripture citations in support of his charge that "all humans are under sin." Such discrete passages, gathered together to illustrate or demonstrate some point with the authority of Torah, can be found both in contemporary Judaism (see, e.g., 4QFlorilegium) and in other early Christian writings (see, e.g., 1 Pet 2:6-8; Heb 1:5-14). The present *catena* is particularly dense and complex, drawing from LXX Qoh 7:20 (3:10); Ps 52:3-4 (3:11); Ps 13:1, 3 (3:12); Ps 5:10 (3:13a); Ps 139:4 (3:13b); Ps 9:28 (3:14); Isa 59:7 and Prov 1:16 (3:15-17); Ps 35:2 (3:18) (see L. E. Keck, "The Function of Rom 3:10-18: Observations and Suggestions," in *God's Christ and His People: Studies in Honour of Nils Alstrup Dahl,* ed. J. J. Jervell and W. A. Meeks [Oslo: Universitetsforlaget, 1977] 141-57).

Such *catenae* are usually organized thematically or by means of word linkage. Here the phrase "there is not one" is repeated five times in 3:10-12, and once more at the end (3:18). Paul may in fact have added one or another instance to the original text of the LXX. The function of these particular lines is to assert the universality of sin according to Torah: "there is not one who is righteous" being equivalent to "everyone is unrighteous." In searching for a reason for including the other verses, we notice that mention is made in succession of throat, tongue, lips, mouth, feet, and eyes. These refer to parts of the body, from top to bottom. The point, then, may simply be that sin is both universal and total, that is, encompassing all human activities.

Paul had shown in 1:18–32 that Gentiles were "under sin." As for the inclusion of Jews, "we know that whatever the law says it speaks to those who are under the law" (3:20). Jews above all fall within the range of the charges made by these texts. Paul adds a purpose clause, "so that every mouth may be stopped and the whole world may be held accountable to God." The effect of Paul's entire argument from 3:1 has been to insist on God's role as righteous judge, with all blame for wrongdoing to be attributed to humans. The *catena* of verses has demonstrated just that point. But by making this statement, Paul is also asserting that both Jew and Gentile are, in fact, responding to the same God, who is One. The positive side of that conviction we will find stated in 3:29.

Paul's final statement in 3:20 is very difficult: "because no human being will be justified [= declared righteous] in his sight on the basis of the works of the law [literally, 'out of works of law']." We can see that Paul has adapted another Psalm verse, this time from LXX Ps 142:2, which reads, "Do not enter into judgment with your servant, for no living being will be declared righteous before you." By choosing this psalm to quote, Paul has already anticipated a transition to the restatement of his thesis, for those able to catch intertextual echoes, since the psalm goes on to emphasize that God's righteousness will accomplish what human weakness cannot: "In thy faithfulness answer me, in thy righteousness" (142:1) (see R. B. Hays, "Psalm 143 and the Logic of Romans 3," *Journal of Biblical Literature* 99 [1980]: 107–15).

Paul has changed the wording of the verse to which he alludes: "no living being" becomes "no flesh," and he adds the critical words "on the basis of works of the law." By so doing, he has complicated things, for at first sight the statement flatly contradicts 2:13, where Paul declared that "the doers of the law will be justified." This is the reason some interpreters find it impossible to think of this section as representing Paul's own views.

It may also be, however, that Paul intends a careful distinction between "doers of the law" and "on the basis of works of the law" (*ex ergōn nomou*). I suggest this because Paul will clearly state in 8:3 that those empowered by the Spirit will "fulfill the just requirement of the law." Furthermore, we shall have to see how Paul contrasts "on the basis of works" and "on the basis of faith" in order to resolve this tension. In the meantime, Paul adds to the confusion by declaring, "because knowledge of sin is through the law." The syntax tells us that Paul intended this statement to clarify the previous one. And I have already pointed out that a commandment can make wrongdoing explicit and turn it into a personal rebellion (= sin). But the further development of this point also—which is really the whole question concerning the problem of the law—must await the discussion of Romans 7.

Summary

This section of Romans has been both dense and filled with difficult concepts. It may be helpful to provide an interpretive summary here, to prepare for our reading of the next part of Paul's argument, which is the restatement of his thesis in 3:21-31. Although the word itself does not occur until 2:12, Paul's real topic in the present section has been *sin*. It is important to clarify, to the extent that we can, what Paul means by sin and why he sees it as the antithesis of faith.

We can begin by observing that, as Paul speaks of it, sin is not a moral category but a religious one. The distinction is of fundamental importance. He does not suggest that every pagan was lost in vice or that every Jew is incapable of virtue. Both Jews and Greeks can be virtuous—they can do good deeds. Immorality may be a result and sign of sin, but it is not itself sin.

As Paul uses the concept, sin has to do with the human relationship with God—or, better, with the breaking of the human relationship with God. In this sense, the opposite of sin is not virtue but faith. Sin and faith are, for Paul, the two basic options available to human freedom vis-à-vis the power and presence of God. Paul makes the disjunction explicit in 14:23—"Whatever is not out of faith (*ek pisteōs*) is sin (*hamartia*)"—but it is presumed throughout. Paul uses the singular *hamartia* for the same reason. It is a matter not of "sinful acts" but of a fundamental disposition of human freedom, a basic rebellion of the will against God.

That is why Paul's appropriate starting point is the analysis of idolatry in 1:18-32. Jews thought of idolatry as a matter of worshiping the wrong gods, and therefore something that only Gentiles could do. Paul thought more deeply on the matter. He saw that idolatry was a disease of human freedom, found as widely among Jews as among Gentiles. Idolatry begins where faith begins, in the perception of human existence as contingent and needy. But whereas faith accepts such contingency as also a gift from a loving creator from whom both existence and worth derive, idolatry refuses a dependent relationship on God. It seeks to establish one's own existence and worth apart from the claim of God by effort and striving ("works") of one's own.

Later, Paul will use the striking expression "the flesh" (*sarx*) and speak of "life according to the flesh" (7:5, 18, 25; 8:3-7). He means by flesh the measurement of life apart from spirit, and specifically apart from the Holy Spirit of God. It is life in denial of transcendence, a life lived on the basis of perceived reality, taken as a closed system. Seeking to establish one's own life and worth within such a framework requires boasting and arrogance. It demands competition and hostility toward others. The reason is simple. Since life as a *gift* is rejected, then life on one's own terms must be by means of having or possessing. I am insofar as I have, own, can claim, "this is mine." And since I view the world as a closed system, there is only so much "having" available. I am inevitably in competition with other humans for life and worth. My self-aggrandizement must be at another's expense. Rivalry, envy, hatred, and murder are the logical expressions of the idolatrous impulse, for the "need to be" that derives from the refusal of the first gift is an endless hunger, an unslakable thirst.

What appears under the form of boasting and haughtiness and arrogance as "strength," however, is what Paul rightly calls the "weakness of the flesh." Idolatry begins in fear, the terror of non-being that is rooted in contingency and non-necessity. In order to overcome that fear, idolatry must ceaselessly labor to control the world and to acquire it as possession. To seek self in created things, however, is to distort everything. That which we make ultimate grows distended and monstrous, for creatures cannot bear the weight of worship. And the idolator becomes enslaved, for only constant effort and service can construct a self on the ground of nothingness. Most destructively of all, relationships are distorted, because everything becomes a means to a single end, namely, my advancement.

Essential to Paul's perception of idolatry as a disease of human freedom is the way it can manifest itself not only in the obvious forms of acquisitiveness—the pursuit of pleasure or possessions or power, as a means of asserting that "I am"—but also far more subtly in what can be taken as "good" behavior. Such is the moral rectitude that exercises a more refined sort of competition. Now one's "virtue" becomes the possession by which superiority is asserted over another. And, in the ultimate distortion, even one's relationship with the true God can be poisoned by the idolatrous impulse, as when I presume to bribe God by my good behavior.

I hope the reader understands that I am using "idolatry" as an analytic concept. I am well aware that Paul does not use this term! But there are good reasons to think that Paul would find the term useful, and why I use it. The first is that Paul in 1:18–32 is clearly and deliberately employing the conventional Jewish polemic against idolatry. The second is that Paul himself distinguishes between "the flesh" and "sin," even though they are related. And it is to get at this distinction that I am using the term "idolatrous impulse," for in my reading this comes close to what Paul is getting at when he speaks of "life according to the flesh."

Where, then, does "sin" come into play? In one sense, everything I have been describing fits under Paul's sense of the human populations "under sin" (3:9). So "idolatry" is part of that rebellion against God, indeed at the heart of it. In Paul's usage, however, "sin" tends to carry with it more of a note of consciousness and deliberation. If, to borrow Freudian terms, idolatry can be seen as the impulse of the id, sin has something of the calculation of the ego, what Paul terms "the hard and impenitent heart" (2:5). Sin can be considered the potentiation of idolatry through consciousness, or the choice of idolatry even when presented with an option.

Paul's argument here, then, has been that "sin" has become such a pervasive and powerful distortion of the human world that no one can escape its influence: all are in one way or another "under sin." A person locked into the idolatrous impulse can make even morality, even the observance of God's commandments, an expression of sin, by using it to assert the self over others. Virtue therefore can actually become a possession that is claimed as one's own and used as a source of boasting over one who is wicked. But such a condemning judgment is itself the expression of hostility and a sign of sin (2:1–3). Observance of God's commands also can be the source of boasting (2:23), even a means of trying to bribe God for a reward (11:25).

Precisely these last remarks, however, call for an important qualification. It is of the first importance to assert at this point that Paul has said nothing about Judaism as a religion. He will in fact affirm in as many ways as he can the validity and greatness of God's revelation through Torah. Law is not the problem. The problem is a disease of the human spirit that can distort even God's good gifts. Paul writes from the side of one who considers himself to have been given the greatest of those gifts, "the love of God poured into our hearts through the Holy Spirit" (5:5), and it is from that perspective that he thinks through what impulse there is in humans that can enable them to resist and even reject such gifts (see E. P. Sanders, *Paul and Palestinian Judaism: A Comparison of Patterns of Religion* [Philadelphia: Fortress, 1977]).

It would be a fundamental mistake to think that Paul is adjudicating religious systems, declaring Judaism inferior to a new religion called Christianity, as though Judaism were a "religion of law" and Christianity a "religion of grace/Spirit." These are caricatures drawn by later theological polemics. Paul never calls himself a Christian. He is a Jew from beginning to end. He seeks the *plērōma* ("fullness") of his people as an eschatological hope. And he will declare that the first thing the power of the Holy Spirit enables "those weakened by the flesh" to do is "fulfill the just requirement of the law" (8:3)! Rather, Paul is trying to show the consequences of God's giving an entirely new gift in Christ and how that gift enables a new perception of both Jews and Gentiles in their relationship to God and to each other.

Paul has sketched a power at work among humans that is virtually personified. Sin is presented in almost mythical terms as a monarch ruling over humans (3:9; 5:21; 6:12). For Paul, human beings are always in obedience to some greater power, whether it is that of idolatry and sin or of the true God (see 6:15–23). Sin makes a real claim over humans demanding their allegiance (6:20; 7:23). Its power is not one that will be ceded but one that must be broken (6:7; 8:10). Paul knows that if a greater power can break through, then the human capacity to achieve genuine freedom can be realized through what he calls the "obedience of faith." The question, of course, is, How can God get through? Once humans have so locked themselves into a world that systemically denies the reality of God, how can God get in? That will be the good news to which Paul now returns.

GOD'S FAIRNESS REVEALED IN JESUS' FAITH

Romans 3:21–31

Having shown by his antithesis that "the wrath of God is being revealed against the wickedness of humans who suppress the truth" (1:18) and that "all people, both Jews and Greeks, are under sin" (3:9), Paul can now return to his thesis, beginning with a restatement of it. We can expect to find in 3:21–26 basically the same points as in 1:16–17, but more clearly and fully displayed. Then, in 3:27–31, Paul provides a transition to the positive demonstration of the thesis by a series of questions, answers, and propositions. The reader begins to get a sense of why Paul is "not ashamed" of the good news (1:16) and is eager to "proclaim the good news also to those in Rome" (1:15), for the message he bears is awesome in its implications.

The Thesis Restated (3:21–26)

Recognizing the role it plays in the diatribal argument is the most important key to interpreting this passage. As the restatement of the thesis, it serves both to respond to the condition elaborated by the antithesis (that "all have fallen short of the glory of God") and to explicate the dimensions of the good news that were expressed so compactly in 1:16–17. In its present form, the passage is clearly and completely the result of Paul's fashioning. Whether some portion of it may have had some antecedent form is of less importance. It has been suggested, for example, that the basic lines of the passage, dealing with the death of Christ, represent a pre-Pauline tradition, into which Paul has inserted his distinctive teaching on the significance of faith (see B. F. Meyer, "The Pre-Pauline Formula in Rom 3:25–26a," *New Testament Studies* 29 [1983]: 198–208). This theory is similar to the one holding that Paul made alterations to traditional hymns in passages such as Phil

50

2:5-11 (see G. Bornkamm, "On Understanding the Christ Hymn, Phil 2:6-11," in *Early Christian Experience* [New York: Harper & Row, 1969] 112-22) and Col 1:15-20 (see B. Vawter, "The Colossians Hymn and the Principle of Redaction," *Catholic Biblical Quarterly* 33 [1971]: 62-81). But language like that in 3:25 is scarcely foreign to Paul or outside his range. Despite being fuller than 1:16-17, the passage is still dauntingly dense, demanding of the reader approaches from several angles.

We can begin by noting the overall points Paul wants to establish, before turning to a more detailed discussion of the role assigned to Jesus and to Jesus' faith.

1. Paul emphasizes that this is something *God* is doing, in sharp contrast to the "doings of humans" that he has enumerated in 1:18-3:20. God is the subject of this action, this good news. It is *God's* righteousness that is being manifested (3:21), *God* who is the giver of grace as a gift (3:23), *God* who puts forward Jesus as an expiation (3:25), *God's* righteousness that is shown by his forbearance of past sins (3:25) and the making of people righteous in the present (3:26). The good news, once more, is not simply a message *from* God but a message *about* God's work in the world.

2. God's action reveals who God is. When Paul declares in 3:22 that "there is no distinction," he echoes the principle enunciated in 2:11, "with God there is no partiality." The same holds true both for judging and for gifting. God is fair to all creatures. Likewise, God's action not only "makes them righteous" but "shows that he is righteous" (3:26). Here is the basis for doing theology: just as from the shape of creation one can "know God," so from human experiences in time, one can hope to trace the lines of God's very nature.

3. Paul stresses the contemporary character of God's revelation. He begins with "but now" (3:21) and ends with "in the now time" (*en tǭ nyn kairǭ*, 3:26). The word "now" will be used repeatedly in Romans, with the same sense of contrast between a former state of affairs and a present reality. The most forceful of all is the solemn summary statement in 16:25-26, which picks up on the same revelatory language Paul uses here: "the revelation of the mystery that was kept secret for long ages but is now disclosed" (see also 5:9, 11; 6:19, 21, 22; 7:6, 17; 8:1, 18, 22; 11:5, 30, 31; 13:11). Precisely this emphasis on the "now time" marks Paul's message as truly "news" and provides Romans with its tremendous energy and sense of urgency: "salvation is nearer to us *now* than when we first believed" (13:11). In Paul's other letters, 2 Cor 6:2 comes closest to the same sense of immediacy: "Behold *now* is the acceptable time, *now* is the day of salva-

tion." I have deliberately cited these two passages in order to make clear that, although Paul does not explicitly use the word "salvation" in 3:21-26, that is very much what he sees God as being up to. As the thesis stated, the good news is the "power for salvation" (1:16).

4. God's revelation in the "now time" is through human experience. We shall see soon how Paul locates the action of God in the obedient death of Jesus. But already in 3:21 he stresses that God's way of making humans right is being revealed "apart from the law and the prophets." What this means first of all is that God's action is really *action*. That is, God's revelation is not simply ideational, or verbal, or textual; it is, rather, anthropological. It is action that happens in and through human freedom. It happened in the real human person Jesus, and it continues to happen in the lives of Paul's readers (3:26), into whose hearts the love of God has been poured through the Holy Spirit (5:5). Here is one of Christianity's most dramatic claims, setting it apart from both Judaism and Islam, namely, that God has entered fully into *human experience* in order to rectify relations with humans. Christianity is in this sense *not* a "religion of the book" in the same way as the other Western monotheistic traditions.

There is another sense in which God's revelation in the now time is "apart from the law and prophets," and that is the way in which this specific human experience—the crucifixion and resurrection of Jesus—appears to *contradict* the scriptural antecedents provided by Torah. This aspect of things is not emphasized in Romans, although we find the essence of it in 9:30-33, where Paul suggests that his fellow Jews' zeal for Torah makes them trip over the stumbling block that was the messiah. The scandalous character of the gospel about a crucified messiah is more explicitly displayed by 1 Cor 1:18-26: the death of Jesus on the cross confounded the messianic hopes of Jews who "looked for signs" of a messiah and did not find them in him whose manner of death was, according to Torah itself, cursed by God: "Cursed be everyone who hangs upon a tree" (Deut 21:23; see Gal 3:13). It is this shocking and paradoxical experience of God's work through the death and resurrection of a failed messiah that demands the "obedience of faith," a response equivalently radical and unreserved. There was simply no *obvious* way in which Jesus fit into the precedents of how God had revealed Godself in the past.

5. Yet Paul also asserts that this revelation of God's righteousness through Jesus is "witnessed to by the law and prophets" (3:21). Here is the dialectical tension established by the experience of God in the crucified messiah. If Torah is read one way, then the experience must be negated: Jesus cannot be messiah if Torah declares him cursed. Yet one can also

approach the matter another way: beginning with the experience of Jesus, Torah can be reread in such fashion as to confirm God's activity in the "now time." It is precisely this new way of reading that will enable Paul to declare in 10:4, "Christ is the *telos* of the law," and to state in 1:2 that the good news was "promised ahead of time through his prophets in the holy Scriptures," and to affirm here that it is "witnessed to by law and prophets." In Paul's rereading of the Abraham story in chapter 4, in his interpretation of the story of the fall of Adam in chapter 5, and above all in his rereading of the story of Israel in chapters 9–11, we shall discover precisely what Paul himself understands this "witnessing" to be.

6. Paul asserts that God's action is both gratuitous in the strict sense of that term—that is, unearned by humans—and is effective for those for whom it was performed. The gift character of God's action is found particularly in three phrases. First, Paul affirms that all "have fallen short of the glory of God" (3:23)—not just Gentiles but also Jews have distorted their relationship with God and thus not "given him glory" (see 1:21; 2:24). Second, Paul states that they have been made righteous "freely by his gift" (3:24)—God was not constrained to act this way but chose to do so. In commenting on 1:5, I noted how thematic the term "grace" (*charis*) is in Romans; this aspect of God's action will be elaborated especially in 5:12–21. Third, God's graciousness is demonstrated by the "forbearance (*anochē*) of God" by which he "passed over the sins of the past" (3:26). Here Paul echoes 2:4, where he spoke of God's forbearance (*anochē*) and long-suffering (*makrothymia*) in extending to humans the chance of repentance. The gift of God is also effective: Paul speaks not of a "hope of righteousness" but of "those who are being made righteous" (3:24).

7. God's gift extends universally to both Jew and Gentile. This is the clear inference to be drawn from Paul's statement in 3:22, "for all have fallen short of the glory of God, being made righteous freely by his gift," which, in the light of the antithesis, must include both Jew and Greek. The thesis statement also had included "the Jew first and then the Greek" (1:16). Precisely such inclusiveness is what prompts the question in 3:29, "Is God the God of the Jews only? Is he not also of the Greeks?"

8. Finally, we need to note the mode of *receiving* the gift by which God makes humans righteous. And with this we come to one of the most ticklish and important points in the interpretation of Romans. Our approach will be correspondingly careful and deliberate. There can be no question that God's righteousness involves *faith* (*pistis*). The critical question is, "Whose faith?" The most undisputed point is that, from the human side, God's gift

is received by faith. Thus, in 3:22: "for all who are believing [having faith/responding in faith]." The Greek *eis pantas tous pisteuontas* echoes the last part of the thesis statement that declared salvation to be "for everyone who has faith" (1:16), as well as the difficult statement "out of faith to faith" (*eis pistin*), about which more will be said shortly. For now, however, we can see that the establishment of a "right relationship" between God and humans involves a transaction consisting of the giving of a gift by God and a receiving of the gift "with faith" by humans.

Since the word group is so central to the argument of Romans, and since Paul nowhere defines what he means by "faith" or "having faith," a short pause here is necessary for present-day readers who may not even be aware that the same Greek roots underlie the English words for "faith" and "belief." Both translate the Greek noun *pistis* and capture different dimensions of the Greek. For some unknown reason, however, English never developed a second verb form to match the Greek verb *pisteuein*, "believing." And since the English "belief/believing" has taken on largely a cognitive, creedal sense ("to believe in something"), it is tempting to read that dimension back into Paul. In fact, however, both the noun *pistis* and the verb *pisteuein* have a rich range of meanings. English could use a word such as "faithing" to capture some of these dimensions.

For Paul, "faithing" (*pisteuein*) certainly includes what we think of as belief, that is, a confession that something is so. Thus, in Rom 10:9, Paul speaks of "believing in the heart that God raised Jesus from the dead." But "faithing" in Paul's usage includes a much broader range of response than simple cognitive assent. It points above all to the innermost response of the "heart" in a fully personal engagement with another, and in this case, *the* Other. Paul therefore will touch on the nuance of faith/faithing as "hearing and responding" (Rom 10:14), as "trust" (Rom 4:3), and as "hope" (Rom 4:18). The special connotation of faith that Paul seeks to develop in this letter, however, is that of "obedience" (see 1:5; 16:26), that is, a deeply responsive hearing in which the claim of God is acknowledged by human freedom. When Paul speaks in 3:22, then, of "all those who are faithing," he means those who respond to God's gift with hearing, belief, trust, hope, and obedience.

The Role of Jesus Christ

Having sketched the basic dimensions of this second thesis statement, we can now turn to its most important element, namely, the role of Jesus Christ. It is striking that Jesus was left out of the first thesis statement (or was there only by implication, as I have suggested), since his role takes the central place in the restatement. Jesus is central to the *gift* that God gives humans who have fallen short of God's glory. His name is repeated three times: in 3:22 in the expression "Jesus Messiah," in 3:24 in the expression "Messiah Jesus," and in 3:26, with the simple name "Jesus."

Paul employs two expressions for describing the reality that God has accomplished through Jesus. In 3:24, he says that all are being made righteous "through the redemption that is in Christ Jesus." Nothing in this expression is easy. The term *apolytrōsis* derives from the social context of slavery. The verb *lytroun* meant basically to provide the means of liberating a slave, as by a ransom or a price (see LXX Lev 25:25). In the LXX, the term takes on the extended meaning of the "liberation" or "redemption" of the people Israel from Egypt, where they had served as slaves (see LXX Exod 6:6; Ps 110:9). The verb *apolytroun* can have the same literal meaning of "buying back" (Exod 21:8) or the extended sense of "liberate/free" (LXX Zeph 3:1). In the New Testament, the cognates *lytrousthai/lytrōsis/lytrōtēs* have entirely the metaphorical sense of "freeing/ liberating" (see Luke 1:68; 2:38; 24:21; Acts 7:35; Titus 2:14; Heb 9:12; 1 Pet 1:18). Only the use of *lytron* in Mark 10:45 and Matt 20:28 retains something of the literal sense of "something given in exchange," when Jesus declares that the Son of man has "come to give his life as a ransom (*lytron*) for many." The term that Paul uses here, *apolytrōsis*, is found also in Luke 21:28 and Heb 11:35 in the metaphorical sense of "liberation/deliverance/freedom." In Heb 9:15, by contrast, the term is placed in the specific context of a sacrificial death that "redeems from transgressions." Outside Romans, Paul connects Jesus to *apolytrōsis* but without much specificity. 1 Cor 1:30 says that Christ is "our righteousness and sanctification and redemption," and Col 1:14 declares "in him we have redemption" (see also Eph 1:7, 14; 4:30). Finally, Paul will speak of the *apolytrōsis* of our bodies as a future expectation.

Against this less-than-clarifying backdrop, how should we read the "redemption that is in Christ Jesus" in Rom 3:24? At the very least, it has the broad sense of "salvation/liberation/deliverance," for "salvation" is the theme established by the thesis (1:16). The term may also retain some nuance of "ransom from slavery," since that is also an important theme in Romans (see 6:6; 7:25; 8:15, 21): people have been freed from sin to become "slaves of God" (7:6; 12:11; 14:8; 16:18). Harder to determine is whether any sacrificial nuance should be read into the term. Does it have any of the sense of "life given for others" suggested by Mark 10:45 and the sacrificial imagery of Heb 9:15? Possibly, in the light of the second phrase used by Paul. At the least, however, Paul's use of *apolytrōsis* identifies Jesus as the means by which God has saved humans from the enslavement sketched so generously by 1:18-3:20.

The term *apolytrōsis* is qualified by the second expression, "whom [God] put forward as an expiation (*hilastērion*) . . . in his blood" (3:25). How pleasant it would be if this term were perfectly perspicuous, but in fact it is even more obscure than *apolytrōsis!*

The reader should be neither surprised nor discouraged, but rather remember that the language of the nascent Christian movement was just in the process of being forged in Paul's letters, which are, in fact, the first evidence for this language, which used older terms in new combinations and with new referents. Paul's words may have been clear to his first readers because they shared his cultural context and something of the same experience. We, on the other hand, are left to the task of excavation, hoping at least to approximate Paul's intended meaning. I emphasize this because the one thing we must not do—especially in passages like this one that have been subjected to so much theological interpretation for centuries—is simply assume that the meanings later theological systems have assigned to Paul's words are the meanings he intended. Far better for us to achieve a "strange" reading that is more tentative, than an assured reading that, because of its familiarity, teaches us nothing we did not already know.

That said, what's the problem with this term *hilastērion?* One difficulty is simple intelligibility. Even if we follow the RSV translation of "expiation by his blood," we are not much farther ahead, since the English term "expiation" has fallen out of all usage except in these specific religious texts. The English word points to a social transaction that even English-speakers do not recognize. Once more, then, we need to try to *construct* a meaning out of the Greek usage.

The Greek noun *hilastērion* is one of a group of words that are cognate with the verb *hilaskesthai*, which from the time of Homer (see *Iliad* 1.386) meant "to appease" either gods or other humans (Plato, *Phaedo* 95A). The basic idea is that one party has wronged another and must do something to rectify the relationship. In the LXX, we find the verb being used in just this context of relations between God and humans (Exod 32:14) and humans among themselves (2 Kgs 5:18). In the Psalms, the verb is used to translate the Hebrew verb *kipper*, which means to "cover over," so that "expiation" means to "cover over" something by overlooking or forgiving or not counting against someone the wrong they did (in the case of the Psalmist, sins against God; see LXX Ps 24:11; 64:3; 77:38; 78:9; see also Luke 18:13).

The noun *hilasmos*, in turn, is used in Lev 25:9 to translate the "day of *kippurîm*," that is, the Day of Atonement (*yôm kippur*). Now we are in the realm not simply of relational transactions, but in the specific context of ritual practice and cultic language. The noun *hilastērion* is used in Exod 25:16-21 to denote the *covering* (in Hebrew, *kappōret*) for the ark of the covenant (the box containing the tablets of the law), which was to be placed in the tent of the wilderness. The choice of *hilastērion* by the LXX translators was no doubt motivated by the fact that the *hilas-* words had been used to translate *kipper* words, and that the ritual here being described did involve appeasement between God and humans. English translators followed suit by calling this the "mercy seat."

In Lev 16:2-15, the rituals for the Day of Atonement (*yôm kippur*) are described. The LXX refers to this as *hēmera hilasmou* ("day of expiation," Lev 25:9). In this ritual, the *hilastērion/kappōret/mercy seat* comes into play. The priest is instructed to kill a bull, take some of its blood, and "sprinkle it with his finger on the front of the mercy seat (*hilastērion*), and before the mercy seat he shall sprinkle the blood with his finger seven times" (Lev 16:14). The text says, "Thus he shall make atonement for the holy place because of the uncleanness of the people of Israel, and because of their transgressions and all their sins" (Lev 16:16). This is the way the sanctuary is purified. The actual rite of atonement for the peoples' sins, however, is found not in the sprinkling of the bull's blood but in the driving out into the wilderness of the "scapegoat" bearing the peoples' sins (Lev 16:20-28).

In the New Testament, 1 John 2:2 and 4:10 refer to Jesus as the "expiation" (*hilasmos*) for our sins. In the letter to the Hebrews, so much of whose imagery revolves around the death of Jesus as the sacrifice that makes atonement, the verb *hilaskesthai* is used in 2:17 and the noun *hilastērion* appears in the description of the furnishings of the tent of the wilderness (9:5).

Much of this discussion may seem pedantic, but it is important to show just how elusive an image Paul is here employing in this critical passage. The passages in the LXX make clear only that the term *hilastērion* could denote the sacrificial sprinkling of blood associated with the Day of Atonement—and could therefore serve as synecdoche for the whole act of atonement—or could, by association, connote some act of atonement carried out for the temple, land, or people, to put them right with God (see S. Lyonnet, *Sin, Redemption and Sacrifice* [Rome: Biblical Institute, 1970] 155-66).

Precisely such a transferred application appears in an important passage in 4 Macc 17:22. Speaking of the martyrdom of the seven Maccabean sons and their mother, the eulogist says, "and through the blood of these devout ones and their death as an expiation (*hilastērion*), divine providence preserved Israel that previously had been afflicted." We note that some people have died on behalf of others; that blood is mentioned; that the result is the "redemption" of Israel from affliction; and that this is termed a *hilastērion*. The connections with Rom 3:25 are close and instructive, as pointed out by S. Williams (*Jesus' Death as Saving Event: The Background and Origin of a Concept* [HDR 2; Missoula, Mont.: Scholars Press, 1975] especially 34-56).

The phrase "in/by his blood" in 3:25 certainly indicates that Jesus' death

is the defining act of redemption. Does it also suggest that Jesus' death was
a sacrifice? Such a position has recently been vigorously opposed by S.
Stowers (*A Rereading of Romans: Justice, Jews, and Gentiles* [New Haven:
Yale University Press, 1994] 206-13). It must be said, however, that three
converging lines of evidence support the suggestion that Paul's language
here has sacrificial overtones. The first is the way the term *hilastērion* has
been used, both in the ritual descriptions of Torah and in the martyrs'
deaths in 4 Macc 22:17. The second is the fact that Paul can elsewhere
speak of Jesus' death in sacrificial terms. Thus, in 1 Cor 5:7 he declares that
"Christ our pasch has been sacrificed" (Stowers's discussion of this passage
in *Rereading Romans* [p. 211] is very inadequate). Third, Paul's statement
in Rom 8:32 concerning "him who did not spare his only son but handed
him over for all of us," is, as most commentators agree, an allusion to Abraham's sacrifice of his son Isaac in Gen 22:16, which Paul has applied to the
death of Jesus.

Whatever further nuances we may discover in these phrases, we can state
confidently that Paul presents the death of Jesus as the central act of libera-
tion/redemption/salvation by which expiation/appeasement/at-one-ment
between God and humans is accomplished and God's righteousness is displayed. The death of the messiah is God's paradoxical "gift" to humans.

The Faith of Jesus

We come now to the most difficult, yet in some ways most important,
aspect of Paul's thesis restatement. It is difficult because the reading I think
is correct goes against a long history of theological interpretation (see, e.g.,
E. Käsemann, *Commentary on Romans* [Grand Rapids: Eerdmans, 1980]
94, 101; and A. Nygren, *Commentary on Romans* [Philadelphia: Fortress,
1949] 150-61), which is monumentalized in widely used translations (the
KJV, RSV, NAB, NEB, NIV, JB). It is important because the proper determination of "whose faith saves" is critical to Paul's entire understanding of
soteriology and Christology (see R. B. Hays, "*Pistis* and Paul's Christology:
What is at Stake?" *SBL Seminar Papers 1991,* ed. D. Lull [Atlanta: Scholars
Press, 1991] 714-29). A small but growing number of scholars have in
recent years taken up the position argued here, that Paul sometimes, and
above all in this passage, speaks of "the faith of Christ" (see M. Barth, "The
Faith of the Messiah," *Heythrop Journal* 10 [1969]: 363-70).

The term *pistis* ("faith") occurs three times in 3:21-26, each time in connection with Jesus. The interpretive issue is whether these constructions
point to other peoples' *faith in Christ* or refer to *the faith of Jesus,* the

human person. I hope my reader will recall the earlier discussion of "subjective and objective genitives" (see pp. 21). Is Jesus here the object of faith or the subject of faith?

My discussion has only to do with Paul's argument in Romans. No one questions that Paul can speak of Christians' confessional faith *in Christ*, as he does in Gal 2:16; Phil 1:29; and Col 2:5. But does he in this case? The translators of the Revised Standard Version (which I have been using as my companion throughout this reading) certainly think so. In 3:22, the RSV reads "the righteousness of God through faith in Jesus Christ for all who believe." In 3:25, it reads, "whom God put forward as an expiation by his blood, to be received by faith." And in 3:26, God is said to "justify him who has faith in Jesus." In each case, Jesus is the object of Christians' faith. These translations, however, are wrong. They fly in the face of grammatical and literary considerations, and they entirely miss the direction of Paul's argument.

We can take up each phrase separately. In 3:22, as I have suggested, we find Paul's restatement of the thesis in 1:17. But there, the movement was "out of faith" (*ek pisteōs*) and "to faith" (*eis pistin*). In 3:22, the phrase "to all who have faith" (*eis pantas tous pisteuontas*) corresponds to the second phrase in the thesis, *eis pistin*. If the phrase *dia pisteōs Iēsou Christou* is then read (with the RSV) "through faith in Christ," it becomes both redundant, and it fails to correspond to the first phrase of the thesis, *ek pisteōs*. The most natural way to read the phrase in 3:22 is "through the faith of Jesus Christ for all who believe." Note that the implication of this translation is that Jesus' human faith is the means of the revelation of God's righteousness.

The expression in 3:25 is even more unlikely if translated objectively. The RSV's "to be received by faith" represents a desperate guess. The phrase *dia pisteōs* is not found at the end of the clause, as the RSV translation would suggest, but right in the middle of it, between two other phrases referring to Christ. Literally, "whom [God] put forward as an expiation through faith in his blood." The phrase "through faith" in other words, is fitted between "expiation . . . in his blood" and is clearly intended to qualify the manner of Jesus' death. It might be possible to read it as referring to *God's* faithfulness: it was out of his fidelity to humans that he put forward Jesus. But it is impossible to take the phrase as referring to the human "reception of the gift in faith." The KJV renders it as "faith in his blood," but this is to miss the character both of the Greek construction and of Paul's argument. The placement of the phrase next to Jesus and the act of his death make me think that the two phrases "through faith" and "in his blood" form what in Greek is called a hendiadys, that is, two phrases that make a single expression. In this case, the two phrases would be the equivalent to "Jesus' faithful death," which is exactly what Paul seems to want to get at here.

The final phrase in 3:25 simply cannot be translated as the RSV has it, "him who has faith in Jesus." The Greek cannot be made to say that. The most natural reading would be "the one who shares the faith of Jesus." Indeed the RSV itself translates precisely the same phrase in 4:16, in reference to Abraham, as "those who share the faith of Abraham," and *not* as "those who have faith in Abraham!" It is striking here that, in the best text tradition, Paul uses only the personal name of Jesus, without any title. The few times Paul does this, he seems intentionally to be referring to Jesus' humanity (e.g., Rom 8:11; 1 Thess 1:10; 2 Cor 4:10-14). The impact of the "subjective" translation is that Jesus' human faith is one that can be shared by others, as the phrase "to all who have faith" in 3:22 already suggests.

The reading of Romans 3:21-26 that I have given, then, places the faith of Jesus at the heart of God's gift to humans. His sacrificial and redemptive death is not simply an offering made of him, but an offering he makes of himself, "faithfully." It is Jesus' faith that reveals God's way of making humans righteous with God. The "faith of Christ" therefore lies at the heart also of Paul's theological argument in Romans (see L. E. Keck, "'Jesus' in Romans," *Journal of Biblical Literature* 108 [1989]: 443-60).

One reason why some have found it difficult to accept this line of argument is that they cannot conceive of what Jesus' faith might have been. And so long as we restrict *pistis* to "belief," the concept does seem odd. But if we recognize that *pistis* can mean the complete human response to God (see R. Bultmann, "*pisteuō*," *TDNT* 6:217-19), then the possibility for speaking realistically about the faith of Jesus increases. I am in basic agreement with R. Bultmann that, for Paul, faith means above all a form of *obedience* (see R. Bultmann, *Theology of the New Testament* [New York: Scribner, 1951] 1:314). We have already seen Paul make "faith" and "obedience" mutually defining terms in 1:5. In his antithesis, we have observed how Paul conceives of sin as both disobedience (*apeitheia*) and faithlessness (*apistia*), as though these terms were also, for him, equivalent (see 1:30; 2:8; 3:3). We know from Phil 2:7-8 that Paul defines Jesus' response to God as an "obedience unto death, even death on the cross." Further, we shall see in 5:12-21 that Paul will contrast Adam's and Christ's response to God precisely in terms of disobedience and obedience (see L. T. Johnson, "Romans 3:21-26 and the Faith of Jesus," *Catholic Biblical Quarterly* 44 [1982]: 77-90).

Paul's restatement of his thesis in 3:21-26, therefore, does not place its emphasis on the human reception of God's gift through faith, although that is clearly stated in 3:22 and 3:26. His main emphasis is on the fact that righteousness comes about on God's initiative by means of a gift, and on the character of that gift, namely, the profoundly human response of Jesus the messiah to God in faith, expressed most perfectly in his obedient death as a means of liberation and reconciliation for others (see also S. Williams, "The Righteousness of God in Romans," *Journal of Biblical Literature* 99 [1980]: 241-90).

Questions, Answers, Assertions (3:27-31)

Aspects of the thesis are now drawn out by a series of short questions, which in diatribal fashion, are given short and abrupt responses, followed by assertions that draw broader conclusions. The series serves to sharpen the point Paul has made in 3:21-26 and to lead to the next stage of the argument.

The first set of questions (3:27) returns to the question of boasting (*kauchēsis*). In the antithesis, we saw that the ungodly were "insolent, haughty, boastful" (1:30), and that the Jews "boast of the relation to God" (2:17). Boasting in these cases proceeds on the assumption that life and worth are possessions that can be claimed as one's own. But now, Paul says, boasting is excluded. He poses another question: "On what principle?" Actually, in a difficult play on words, he asks "By what law (*nomos*)?" He asks a third time, "by works?" and responds, "No, but through the *nomos* (law/principle) of faith."

His language is typically dense, but it serves to point to the centrality of *faith* as the principle of right relationship between God and humans. And he adds by way of explanation, "for we reckon that a human being is made righteous by faith apart from the works of the law" (3:28). The phrase "apart from" (*chōris*) is the same used in 3:21 when Paul stated that righteousness was being revealed "apart from law and prophets." The proposition seems to follow logically from his thesis. If humans are established in righteousness by *gift*, they certainly cannot boast of it as though it were their possession or accomplishment (though Paul will show a way it can be the basis of boasting in 5:1-5). And if the gift is given through the faithful death of Jesus (a death cursed by Torah), and is received by faith, then it certainly bypasses the observance of the law entirely. The transaction has taken place through the giving and receiving of a gift. In Jesus, God has said yes to humans once for all, and, in Jesus, humans have likewise said yes to God. Paul states it beautifully in 2 Cor 1:20: "all the promises of God find their yes in him. That is why we utter the Amen through him to the glory of God." This states precisely what Paul means by "out of faith to faith": Christians claim the faith of Jesus as the yes through which they can also say yes to God.

Paul's next question in 3:29 is possibly the most radical and far-reaching statement in the letter: "Is God only for the Jews? Is He not also for the Gentiles?" He responds resoundingly, "Yes, for the Gentiles also!" With this statement, Paul plumbs the deepest meaning of two theological convictions that he shared with his fellow Jews and applies them with a boldness that no other Jew ever approached.

The first conviction is that God is One. Serious monotheism must be radical monotheism; that is, it cannot be the refinement of a tribal henotheism which says that our god is better than other gods. Radical monotheism asserts that there is only one absolute, originative power at the root of reality, the One God who is the creator, sustainer, and judge of all. If this is so, then there can only be "one God" for all the peoples of the world.

The second principle is that God is fair (righteous). If there is but one God for all peoples, and if that one God is fair, then it follows that God cannot rig the salvation game. God cannot be both one and fair if God arranges matters so that only some part of the world's population can respond to God. That would be like creating a board game, distributing it to everyone, but handing out the rules only to a few. Such would be the case, however, if it were necessary to perform all the "works of Torah" in order to be in proper relationship with God, for Torah was revealed only to one part of the world's population.

If right relationship with God were possible only on the basis "of the works of the law," then most of the world would be excluded from the game. The only possible conclusions, then, would be either that God was not truly "One" (but only a tribal deity who looked out for his own) or not truly "righteous" (but one who cheated at the game he created). But Paul has stated emphatically that "there is no favoritism with God" (2:11). Now he states that God is the God also of the Gentiles, "since God is One."

But if God is both one and fair, then God must make it possible for all humans to respond to God. There must be some principle by which all humans can be in "right relationship" even if they never heard of Torah. This principle ("law") Paul calls "faith." It is through such a process of reasoning that Paul can conclude, "Since God is one, he will make the circumcised righteous out of faith, and the uncircumcised righteous through faith" (3:30). For an effort to exploit the difference in prepositions here, see S. Stowers, "*ek pisteōs* and *dia tes pisteōs* in Rom 3:30," *Journal of Biblical Literature* 108 (1989): 665–74.

Two further comments on this remarkable set of statements. The first concerns the role of Jesus. Paul's position makes it even more plausible that *pistis Christou* in Romans must refer to the faith of Jesus rather than faith *in* Christ. As Paul will show, Jesus responded to God in the way that the Gentile-then-Jew Abraham did, in trust and hope and obedience. Jesus' faith is therefore exemplary for all others, both Jews and Gentiles. Certainly, for Paul, Jesus' faith is also causative in a way that Abraham's was not. In other words, because Jesus was not just another human person but was God's Son, and the new Adam, he opened up a possibility for *all* humans to respond in the way he did. We will follow this part of the argument as Paul develops it in chapters 5-8.

This brings us to the second observation. If saving faith meant faith *in* Christ, then Paul would logically be back in the same position against which he is arguing. In other words, just as only Jews would have access to God if access were available only through Torah, so could only Christians have access to God if access were available only through the confession of Christ. Paul probably thought it a real possibility that all humans *would* have the chance to confess Christ. His world was a smaller one than ours, and his mission had a chance of encompassing the *oikoumenē* (see 13:11-14). Paul, furthermore, could not have conceived of a global humanity, most of which would never be exposed to the good news about Christ. In 3:29, however, Paul planted an insight that Christian theology itself has never fully dealt with. Certainly it would be inconsistent with Paul's whole argument to claim that one had to be Christian in order to have access to God— for then God could neither be truly one nor truly fair. Then the particularity of the Christian religion would simply replace the particularity of Judaism, providing an expanded but in principle equally restricted range of accessibility to God. There are strong reasons for supposing this to run completely counter to Paul's most profound insight into God's way of righting relations with humans (see also H. Boers, *The Justification of the Gentiles: Paul's Letters to the Galatians and Romans* [Peabody, MA: Hendrickson, 1994] especially 221-27).

Paul's final question and answer provide the transition to the next part of his argument, in which he will show Abraham to be the model of faith. His question follows logically from the establishing as the principle of righteousness "faith apart from the works of the law." He asks, "Do we therefore destroy the law through faith?" (3:31). His first response is quick: "By no means!" It is unthinkable for Paul the Jew for Torah to be utterly negated, for to negate Torah would be to nullify the entire story of God's dealings with humans. Yet he has himself certainly relativized Torah. We are therefore startled to see his second answer: "Rather, we are establishing/upholding the law." Here is paradox, indeed, and we will need Paul's next stretch of argument to comprehend how this can be so (see C. T. Rhynne, *Faith Establishes the Law* [SBLDS 55; Chico, Calif.: Scholars Press, 1981]).

HOW FAITH WORKS:
THE EXAMPLE OF ABRAHAM

Romans 4:1-25

The literature of the ancient Mediterranean world makes heavy use of examples from the past, out of the conviction that some things were best learned through the hearing of a story rather than through a maxim or principle. Some examples were adduced simply to illustrate a point; sometimes they were employed as models for people to imitate in their behavior. In the normal order of things, children could see in their parents living models of virtue to emulate (see Pseudo-Isocrates, *To Demonicus*).

Moral teachers also made frequent use of figures of the past, often derived from the classical texts of Homer, Hesiod, and the Dramatists, whose poetry formed the "scriptures" of the Greco-Roman world. Thus Epictetus, whose *Discourses* so resemble Romans' diatribal style, makes frequent use of the mythic figure Herakles (2.16.44; 2.18.22; 3.24.13) as well as philosophical antecedents like Socrates (1.9.22; 1.12.23; 1.19.6) and Diogenes (2.22.58).

Jewish literature from that period also exploits scriptural characters for purposes of praise (see Sir 44:1-50:29) and instruction. The *Testaments of the Twelve Patriarchs*, for example, presents the sons of Jacob as living embodiments of various virtues and vices for the reader to imitate or avoid. The encomiastic 4 Maccabees offers the martyrdom of the Maccabean brothers and their mother as the expression of heroic virtue to be admired and imitated. Philo Judaeus uses Abraham, Joseph, and Moses, to illustrate various virtues (see *On Abraham*, *On Joseph*, *Life of Moses*). It is no surprise, then, to find Paul employing an *exemplum* from Torah for purposes of illustrating his argument concerning faith.

For one writing within the symbolic world of Torah, furthermore, no more obvious figure could be found than that of Abraham. The most obvious reason is simply that Abraham is the founding figure of the tradition, as Paul says, "our forefather according to the flesh." As it was natural in that world for children to look to their parents for models of virtue, so it was instinctive to look to this (literal) father of the people for such a model as well. The narrative concerning Abraham in Genesis 12-25, furthermore, is particularly vivid and detailed, making it attractive for a variety of appropriations by later Jewish writers, within Torah itself (LXX Ps 104:6; Mic 7:20; Isa 29:22; 41:8; 51:1-2; 63:16; Ezek 33:24), the expanded texts of the LXX translation of Torah (Jdt 8:26; Tob 4:12; Sir 44:19-21; 1 Macc 2:52; 4 Macc 6:17-22; 7:19; 9:21; 13:12; 14:20; 15:28; 16:20-25; 17:6), and in the extensive Jewish literature produced between 200 B.C.E. and 300 C.E. Thus, Abraham figures prominently in the retelling of the biblical accounts by Josephus (*Antiquities of the Jews* 1.149-242), Pseudo-Philo (*Biblical Antiquities* 6.1-8.3), the book of *Jubilees* 11:14-23:8, and the *Genesis Apocryphon* from Qumran. Abraham is also vigorously exploited by the rabbinic tradition that emerged as the heir to Pharisaism.

These accounts emphasize two aspects of the Abraham story: his fidelity to God through the process of being tested, especially by his willingness to offer his only son, Isaac, in sacrifice (Gen 22:1-14; see, e.g., 1 Macc 2:52; Sir 44:20; *Jubilees* 17:17; 18:15-16; 4 Macc 16:20; *Pirqe Aboth* 5:3; *Aboth de Rabbi Nathan* 33), and his hospitality, demonstrated by his reception of the messengers from God (Gen 18:1-15; see, e.g., Philo, *On Abraham* 167; *Aboth de Rabbi Nathan* 7; *Testament of Abraham* 1:2; 4:1-11; *Genesis Rabbah* 49.4; 55.4; 61.5). As claimants to the heritage of Israel, it was natural for Christians also to connect themselves to the figure of Abraham (e.g., Matt 1:1; 3:9; 8:11; Luke 1:73; 16:22-30; 19:9; John 8:33-58; Acts 3:13, 25; 7:2-26; 1 Pet 3:6).

Two New Testament writings apart from Paul make particular *exemplary* use of Abraham. In Jas 2:20-24, Abraham is presented as the example of how faith reaches its perfection in deeds: "faith was active along with his deeds and was perfected by his deeds" (Jas 2:22). The incident cited is Abraham's offering of his son, Isaac (2:21). James sees this action as "fulfilling" the text of Gen 15:6, "Abraham believed God and it was reckoned to him as righteousness," and for this reason Abraham was called "friend of God" (Jas 2:23). The Letter to the Hebrews focuses on Abraham as a hero of faith together with all the "cloud of witnesses" (12:1) cited from Torah in the great encomium of Hebrews 11. Abraham's faith is a kind of obedience (11:8) shown by his willingness to go to another country as an alien. Sarah's faith in the promise that she would bear Isaac is also singled out (11:11), as well as the fact that Abraham was "as good as dead" at the time Isaac was born (11:12). Abraham showed his faith in his willingness to "offer up his only son" (11:17). Hebrews connects Abraham's receiving back of Isaac to God's ability to "raise men even from the dead" (11:18-19). The treatment of Abraham in these two writings is distinctive, yet resembles Paul above all in their shared emphasis on Abraham's *faith*. The same is true in the extended consideration given Abraham in the extracanonical *1 Clement* (ca. 95 C.E.), which emphasizes Abraham's obedience and hospitality under the rubric of faith (*1 Clem.* 10; see R. Longenecker, "The 'Faith of Abraham' Theme in Paul, James, and Hebrews: A Study in the Circumstantial Nature of New Testament Teaching," *Journal of the Evangelical Theological Society* 20 [1977]: 203-12).

Paul's Use of Abraham in Galatians

Paul refers briefly to his Jewish pedigree in 2 Cor 11:22 (replying to the claims made by his rivals) by asking, "Are they of the seed (*sperma*) of Abraham? I am too!" Otherwise, he makes mention of Abraham only in Galatians and Romans. Although there are undisputed points of contact between the letters, and it is possible to argue for a deep structural unity to Paul's religious perceptions underlying the discrete accounts (see, e.g., H. Boers, *The Justification of the Gentiles: Paul's Letters to the Galatians and Romans* [Peabody, Mass.: Hendrickson, 1994] 143-220), it is important also to distinguish the argument being made in the respective letters and the role played by Abraham in each.

Galatians is a polemical letter generated by a real crisis among churches Paul founded in the region of Galatia. After Paul preached the crucified messiah to these Gentiles and they experienced the power of the Holy Spirit (3:1-5), some agitators tried to convince Gentile believers of the necessity of undergoing another ritual of initiation besides baptism (3:27), namely, the Jewish rite of circumcision (5:2, 12; 6:12). The implication was that this would make them truly "children of Abraham" and members of the covenant. It would also represent a commitment to the "yoke of Torah" by the keeping of the commandments revealed by God to Moses at Sinai.

Paul's argument in Galatians is intended to persuade the Gentile believers of the sufficiency of what they have been given "by faith" and the foolishness of giving up their freedom for a "yoke of slavery" (5:1). What they apparently see as doing more, Paul regards as abandoning what they have been given as gift. Galatians pushes to the surface the impossibility of combining an absolute adherence to Torah and a commitment to Jesus: "You are severed from Christ, you who would be justified by the law, you have fallen away from grace" (5:4). The reason? Circumcision obliges one to "keep the whole law" (5:3). But part of the law states that anyone hanging upon a tree is cursed by God (Deut 21:23; Gal 3:13). If, then, one affirms the law as absolute norm for life, then one cannot have Jesus as messiah and proclaim that through him God has sent the Holy Spirit, for he surely was hanged on a tree by crucifixion.

If one lives by means of "gift" (= grace), that is, as Paul states in 2:20, "by the faith of the son of God who loved me and gave himself for me," then one cannot also affirm of the commandments of Torah, "the one who does them shall live by them" (3:12, citing Lev 18:5). Something has to give. Either Torah needs to remain as the absolute frame for God's activity, or the experience of God in Christ must be absolute and Torah thereby relativized. Paul's answer, as we know, is that the experience of God in Christ is the absolute, experientially based reality that cannot be forsworn (3:1–5). What, then, can be said about Torah? It is in the section of Galatians beginning in 3:6 that Paul addresses this issue through use of the figure of Abraham.

To grasp Paul's argument in Galatians, we must remember that for him it is not merely a matter of interpreting texts or maintaining logical consistency. Something has happened to him and to his readers (2:20–3:5) that has radically transformed their lives (see D. Lull, *The Spirit in Galatia* [SBLDS 49; Chico, Calif.: Scholars Press, 1980]). They received the Holy Spirit "out of the hearing of faith" (3:5). On the basis of this *experience*, Paul draws an immediate connection to Abraham: "just as Abraham believed God and it was counted to him as righteousness" (Gen 15:6). You know therefore that those who are out of faith are the children of Abraham" (3:6–7). We should note parenthetically Paul's use of "out of faith" (*ek pisteōs*), which we have met also in Romans, and then recognize how bold a move Paul has here made, making *faith in God* the defining element in belonging to Abraham's family. This enables him to declare that Scripture "foresaw that God would justify the Gentiles by faith," and "promised beforehand that 'in you all the nations will be blessed'" (3:8). We recognize here the same preemptive strike as in Rom 1:2, where Paul asserts that the good news was "promised ahead of time through the prophets in the writings." Paul can therefore now conclude, "so those out of faith are blessed together with Abraham" (3:9).

He then puts this principle of righteousness through faith in opposition to the situation under the law (3:10–14). The law claimed the ability to give life to the one who practiced it (Lev 18:5). Likewise, it put under a curse anyone who did not keep everything written in it (Deut 27:26). But the curse was imposed explicitly on anyone who was hanged on a tree (Deut 21:23), which would include crucifixion. But Jesus was crucified and then raised from the dead. This is the experiential wedge that breaks the perfect system of Torah. Furthermore, despite his horrible death, Jesus had *faith in God* and, by his resurrection, now *lives* (see 2:20).

The claims of the law therefore must be countered on the basis of this truth. As one trained in midrash, Paul knows that texts require relativization by other texts, and he finds one critical to his position in the prophet Habakkuk 2:4: "the righteous one will live on the basis of faith" (a text we saw figure in Paul's thesis statement in Rom 1:17). Here, then, is a classic case of contradiction between Scripture texts that will be resolved on the surface by the negotiation of the texts, but will be motivated by powerful religious experiences that breathe life into textual witness (see N. A. Dahl, "Contradictions in Scripture," in *Studies in Paul* [Minneapolis: Augsburg, 1977] 159-77). The resolution in this case comes from the conviction that the faith of Jesus expressed itself in "loving me and giving himself for me" (2:20). Paul can therefore declare, "by being cursed for us, Christ redeemed us from the curse that is leveled by the law" (3:13).

Christ did this "so that the blessing of Abraham might come upon the Gentiles in Christ Jesus, in order that we might receive the promise that is the Spirit, through faith" (3:14). Beginning with their experience, the argument has come full circle *back* to their experience of the Holy Spirit. Thus, Paul's implicit logic can be seen once it is granted that the blessing is through the gift of the Holy Spirit: (1) Abraham had faith/all nations would be blessed through him; (2) Gentiles have faith/Gentiles are blessed with Holy Spirit; (3) *therefore*, Gentiles are children of Abraham!

Paul also establishes a textual link between Abraham and the Christian experience by his exploitation of the ambiguity of the Greek noun *sperma* ("seed"). It is obviously a collective noun, but Paul insists on its singular character, thereby referring it to the single person of the messiah. The promises were therefore spoken "to Abraham and to his seed," which for Paul means "the seed who is messiah." By this logic, he is able to assert that those who live by the faith of the messiah are partakers in the blessing that was promised to "Abraham and his seed" (3:15-16). Paul exerts considerable effort on this point in order to show that this entire relationship with God, this making of covenant, happened 430 years before the law was revealed at Sinai, and is therefore not affected by the giving of the law (3:17): "if the inheritance is by the law, it is no longer by promise, but God gave it to Abraham by a promise" (3:18).

Because of the polemical context of Galatians—agitators are trying to impose the observance of the law as a necessity—Paul is unusually harsh toward the claims being made for Torah. He relativizes its normative force by showing that it was revealed later than the promise of the blessing (therefore it cannot be considered *necessary* for a relationship with God [3:17]), that it was revealed through intermediaries and not directly by God (in contrast to the promise revealed directly by God to Abraham [3:19-20]), and that it was of only temporary force until the coming of the messiah (in contrast to the promise which reached its fulfillment in the Messiah [3:24]; see T. Callan, "Pauline Midrash: The Exegetical Background of Gal 3:19b," *Journal of Biblical Literature* 99 [1980]: 549-67). On the other hand, he does not deny its significance entirely and denies that the law is against the promise—it simply could not itself fulfill the promise, which could only reach fulfillment in persons. It was, Paul says, the law's role to act as a custodian or pedagogue until the messiah came, and "faith should be revealed" (3:23), "so that we might be justified by faith" (3:24). And in a statement that combines the points of Rom 3:19-20 and 3:21-26, he declares, "Scripture closed up all things under sin, so that what was promised to faith in Christ Jesus might be given to those who believe."

In Galatians, therefore, Abraham serves to show how Torah itself places the covenant established by promise through faith prior to that of the law revealed through Moses, how the principle of faith established him in right relationship with God without any mediation of law, and how those who by faith have accepted God's gift of a crucified and raised messiah are truly his children. As a corollary, Paul assigns the law a subsidiary and basically negative function.

To spend so much time on Galatians may appear excessive, but it is necessary in order for us to grasp the distinctiveness of Romans' treatment of Abraham and of the law. The two discussions should not simply be collapsed into one. Above all, the shape of Paul's argument in Galatians, based as it is on the *experience of transformation* in the Holy Spirit through the "hearing of faith" of the crucified messiah, must be seen as the implicit backdrop to his magisterial argument of Romans, showing that Paul's thought is not abstractly theoretical but is based on the specific religious experience of his Gentile communities.

Abraham the Father of Us All

We note at once the distinctiveness of the approach in Romans. Here Paul has declared that faith "establishes the law" (3:31), and we should read what is said about Abraham in that light. He begins with the most obvious truth for Paul and his fellow Jews, that Abraham is "our forefather." In terms of earthly descent all Jews claim Abraham as their father. Paul's opening question in 4:1, then, might be read in one of two ways. The first would be more neutral, as rendered by the RSV, "what then shall we say about Abraham, our forefather according to the flesh?" In this translation, "according to the flesh" would mean simply earthly descent, as in 1:3 and 9:5. Other renderings take a bit more seriously the specific nuances offered by the Greek "find" (*heurkenai*) and read "according to the flesh" in Paul's more specifically negative fashion (see 6:19; 7:5; see R. B. Hays, "Have we Found Abraham to be our Forefather according to the Flesh? A Reconsideration of Rom 4:1," *Novum Testamentum* 27 [1985]: 76-98). One possibility—attractive in light of the immediately following statements—is that Paul asks whether

Abraham, operating at the level of the flesh, "found" something. At issue in every reading is the manner in which Abraham is to be considered as ancestor, and for whom.

Paul immediately asserts that if Abraham had been made righteous "on the basis of works" (*ex ergōn*), then he would have had reason to "boast, but not toward God" (4:2). This is a key statement. It shows that Paul's thought is not moving simply on a social or political plane but at a theological one. Obviously, the law had not yet been revealed to Moses, so Paul's reference to "works" must include any efforts on Abraham's part, not simply the "works of the law" signified by circumcision. Any human accomplishment can give rise to boasting, an assertion of self over against others: my pile of possessions is bigger than yours, therefore I am more than you are! But, Paul asserts, no such human accomplishment can legitimate boasting "toward God." Nothing any creature can do will bridge what Kierkegaard called the "infinite qualitative distance" between God and creation (see 9:19-21). No creature can purchase a relationship with God or improve one's position with God through bribery: "Who has ever given a gift to him that he should be repaid?" (Rom 11:35).

Paul now quotes from Gen 15:6, as he had in Gal 3:6: "Abraham had faith in God and it was reckoned to him unto righteousness." The language of "reckoning" (*logizesthai*) deliberately evokes the calculations on a tally sheet, allowing Paul to continue that transactional metaphor: "to the one working, wages are not reckoned as a gift but as what is owed" (4:4). The point here is that Abraham had done nothing vis-à-vis this God who had called him and given him a promise *except* to believe. The transaction was not one of earning but one of gifting, or gracing (*charis*). The Genesis story must be remembered in order to grasp Paul's argument. Before God's call, Abram was a Gentile. His father lived in Ur of the Chaldeans (Gen 11:27-28), and when Abram left with his wife and possessions from there to the land of Canaan, he was still a Gentile (Gen 11:31). God's call to Abraham was to "go from your country and your kindred and your father's house" (Gen 12:1). To answer that call meant leaving behind all that ancestral worship and putting his trust in the one who told him, "I will bless you and by you all the families of the earth will bless themselves." In other words, Abraham was an *idolator* until he was called by God, a fact implicit in the Genesis account and argued away by later Jewish writings (Pseudo-Philo, *Biblical Antiquities* 6.3-18; *Jub.* 11:14-17; Josephus, *Antiquities* 1.155). But it is assumed here by Paul.

Paul therefore declares in 4:5: "To the one not working but who has faith in the one who makes the ungodly (*asebē*) righteous, his faith is unto righteousness." The statement echoes 1:18, where Paul had described the wrath coming over all "ungodliness" (*asebeia*). By implication, Abraham was, at the time of his call, in the position of those Gentiles Paul described in 1:18-32. How did he come to be righteous? Through God's initiative in giving to him an unmerited *gift*, and by his trusting and obedient acceptance of that gift. In Abraham, therefore, we see what Paul understands as the basic pattern for the divine-human relationship. It begins always with God's gift and is received by human trust. Since the initiative comes from God, the gift cannot be seized or clung to as a possession. It can never become the basis for self-assertion over against other humans, and certainly not God.

To show that this pattern is, in fact, generalizable beyond the single case of Abraham, Paul elicits the testimony of David in LXX Ps 31:1-2, prefacing it with the interpretive gloss, "So also David speaks of the blessedness of the human being to whom God reckons righteousness apart from works" (4:6). Paul's choice of the Psalm may be connected to its containing the key word "reckon" (*logizesthai*), which appeared also in Gen 15:6. The psalm declares the person blessed, or happy, whose lawless deeds are forgiven (Ps 31:1), whose sins are covered over (31:1), and whose sin (singular) the Lord does not "reckon" (31:2). The terms used by the psalm fit perfectly the situation Paul addresses. As we have seen, Paul's thesis statement in 3:21-26 contained the notions of "covering over" and "not counting" sins. The psalm works not only to connect David to Abraham but also Abraham to the Christian experience.

By focusing on the very first part of the Abraham story as the most critical, Paul succeeds in defining the drama of idolatry and sin, grace, and faith, in a context that is Gentile (that is, universal) rather than Jewish (that is, particular). He now moves to exploit that implication. Paul insists in 4:9 that the blessing was pronounced on Abraham when he was still uncircumcised—we can infer that it is possible for other uncircumcised persons to have a right relationship with God based on *gift* (see 3:24). The statement in Gen 15:6, "his faith was reckoned to him unto righteousness," was written before the account in Genesis of Abraham's performing circumcision on himself and all his relatives and possessions (Gen 17:9-27). Paul concludes, therefore, that the reckoning of righteousness took place "not after, but before he was circumcised" (4:10).

In a significant bit of interpretation, Paul asserts that "he received the sign of circumcision as a seal of the righteousness through faith which he had while uncircumcised" (4:11). We notice that Paul has used the narrative sequence of Genesis to make a point similar to the one in Gal 3:6-15. There he had argued that the promise occurred 430 years before the giving of the law and therefore had priority over the law, which came later. Here, he takes Abraham's circumcision as metonymy for the law and argues the same point: first came faith, then circumcision. Therefore faith is a more fundamental principle than law for a right relationship with God. Another aspect of Paul's interpretation of Abraham's circumcision, however, is that circumcision is related integrally to *faith* and not to *law*. This is a more decisive reinterpretation and reminds us of his argument in 2:25-29 concerning "true circumcision" as a matter of the heart. It will also follow from this that a "faithful obedience from the heart" is the living response that gives observance of the law its meaning.

Paul concludes this part of his exposition with an extended purpose clause. Things happened this way *in order that* Abraham would be "the father of all those who have faith without being circumcised and who thus have righteousness reckoned to them [viz., the Gentiles], and *likewise* the father of the circumcised who are not merely circumcised but also follow the example of faith which our father Abraham had before he was circumcised" (4:11-12). Abraham has thus been demonstrated to be the father of *both* Jewish and Gentile believers. More importantly, it is the principle of *faith* that establishes righteousness in both situations. What is perhaps most startling here is that Paul has made the pattern of Gentile righteousness by faith normative for Jewish righteousness, rather than the reverse (see M. Cranfield, "Abraham in Romans 4: The Father of all who Believe," *New Testament Studies* 41 [1995]: 71-88). Those Jews who (literally) "align themselves with the footsteps of the faith Abraham had before he was circumcised" are allowed to call him "father." In no sense, then, is descent from Abraham to be considered "according to the flesh," either by genealogical descent or by human effort (4:1). And Torah itself demonstrates this, showing in the narrative of Abraham how the principle of faith "establishes the law" (3:31).

By Gift and Not by Law (4:13-17)

Paul continues to work out the implications of Abraham's example, now returning to the framework of Gal 3:6-15, which had opposed promise/inheritance/and faith, to the law. He now repeats that the promise that Abraham would inherit the earth came about "through the righteousness of faith" and not "through law" (4:13). For the first time in this chapter, Paul connects "works" and "law" through the symbol that joined them, namely, circumcision. He poses a question that reverses that in 3:31. The issue is not whether faith destroys the law but the opposite: "for if the heirs were on the basis of law, then faith would be made empty and the promise would be destroyed" (4:14). If, in other words, the relationship with God could be secured by means of human observance, then it would not be according to an initiative that is from God (the promise) to be received by faith. This is plain enough. But Paul adds to it one of those odd and apparently unmotivated asides concerning the law that we will be able to consider in detail only in discussing Romans 7: "for the law works wrath, but where there is no law, there is no transgression" (4:15).

Paul now moves to a contrast between gift and law. Once more, righteousness was "on the basis of faith" (*ek pisteōs*) for this reason, "in order that it might be according to a gift, to secure the promise to all his seed, not only to those out of the law, but also to those out of the faith of Abraham" (4:16). I have translated very literally here to give some sense of Paul's tight use of prepositional phrases. This is the place where the RSV translates "those out of the faith of Abraham" as "those who share the faith of Abraham," and that is accurate enough. What is surprising is that the same translation was not made in the case of 3:26, where the phrase *ton ek pisteōs Iēsou* was translated by the RSV as "the one who has faith in Jesus," rather than "the one who shares the faith of Jesus." The overall implication of Paul's compressed statement is that right relationship with God is a matter of gift for both Jew and Gentile, which means that the response of faith is also the same for both. It is for this reason that God declared to Abraham in Gen 17:5, "I have made you the father of many nations." Paul has shown Abraham to be not simply father of the Jews, but father of the Gentiles as well.

Paul's statement in 4:17 is a hinge that connects the argument he has been making with what follows. But it is much more than a transition. The statement reveals the very heart of Paul's religious perceptions. Abraham's faith, he says, was in "the presence of the God who gives life to the dead and calls into existence things that do not exist." This understanding of God undergirds everything that Paul has argued to this point. For Paul, God is the living one, the absolute source of all that exists: "From him and through him and in him are all things" (11:36). God's power is shown first in creation: "he calls into being that which does not exist." Notice that Paul makes creation both absolute and continuous. The participle is present: God goes on calling into being, it is his characteristic act. And God calls into being out of nothing. Paul invokes the same conviction in 1 Cor 1:28 in spelling out the call of God: "God chose what is low and despised in the world—even things that are not—to bring to nothing things that are," and he draws from that conviction precisely the point of the argument in Romans: "that no human being might boast in the presence of God" (1 Cor 1:29). In 1 Cor 1:31, Paul adds, quoting Jer 9:23-24, "Let the one who boasts, boast in the Lord." If God is the source of all reality, then God is also the source of all gifts, and therefore the only true ground of boasting.

God's ability to raise the dead to life by resurrection is continuous with his act of creation, of calling into being out of nothing. This is the connection Paul tries to make for the Thessalonians. Their hope for the resurrection of their loved ones is based on their experience of the resurrection of

Jesus (1 Thess 4:14) who was raised by the "true and living God" (1 Thess 1:9-10). It is sometimes amusing to hear people say that they can believe that God created the world but cannot believe in resurrection. But if they cannot believe in resurrection, neither do they really believe in what Paul thought of as God's creation. For God to call into being at every moment that which is not, that is, for God to be the source and sustainer of *being* itself, is so radical a notion that resurrection, by comparison, is not much more than an obvious corollary.

If this, then, is God's nature, two things follow. The first is that God (*ho theos*) is the only appropriate object of faith. Thus, Abraham's trust and obedience were not directed to anything but "the God who gives life to the dead" (4:17). Such a conclusion is important for Christian faith as well, as Paul will shortly make clear in 4:24. The second is that if faith is directed to the "living God" who is creative at every moment, then faith must be responsive and adaptable to the way God reveals God's self at every moment.

If God is the living God, then revelation must be continuous by definition, and faith cannot be static and fixed, but rather must be open and flexible. Faith, in a word, is directed not to God's past actions, and still less to the human record of God's past, but to God's present self-disclosure, which is always new and often surprising. This point is critical to Paul's argument, for he will state in 9:31 that at the new revelation of God's gift in the messiah Jesus, his fellow Jews allowed their commitment to Torah to block their ability to respond in faith to this "good news from God." For Paul, God's action in the world cannot be constrained by textual precedents. The "now time" revelation of God in Jesus took place "apart from the law and prophets" (3:21). Only when faith responds to what God is now doing in the world can it begin to try to connect this new understanding with scriptural precedents and figure out how "law and prophets witness to it." But the reverse could not happen. By reading Leviticus, Deuteronomy, or even Isaiah, one would not conclude to the scandalous death of Jesus on the cross.

The Structure of Faith (4:18-25)

The most properly "exemplary" aspect of Abraham is now considered, as Paul turns to the description of the internal structure of his response to God. This short yet vivid depiction of the specifically human dimensions of Abraham's example provide insight into Paul's understanding of what faith is and prepares for the further development in 5:12-21. Paul's language here is entirely encomiastic. He holds Abraham up for praise and for emulation. In good rhetorical fashion, he heightens our appreciation for Abraham's behavior by accentuating the circumstances working against it. Paul shows that for Abraham to believe in God's promise "thus shall your seed be" (Gen 15:5), that he would be the father of many nations (Gen 17:5), he would have to go beyond the evidence available to him. In Paul's paradoxical expression, Abraham needed to "hope against hope," that is, to place his trust in an unseen power beyond what any human "hope" could offer.

In human terms, "according to the flesh," it was impossible for Abraham to become the father of even one child, much less a multitude of nations. He could "look at his own body which was as good as dead since he was about a hundred years old" (4:19; see Gen 17:17). Paul's choice of adjectives (the participle *nenekrōmenon*) is clearly deliberate. For life to come from this body, for "seed" to spring from these loins, it would be like "life from the dead." But that was not the only empirical evidence arguing against believing God. Abraham's wife, Sarah, was also ninety years old (Gen 17:17) and had been barren from the time Abraham had married her (Gen 11:30). Paul's language is once more deliberately shocking: Abraham could see "the deadness (*nekrōsis*) of Sarah's womb" (4:19). And once more, the implication is clear: the birth of Isaac would literally have to be "life from death." Now we see the pertinence of Paul's speaking of the God "who gives life to the dead and calls into existence the things that do not exist" in 4:17, for only such a God could accomplish what had been promised in the face of such human impossibility.

Despite the evidence before him, Paul says, Abraham "did not weaken in faith" (4:19). The word choice here is once again important. Paul will later use the term "weakness" (*astheneia*) as something that is contrary to "faith" (6:19; 8:3, 26), and in his discussion of the "weak" and the "strong" in chapter 14, "weakness" will be characterized as a lack of a robust faith and trust (see also 1 Cor 8:7–12). How would weakness be manifested? If Abraham were to have "lack of faith" (*apistia*) or were to "waver" (*diakrinein*) concerning God's word in light of the evidence. But this did not happen. Instead, Abraham "grew strong in (= was empowered by) faith" (4:20).

Note now the two characteristics of Abraham, model of faith. First, he "gives glory to God" (4:20). This is the exact opposite of those idolators who, despite knowing God, "did not glorify him or give him thanks" (1:20). To glorify God, as I have suggested, means to recognize and acknowledge God's presence and power. What we learn from Abraham is that such acknowledgment sometimes (perhaps most often?) involves going beyond evidence that appears to point the other way. So Abraham, despite knowing full well what he and Sarah cannot do, recognizes what "he who gives life to the dead" *can* do. Thus, Paul notes, second, that Abraham was "fully convinced that God was able to do what he had promised" (4:21). He trusted the power and fidelity of the God he could not see or control rather than the weakness and frailty all too obviously before him. Paul concludes that *this* was why (*dio*) it was credited to him as a right relationship with God, "counted unto righteousness."

Paul has one more turn to take with Abraham, which is to connect his faith with that of Paul and his readers (4:23–25). He asserts that the words "it was reckoned to him" apply equally to those "who are believing in the one who has raised Jesus our Lord from the dead" (4:24). The faith of Christians, we see, is also *in God*, just as Abraham's was. Paul does not here speak of confessional faith in Christ. The faith that makes righteous is the fundamental response to reality as defined by the creating God, and this response is the same for Abraham, for Jesus, and for all humans, including Christians. In Paul's "now time," however, the living God has not called them out of one country into another or promised the birth of a child out of "dead" parents, but has, rather, "raised Jesus from the dead." Paul has deliberately structured the description of Abraham's faith in "the God who gives life to the dead" so that it matches precisely the shape of Christian faith. Now God's gift is the death and resurrection of the faithful son Jesus. Responding in trust and obedience to *this* action of the living God now represents the possibility of having "faith like Abraham's."

The discussion ends with a carefully balanced statement concerning the Jesus whom God raised: "he who was handed over on account of our transgressions, and raised on account of our being made righteous" (4:25, in a very literal translation). The balanced clauses, together with the use of the relative pronoun *hos* ("who") remind us of other traditional kerygmatic statements concerning Jesus (see, e.g., Phil 2:6; Col 1:15; 1 Tim 3:15). Despite the precise balancing of the clauses, however, the exact meaning is not entirely clear. Paul certainly considers both the death and resurrection of Jesus to have a vicarious character, that is, they were carried out "on account of us" or "for us." As in 3:24–25, we see Paul's understanding of Jesus as a representative figure, whose death—and now, his resurrection—is portentous for all humans. The resurrection here is also certainly understood as part of God's action in and through Jesus that worked for their vindication/acquittal/righteousness (all these translations are possible; see 5:18).

The first clause, however, remains obscure. The verb *paradidōmi* must be taken as referring to Jesus' death. It is used for arresting, or "handing over" someone to execution in such passages as Matt 4:12; 5:25; 10:19; 17:22; 26:2; Luke 22:6; 24:7; John 19:16 (compare 2 Cor 4:11 and especially Gal 2:20). In the present context, the verb takes on an added nuance because of Paul's threefold repetition of "God handed them over" in 1:24, 26, 28. Now Jesus is being "handed over." Paul will also declare in 8:32 that God "did not spare his only son but handed him over (*paradidōmi*) for all of us." So far, so good. But what is the connection between Jesus' death and "our transgressions"? The noun *paraptōma* is not itself particularly difficult. It is used for any sort of sin, trespass, or transgression (see Matt 6:14-15; Gal 6:1; Eph 1:7; Col 2:13). It plays a prominent role in Romans immediately after this passage; Paul will use the same term in 5:15, 16, 17, 18 and 20, when contrasting Christ and Adam.

There are two possible meanings for "on account of our sins." The first is that the sins of all humans made the death of Jesus necessary as a kind of repayment or penalty. But there is nothing in Paul's language elsewhere to support that sort of reading. The second meaning is more likely: "our sins" put us humans in such a position of alienation from God that only the "handing over" of the Son of God in our behalf could reach us to rescue us. Paul is comfortable with this sort of "language of exchange." In 2 Cor 5:21, for example, he says, "For our sake he made him to be sin who knew no sin, so that in him we might become the righteousness of God." Something close to that is meant here, I think, especially in light of two passages on either side of it. In 3:22-23, Paul said that "since all have sinned and fallen short of the glory of God, they are justified by his grace as a gift through the redemption which is in Christ Jesus." And in 5:6 and 8, Paul will state, "while we were still weak, at the right time, Christ died for the ungodly . . . while we were yet sinners, Christ died for us." It is in this sense that "Jesus was handed over on account of our sins"—not that every human is responsible for the death of the messiah, but that the death of the messiah was necessary to reach those so lost under the power of sin.

In chapter 4, Paul has masterfully employed the figure of Abraham to demonstrate how Torah itself, when read from the perspective of the "now time" experience of the messiah, reveals how righteousness is established by faith, and therefore that "faith establishes Torah" (3:31). Paul has also demonstrated again that Jew and Gentile are on the same footing with God. Abraham is the father of all who believe, showing how faith is possible to Gentiles as well as to Jews. Finally, Paul shows the inner structure of faith as response to the living God who challenges humanity with surprising revelations of presence and power.

GOD'S GIFT IN CHRIST JESUS

Romans 5:1–21

In a very real way, Romans 5 is the heart of Paul's argument, for it is where he brings to a climax the positive demonstration of his thesis concerning how "God's righteousness" has worked to make humans righteous through faith. The chapter falls naturally into two sections which are intimately related. In 5:1–11, Paul emphasizes the *reality* of the gift that God has given us in Christ. In 5:12–21, he stresses the *greatness* and *character* of that gift. It is in this second section that we come to understand what Paul means by the "faith of Jesus": the obedience toward God by which Christ reversed the reign of sin begun by Adam.

Chapter 5 will provide us with one more glimpse of the complex symbolic world within which Paul constructs his argument concerning God. We will find Paul employing classic tropes from Greco-Roman rhetoric, but they will be put in service of a midrashic reading of Torah, generated in turn by the specific religious experience shared by Paul and his readers, of Jesus, the crucified and raised messiah (see N. A. Dahl, "Two Notes on Romans 5," *Studia Theologica* 5 [1951]: 37–48).

The Gift Has Been Given and Received (5:1–5)

Once more, the present-day reader may need reminding that the chapter divisions in our New Testament are a later invention. We should not be surprised, therefore, to find the *beginning* of our chapter 5 taking the form of a solemn *conclusion* to what is our chapter 4! Paul declares, "Therefore, since we have been made righteous on the basis of faith." The participle he uses here is in the aorist tense, which signifies that the action has already happened. Being in right relationship with God is not something Paul and his readers long for, but is a present reality.

Recognizing this emphasis also helps to resolve a textual problem in the Greek phrase that follows. Some manuscripts read, "we have peace," and others, "let us have peace" toward God through our Lord Jesus Christ. The difference in the Greek is a matter of one letter, so it is easy to understand how scribes (especially taking dictation) might have mistaken one for the other. I think the indicative found in the best critical editions is undoubtedly the form chosen by Paul, even though the manuscript evidence itself is evenly divided. The reason for considering it the best text is simply that it fits Paul's point better. He is not, in this place, exhorting his readers, but rather expounding to them the situation they are in.

The result of being put in right relationship through faith, Paul declares, is "peace toward God." When discussing the greeting to the letter, I pointed out that the term *eirēnē* was not only a common Jewish greeting but also the specific quality of a proper covenantal relationship (see above on 1:7). In contrast to the wicked, who "do not know the paths of peace" (3:17), those who are in right relationship with God have *šālôm* ("peace"). Things are, in a word, as they should be. The next phrase makes clear once more that this is a state of affairs that God has accomplished "through our Lord Jesus Christ." The designation "Lord" (*kyrios*) is specifically attached to Jesus as the risen one (see Phil 2:11; 1 Cor 12:3; Rom 10:9) and picks up from the immediately preceding statement, "the one who raised our Lord Jesus from the dead" (4:24). More significant for the argument, it focuses the reader's attention on the figure of Jesus, who dominates this section of Romans more than any other. Paul will argue that Jesus is the means by which God's gift is given to humans and, in a very real sense, is himself the gift.

Indeed, Paul immediately states, "it is through him that we have obtained access to this gift/grace (*charis*) in which we stand" (5:2). Before we can discuss this further, we need to take note of another textual variant. A good many ancient manuscripts contain the phrase "by faith" after the phrase "access to this gift." I agree with those critics who see this as a later addition influenced by Eph 3:12, even though the presence of the phrase would accord perfectly with Paul's argument. We find here, in any case, a restatement of 3:24, with a stronger emphasis on Jesus as the instrument of God's gift and the reality of its reception: Jesus "gave access" to the gift, in which "we are standing."

There is some possibility that Paul deliberately used the term "access" (*prosagōgē*) for its cultic connotations, since the verb "approach" (*prosagein*) is used by the LXX both for the specific rituals of the day of atonement and generally for access to the divine presence (see Exod 29:4, 10; Lev 16:1–21; Num 5:16; Deut 2:19). If so, this would further strengthen the argument that Paul used sacrificial imagery in 3:25. Certainly, Eph 2:18 and 3:12 use the term in just such a connection, and, using a different word,

Heb 10:19 sounds the same note of "access through the blood of Jesus." We can speak more confidently about "standing," for Paul uses it in other places with the same meaning as here, namely, to indicate the position one takes as the basis for claiming one's life (see, e.g., 1 Cor 15:1 and Rom 10:3; 11:20; 14:4).

Since where one "stands" is, for Paul, the ground on which one "boasts," he immediately declares here, "and we make our boast on the hope of the glory of God" (5:3). Such a literal translation is more accurate than the RSV's "we rejoice," which misses the important thematic connections of "boasting" in Romans. As I noted earlier, Paul does not reject boasting as such. The issue is the ground on which one boasts. The idolator/sinner "boasts" on the basis of what that person has done. For Paul, the proper ground for boasting is what *God* has done: "Let the one who boasts, boast in the Lord" (1 Cor 1:31; 2 Cor 10:17). He can therefore declare unselfconsciously in Phil 3:3, "we are those who boast in Christ Jesus."

Paul therefore contrasts the boasting in one's own efforts and possessions that is characteristic of idolatry's self-aggrandizement to the boasting in the hope of the glory of God, rooted in the gift of God. Note again, how "the glory of God" picks up from 4:20, which characterized Abraham's faith as "giving glory to God" and stands in opposition to the refusal to "give glory to God" by idolators (1:20). It is in this light that Paul's use of the term "hope" must be understood. Of all the words in the Christian lexicon, this one is perhaps the least adequately defined or appropriately appreciated. It tends to be regarded as an expectation concerning the future, and it does have that dimension. But as Paul uses the language of hope, it has less to do with the future than with the present. Hope is a perception of the present based on the premise of God's presence and power. Hope is that which enables us to move into the future because of the reality of God's presence in the "now time."

In 5:3-5, Paul builds on these opening statements, using the rhetorical device known as the *sorites* or *climax*. The device consists of a chain of phrases in which the last word of one is picked up by the first word of the next. When properly constructed, the phrases create a sense of urgency and, at the end, of satisfying "climax." The technique is widely used in antiquity (see H. Fischel, "The Uses of the Sorites [*Climax, Gradatio*] in the Tannaitic Period," *Hebrew Union College Annual* 44 [1973]: 119-51). The most impressive example in the New Testament is 2 Pet 1:5-7. There is a *sorites* similar to this one in Jas 1:2-4, and in 1 Pet 1:5-7 a less striking combination involving testing and faith. It is possible that all three authors were working with a common tradition. Certainly the theme of "joy in suffering" finds its oxymoronic place in the religion of a crucified and raised messiah! In light of what has been given in Christ, Paul says, Christians can boast "even in tribulations." The term suggests the sort of afflictions that are imposed from the outside, as by oppressors or opponents (see 1 Thess 1:6; 3:3; 2 Thess 1:4; 1 Cor 7:28; 2 Cor 1:4; 7:4). Paul will pick up this same term again in 8:35, when he declares that "tribulation or distress or persecution" will not separate them from the love of Christ. The experience of affliction instigated by others is deeply ingrained in the Christian experience, beginning with Jesus himself, of whom Paul says in 15:3 (quoting LXX Ps 68:9), "the reproaches of those reproaching you fell on me." Here Paul affirms that tribulation can be "boasted on" because Christians *know* something that it can accomplish: "tribulation produces endurance and endurance produces character, and proven character, hope."

Paul's remarkably optimistic assessment of suffering has two possible roots. The first is the tradition of Greco-Roman philosophy, which, especially in Stoicism, gave a positive valuation to suffering as an element in the formation of character. The conviction that "to learn meant to suffer" (*mathein pathein*) enabled otherwise negative human experiences to be given a positive appreciation (see Herodotus, *Persian War* 1.207; Seneca, *On Providence* 1.6; Epictetus, *Discourses* 1.29.33; and C. H. Talbert, *Learning through Suffering: The Educational Value of Suffering in the New Testament and in its Milieu* [Collegeville: Liturgical Press, 1991]). More proximately, however, the suffering of Jesus (which Paul saw as continuing in his own sufferings and those of his readers [see Col 1:24; Gal 2:20; 4:19]) guides his perception of suffering as yielding endurance and endurance, proven character, and finally, hope. Jesus' death on the cross showed how, at the depths of human shame, foolishness, and powerlessness, the glory and wisdom and power of God could most effectively be at work (1 Cor 1:18–25). This conviction concerning the crucified messiah enabled Paul to view all of life's experiences in this complex, relational fashion, so that suffering takes on entirely new dimensions (see 2 Cor 1:5; 4:11–12). Jesus' death on the cross then becomes paradigmatic for faith in God's presence and power despite human appearances: "we felt that we had received the sentence of death; but that was to make us rely, not on ourselves, but on the God who raises the dead" (2 Cor 1:9).

If this is so, then "our hope does not shame" (5:5). The RSV translation of *kataischynei* as "does not disappoint us" is certainly possible, but it again misses the literary interconnections of this term (as did its translation of *kauchasthai* as "rejoice" in 5:3). The term echoes Paul's statement in 1:16 that he was not "ashamed" of the good news, because it was the power of God for salvation. This hope does not shame because it is based in that which is most real: "for the love of God has been poured into our hearts by the Holy Spirit that has been given to us" (5:5). What a remarkably rich statement, and deserving of a closer look at its language.

This is Paul's first use of the word *agapē* ("love") in the letter. The genitive construction is surely subjective, since Paul is talking about God's love for humans, rather than the reverse (see 5:8). The love that God shows humans, as well as the love of Christ for his fellow humans, is one of the powerful themes in Romans. Paul will exclaim in 8:35, "Who can separate us from the love of Christ?" and in 8:39, "nothing will be able to separate us from the love of God in Christ Jesus our Lord." The term Paul uses for love, *agapē*, was a favorite with Christian writers, for whom it expressed better than other Greek expressions for love what they meant by God's disposition toward humans. Unlike the term *eros*, which denotes the passionate love that seeks unity with the one desired, and unlike *philia*, which denotes the binding of people with like interests, the term *agapē* (as the New Testament writers employ it) refers to disposition of the will in which the good of the other is sought for the other's sake. For Paul (as for other New Testament writers), the *agapē* shown by God toward humans becomes, in turn, the model for the way Christians are to dispose themselves toward each other (see Rom 12:9; 13:10; 14:15; see C. Spicq, *Agapē in the New Testament,* trans. M. A. McNamara and M. A. Richter [St. Louis: Herder, 1963]).

Most striking in the present case is that Paul connects this *agapē* that God has toward "us," with the Holy Spirit. The Holy Spirit here appears as the means or agency by which God's *agapē* reaches us "in our hearts." In 15:30, Paul will feel equally comfortable speaking of the "love of the Holy Spirit." Out of such coalescences did later trinitarian doctrine develop!

No New Testament writer speaks more frequently about the Holy Spirit or insists more emphatically on the immediacy of its presence in the Christian community (see, e.g., 1 Cor 12:3-13). But what does Paul mean by "the Holy Spirit"? The two constitutive terms give us a clue. Spirit denotes a form of power or energy that is at once personal and transcendent—it touches and transforms human "spirit," that is, the human capacity for knowing and loving, human freedom. The term "holy" denotes that this energy field is not generated by human desire or longing but comes from the Other, the source of all being, all life, "the Holy One." Paul consistently connects the presence of this Holy Spirit among believers with the resurrection of Jesus, so that the two realities are mutually defining. We have the Holy Spirit because Jesus is raised; we know Jesus is raised because we have his Holy Spirit. Thus, in 1 Cor 12:3, "No one can say, 'Jesus is Lord,' except by the Holy Spirit." With the resurrection of Jesus, this power for transformation has been made intimately available: "we have all drunk from the same Spirit" (1 Cor 12:13). The same sort of "fluid imagery" is used for the energy transference Paul envisages as the gift of *agapē* in the present passage: the love of God "has been poured into our hearts" by the Holy Spirit. That Paul is speaking metaphorically, however, is shown by his use of the term "heart," which for him as for the entire biblical tradition refers to the seat of human knowing and affection (see also 1:21, 24; 2:5, 15, 29). In a word, God's love has touched the human spirit by the transforming power of the Holy Spirit. A real exchange has taken place within human freedom.

The richness of Paul's language here should not deflect us from appreciating his most important, indeed overwhelming, point. The gift that God gave in the death and resurrection of Jesus, the gift that Jesus gave in his faithful death, *has reached us*. Being in right relationship with God is not a fond desire or wistful hope. It is present and real and the basis for all hope. This is, indeed, the best of news.

God's Reconciling Action (5:6–11)

Paul now spells out the grandeur of God's gesture of love in Christ. He begins in vv. 6–8 by showing what a chasm God's love had to cross in order to reach God's creatures. By emphasizing the alienation and powerlessness of humans, Paul magnifies the greatness of God's power for reconciliation. But notice the shift in grammatical subject in v. 6. Although it is God's love that is being expressed, Jesus' faithful death is the expression of it. So Paul declares, "while we were still weak, at the right season, Christ died for the ungodly." We have seen already in the case of Abraham how the designation of "weakness" stands in opposition to the "faith that empowers" (4:19–20). Humans cannot do this for themselves—they cannot leap the infinite qualitative difference between themselves and God. But Paul also uses the term "ungodly," which recalls both 1:18 (the wrath being revealed over all ungodliness), and especially 4:5 (God justifies the ungodly). Paul makes no distinction here between Jew and Greek; the "us" includes both Jew and Greek. Humans are not only too weak to reach God, Paul suggests; they don't even want to, having "suppressed the truth." For such creatures as these, Paul says simply, "Christ died." He thereby makes explicit what was implied in such terms as "redemption" (3:24) and "expiation" (3:25), namely, that Jesus' death was a vicarious sacrifice, a self-donation in behalf of others who neither wanted nor could accomplish reconciliation with God.

Using the rhetorical device of amplification in another way, Paul heightens God's act by means of a concessive contrast: "One will hardly die for a righteous person—though perhaps for a good person one might make bold to die" (5:7). Paul seems to recognize here those in Judaism who died the "noble death" of martyrdom in behalf of Torah and for their fellows (see 4 Macc 17:22; and A. J. Droge and J. D. Tabor, *A Noble Death: Suicide and Martyrdom among Christians and Jews in Antiquity* [San Francisco: HarperSanFrancisco, 1992]). The author of Hebrews also offers such as these fulsome praise (Heb 11:32-40). But Paul has argued that the people for whom Christ died were anything but "good." They were among the "godless." Indeed, what "commends God's love for us" is this remarkable fact: "while we were yet sinners, Christ died for us" (5:8). We note again how Paul has personalized the entire transaction. Not "others" were the sinners, but "we were sinners." Christ died not in behalf of a faceless humanity but for each individual human person. This is the defining truth about Jesus for Paul, that "he loved me and gave himself for me" (Gal 2:20). This is the realization that shapes the language of exchange that is so characteristic of Paul's rhetoric—foolishness for wisdom, weakness for strength (1 Cor 1:25; 2 Cor 13:4), poverty for wealth (2 Cor 8:9), sin for righteousness (2 Cor 5:21)—as he struggles to give expression to a death of a human person that meant life for others (2 Cor 5:14).

Then, in vv. 9-11, Paul extols the gift of God by showing the consequences of the reconciliation won through the faithful death of Jesus. These next statements use a construction that Paul will employ also in 5:12-21, to emphasize how one thing is greater than another. Paul uses the adverbial phrase *pollō mallon*, which can be translated approximately as "how much the more." It structures the sort of argument that in Greek rhetoric was known as *a minore ad maius* ("from the lesser to the greater"), and in rabbinic Judaism was called *qal we ḥomer* ("light and heavy"). The basic logic is that if something is true in a small instance, it will also be true in a large instance, or even more true! If a child is a bully, the adult will be a monster. Or, as Jesus said to the women in Jerusalem on the way to Golgotha, "If they do this when the wood is green, what will happen when it is dry?" (Luke 23:31).

Thus Paul argues, "since we have been made righteous now by his blood" (that is, the death of Jesus), "how much more will we be saved by him from the wrath" (5:9). Paul clearly has in mind here the scenario sketched in 1:18, where the wrath of God comes upon all ungodliness. A similar statement is found also in 1 Thess 1:10, where Paul speaks of "waiting for [God's] son from heaven, whom he raised from the dead, Jesus who delivers us from the wrath to come." I spoke earlier about Paul's understanding of salvation in social terms. The use of the plural "us" here supports that social perception. But his language also clearly suggests a future crisis from which he and his readers expect to be "delivered."

His expectation, based on what God had already done for them through the death of Jesus, is that this hope is secure. In v. 10, he provides the premise: "For if while we were enemies we were reconciled to God by the death of his son, how much more shall we be saved by his life now that we are reconciled." Besides providing the ground for the hope that Paul expressed in the previous statement, this declaration also introduces a number of concepts we need to consider individually, if we are to grasp the next part of Paul's argument in chapter 5.

Four new things are introduced by 5:10. The first is Paul's description of those now gifted by God as "enemies." Later, he will call living according to the flesh "enmity toward God" (8:7). In the ancient Mediterranean world, enemies were just that, people one opposed and tried to destroy. Hatred of enemies was not only considered morally justified; it even had, in contrast to vices such as envy, a certain nobility to it (Plutarch, *On Envy and Hate* [*Mor.* 536E–538E]). By describing sinners as enemies of God, Paul at once shows how active and hateful the power of sin is (Rom 1:18–32) and at the same time, how powerful God's love was to overcome such deep estrangement. They were not only weak and unwilling to be in relationship with God; their lives were actively working against God.

The second thing to notice here is that Paul's language shifts from that of the courtroom to that of diplomacy. The relationship between God and humans is described not in terms of "righteousness/justice" but in terms of *reconciliation*, the act of bringing hostile parties into agreement or accord (see 1 Cor 7:11; 2 Macc 1:5, and "peace" in 5:1). On reconciliation, see F. Büchsel, "*alassō*," *TDNT* 1:251–59. Paul uses this metaphor theologically only here and in 2 Cor 5:18–20, but it obviously expresses a fundamental perception: "God was in Christ reconciling the world to himself" (2 Cor 5:19).

Third, we see that Paul once more correlates the sequence of death and resurrection in the redeeming act of Jesus to stages in the believers' existence: reconciliation through Jesus' death, and salvation through his resurrection life. Fourth and finally, Paul designates Jesus as "his son." This is the first time Paul has alluded to Jesus as "son of God" since the greeting (1:4). For Paul, the facts that God "sent his son" (8:3; see Gal 4:4) to save humans and "did not spare his own son" (8:32) are irrefutable evidence of the radical character of God's love for humans. As we shall see, he suggests also that God thus responds to the faith of Abraham, who "did not spare his only son" when called to sacrifice him by God (N. A. Dahl, "The Atonement: Adequate Reward for the Akedah?" in *The Crucified Messiah* [Minneapolis: Augsburg, 1974] 146–60).

What does Paul mean by calling Jesus "son of God?" It is a vexing problem in interpretation, one complicated by the doctrinal developments in Christianity that used such passages within a philosophical framework to work out a metaphysically exquisite balance between "two natures in one person." The first thing that present-day readers ought not to do, therefore, is read all this development back into Paul. On the other hand, Paul's use of such language is scarcely casual. He does not use the full title *huios tou theou* often (Rom 1:4; 2 Cor 1:19; Gal 2:20; Eph 4:13), although the expression "his son" appears more frequently (Rom 1:9; 5:10; 8:3, 29, 32; 1 Cor

15:28; Gal 4:4, 6; Col 1:13; 1 Thess 1:10). In passages such as the present one, which speaks of Jesus' death, or 2 Cor 1:19, which refers to his yes to God, or Gal 2:20, which speaks of his faith, Paul clearly focuses on the *humanity* of God's son and especially his human response to God. In Rom 1:4 as well, in the phrase "designated son of God in power through the Spirit of holiness" the emphasis is on a human person who is elevated to a certain status by resurrection. Other passages, however, such as Rom 8:3 and Gal 4:4, speak of God "sending his son," which suggests having a place with God before the sending. Certainly Paul does not shy away from some sense of pre-human existence for the Christ (see, e.g., 1 Cor 8:6; 2 Cor 5:21; 2 Cor 8:9; Phil 2:6; see J. A. Fitzmyer, *Paul and His Theology: A Brief Sketch* [2nd ed.; Englewood Cliffs, N.J.: Prentice Hall, 1989] 49–54).

Precisely such complexity gave rise to the later doctrinal development I have mentioned. The point for our present discussion is this: for Paul, Jesus is not simply another human being. However he might have understood it, metaphysically, Paul considered Jesus to be "son of God" in a sense no other human being could claim, as his later use of the language of "adoption" itself indicates (Rom 8:14–15). Because of his distinctive status, Jesus is able to say yes both for humans and for God (2 Cor 1:19). This special role becomes critical in the next section, where Paul will contrast Jesus to Adam.

Paul closes this praise of God's act in Christ by turning from the expectation for the future to the celebration of the present: "not only that, but we also are boasting in God through our Lord Jesus Christ, through whom we now have received our reconciliation" (5:11). The theme of "boasting" responds to the same term in 5:1, to create a bracket around the section. The language here also echoes that in 2:17. There Paul had addressed the Jew who "boasted in God" because of the knowledge of Torah. Paul's "boasting in the Lord" is based not in the knowledge of texts but in the experience of God's love, which has reconciled them *now* through Jesus.

The Reign of Sin (5:12–14)

In these verses, Paul begins to expound the radical and indeed cosmic implications of the death and resurrection of Jesus. He does this by focusing once more on sin. Now, however, he goes back to the origin and pervasiveness of sin from an angle other than that of idolatry. He engages another biblical character, not Abraham but Adam, who in an even more obvious way can be called "father of us all" (see W. D. Davies, *Paul and Rabbinic Judaism* [New York: Harper & Row, 1948] 36–57).

Paul's focus on Adam is not unprecedented, but it is exceptional. After the Genesis account, Adam is not mentioned in the Hebrew Torah as an individual figure. He does appear in LXX Sir 33:10 and 40:1, as well as in Tobit 8:6, but these texts make no mention of Adam's sin. Philo Judaeus paid more attention to the creation of Adam than to his fall, emphasizing the way in which Adam represents humanity as a whole (*On the Creation* 142). In Jewish texts subsequent to Paul, we find a certain amount of speculation on Adam, particularly with regard to his cosmic significance (see *m. Sanh.* 4:5; *b. Sanh.* 38a-b; *b. Bab. Bat.* 75a; *Exodus Rabbah* 40.3) and the consequences of his sin (*4 Esdras* 3:7; *Apocalypse of Moses* 10; *2 Baruch* 17:3; *Midrash Qoheleth* 43; see J. DeFraine, *Adam and the Family of Man* [New York: Alba House, 1965]).

In Paul's view, Adam was more than one in a series. As the first human, he had a representative role, so that what happened to him was of decisive and defining importance for all those following him. For Paul's comparison and contrast to make sense, I think we need to take seriously how he viewed Jesus' resurrection as a fundamentally new beginning for humanity. In 4:17, we saw how Paul put God's capacity to "give life to the dead" in the same line as "calling into being that which did not exist." Creation and resurrection are variations of the same theme. And Paul unequivocally regarded Jesus' resurrection as a new creation: "If anyone is in Christ, there is a new creation; the old has passed away, behold, the new has come" (2 Cor 5:17). Likewise, in 1 Cor 15:45-50, Paul contrasts the two representatives of humanity in terms of the first creation and the resurrection: "thus it is written, 'the first man Adam became a living being' [Gen 2:7]. The last Adam became a life-giving Spirit." Once this is granted, then a comparison to the first human in the old creation makes sense as a way of dramatically illustrating the radical character of what has happened through Jesus (see K. Barth, *Christ and Adam* [New York: Collier Books, 1962]). In the present case, the contrast is between sin and grace and the power exercised over humanity by each.

The connection is made to 5:1-11 by the connective phrase "because of this" (*dia touto*)—he is now going to describe the situation that required the reconciling act of the death of God's son (5:12). He begins with a chiastic proposition linking sin and death through the grammatical hooks "just as" (*hōsper*) and "and so" (*kai houtōs*). Paul asserts: (a) that sin came into the world through one man, and (b) that through sin came death, and that (b') thus death spread to all humans, because (a') all humans have sinned. Before going into the logic of this, we should grasp the overall significance of the equation: Paul is positing a universal situation within humanity of sin and death, which can be reversed by a death that is a faithful act of obedience carried out by a human of a status equal to or greater than Adam (5:12-21).

That "sin came into the world through one man" is unarguable from Gen 3:6, although one can note parenthetically that Paul here avoids statements concerning the "deception of Eve" that he makes elsewhere (see 2 Cor 11:3; 1 Tim 2:14-15). But what about "through sin, death"? It might be thought that since Adam was made from earth (Gen 2:7), his mortality would be implicit in his creation. But since the sanction attached to disobedience of God's command not to eat "of the tree of knowledge of good and evil" was "on the day that you eat of it you shall die" (Gen 2:17), Paul is able to connect the human experience of death directly to Adam's sin of disobedience. This is confirmed by the curse that accompanies the couple's expulsion from the garden—an exile defined as protection against their eating the tree of life and "living forever"—namely, "you are dust and to dust you shall return" (Gen 3:19). The Genesis story strongly implies that death is not natural, a perception that coincides with the deep human longing for immortality (see Philo, *On the Creation* 134-135). The same sort of understanding is found in Wis 2:23-24: "God created men for incorruption, and made him in the image of his own eternity, but through the devil's envy death entered the world, and those who belong to his party experience it." The issue here, however, is not so much biological as axiological: not so much whether humans naturally die as whether humans' death as marked by sin is "natural." With Adam, death becomes a sign of sin, of an alienation from God brought about by disobedience (see C. C. Black, "Pauline Perspectives on Death in Romans 5-8," *Journal of Biblical Literature* 103 [1984]: 413-33).

Paul's next statement, "death spread to all humans because all humans sinned" (5:12), is one of the most hotly disputed in the history of the interpretation of Romans (see J. T. Kirby, "The Syntax of Romans 5:12: A Rhetorical Approach," *New Testament Studies* 33 [1987]: 283-86). The reason is the patristic debate over "original sin," which involved connecting this "sin of Adam" with the "all have sinned." The issue is extremely complex and need not concern us here, for it is really raised not so much by Paul's text as by the need to find in Paul's text support for divergent interpretations of the human situation. Is human nature scarred from conception by the effect of Adam's sin, or is it possible for humans not to sin (see, e.g., Augustine, *On Forgiveness of Sins and Baptism*). In the context of this debate, much attention was given to the Greek construction *eph' hō*, which the RSV correctly translates as "because." Some Latin translations, however, rendered this as *in quo*, which could be read by those not knowing Greek as "in whom." Now, Paul was understood to be saying, "death spread to all men, for *in him* we have all sinned." Thus, Adam's sin would be one that did not only influence all others, but actually ontologically contained all others. From this sort of premise came various patristic theories concerning how that "original sin" was transmitted, whether through male sperm, for example, or the concupiscence that accompanied sexual intercourse (see F. R. Tennant, *The Sources of the Doctrines of the Fall and Original Sin* [New

York: Schocken Books, 1903]). All such speculation is exegetically beside the point, for in Greek Paul is simply stating that everyone has sinned the way Adam did, so that the effect of Adam's sin continues, and continues to be symbolized by the death experienced by all humans.

In 5:13, Paul issues one of those asides on the law that have puzzled us from the early part of the letter, and concerning which we must here once more delay full consideration: "sin was in the world until the law [or: before the law was given] but sin is not reckoned where there is no law." His main point, though, is a return to 1:18–32: sin is a pervasive and systemic disease of the human spirit. It goes much deeper and much farther back than transgressions against a written law. By so saying, Paul has once more bypassed the religiously critical function of the law. Just as Abraham shows that *faith* was active in the world before the law, Adam demonstrates that *sin* was, as well. The law will enter into the equation, but more as a variable than as a constant.

But now in 5:14, Paul makes an even stronger claim concerning the effects of sin: "But death reigned from Adam to Moses, even over those who did not sin the way Adam did." Remember how Paul thinks of humans as inevitably "subject" or "obedient" to some power above themselves, either the true God or the distorted projections of their own self-striving. In a dramatic collapsing of terms, Paul equates the rule of sin with the rule of death: death rules! This is the logical corollary of Paul's description of humanity under sin. People are filled with "malice . . . envy, murder, strife" (1:29). It is not simply that people die; it is that they put each other to death, wickedly and violently, because of their competition for life and worth, driven by the refusal to accept contingency as a gift. Such people as these, Paul notes soberly in 1:32, "deserve to die." But it is also the fear of death that drives them to such compulsive striving, such fierce competition to endure, survive, live! From beginning to end, therefore, in the reign of sin, death rules. And, Paul says, this has been the case long before the giving of the law, with its curses and threats of death, even for those whose sins were not (according to the best manuscripts) like that of Adam.

But then, if sin and death have come to rule even over those who do not sin as Adam did, why focus on Adam? Because, says Paul, he is the "type of the one to come" (5:14). By speaking of Adam as a "type" (*typos*), Paul seems to be employing the imagery that is broadly associated with the Platonic tradition of Greek philosophy, which used such terms for the distinction between material and spiritual realities. Philo, for example, distinguishes between the Adam of the first Genesis account, who was created in the image of God (Gen 1:26), and the Adam of the second creation account, who was made from the earth (2:7). For Philo, the "first Adam" was the heavenly prototype of the "second" or earthly Adam, who was inferior because made up of material elements (see *On the Creation* 134-35).

As we have seen earlier, Paul uses the same distinction but in a completely different way, by applying the imagery of the "two Adams" to Christ. In 1 Cor 15:45, he asserts that the "first Adam" was the one who was of the earth and that the "second Adam" (i.e., Christ) is heavenly. In other words, Paul does three things with the language of typology. He makes it apply to two different people; he puts it on the plane of history rather than cosmology; and he makes the second figure greater than the first. This enables him in what follows to draw the most immediate connection between the characteristic actions of Adam and Jesus, together with the consequences following upon each.

Obedience and Disobedience (5:15–21)

This last part of Romans 5 makes use of a rhetorical trope called *synkrisis*. It is a technique used especially in epideictic speeches to increase praise or blame by means of comparison or contrast. In the present case, the gift of God in Christ is contrasted to the sin of Adam. Paul has set up the comparison by proposing Adam as "the type of the one who is to come" (5:14). The specific object of praise is the gift by which God reversed the human condition and established humanity in right relationship with himself. In the process, Paul also reveals his own understanding of the "faith of Christ" as Jesus' human obedience to God.

The section is structured by a series of eight comparisons, all of them ringing changes on the same theme and clarifying the basic contrast stated in 5:15, "the free gift (*charisma*) is not like the trespass." Although Paul uses a number of different terms, we should see them as synonyms lined up on either side of the ledger. Thus, on one side, he speaks of "trespass" (*paraptōma*), "sinning" (*hamartanein*), and "sin" (*hamartia*), and on the other side of "free gift" (*charisma*), "grace" (*charis*), and "gift" (*dōrea*). But they all point to the same contrast between what was done through Adam's disobedience (*parakoē*) and Jesus' obedience (*hypakoē*).

The first contrast is unbalanced: "for if many died through one man's trespass, how much more have the grace of God and the free gift in the grace of the one man Jesus Christ abounded for many" (5:15). We might have expected a contrast between life and death, but instead Paul focuses on the *gift* given through Christ. This is how God got through all the web of human idolatry and the systemic influence of sin, by giving a gift so powerful that it could disrupt those patterns and restructure them on the basis of a new way of responding to God. He uses three separate terms for "gift" to make the point. His second emphasis is how the *effect* of this gift exceeds that of the sin: "how much more" has it "overflowed/abounded" for many.

In 5:16, Paul continues this thought and refines it: "and the free gift is not like the effect of that one man's sin. For the judgment following one trespass brought condemnation, but the free gift following many trespasses brings a righteous deed." The last word of this sentence is difficult. Paul uses the noun *dikaiōma*. The RSV translates it as "justification," relying on the metaphor of judgment and condemnation, and that rendering may be correct. It is also possible, however, for Paul to have in mind here the "righteous deed" worked by Jesus that enables others to perform the "righteous requirement" of the law (see the use of *dikaiōma* in 2:26, 5:18, and 8:4). In either case, Paul returns here to the forensic language that dominated chapters 1-4.

At this point Paul draws the contrast between death and life that we had been expecting: "If, because of one man's trespass, death reigned through that one man, much more will those who receive the abundance of grace and the free gift of righteousness reign in life through the one man, Jesus Christ" (5:17). Paul here makes explicit that death's rule over humans was effected through sin: "The sting of sin is death," he declares in 1 Cor 15:56, "but thanks be to God who gives us the victory through our Lord Jesus Christ" (1 Cor 15:57). In the contrasting member, he makes "the abounding gift" and "the free gift of righteousness" equivalent. Those who have received it "will reign in life." Here Paul seems to mean a sharing in the resurrection life that is initiated through Jesus. 1 Cor 15:21-22 is a perfect gloss on this passage: "For as by a man came death, by a man has come also the resurrection of the dead. For as in Adam all die, so also in Christ shall all be made alive."

As the tense of Paul's verbs indicates, the "reigning" of believers is a future rather than a present reality. Indeed, he chided the arrogance of the Corinthian Christians, who considered themselves to "already rule" in the kingdom of God (1 Cor 4:8). In the next chapter of Romans, Paul will also admonish his readers not to let sin "reign" in their mortal bodies. The rule of God is effectively active and powerful through the resurrection of Jesus and the gift of the Holy Spirit (1 Cor 4:20; 6:9-10; Col 1:13; 4:11; Eph 5:5; Gal 5:21; Rom 14:17), but it is not yet fully realized (1 Cor 15:24-57).

In 5:18, Paul shifts attention to the specific acts of Adam and Christ: "Then just as one man's trespass led to condemnation for all people, so one man's act of righteousness leads to acquittal and life for all people." Now the gift of God through Christ is described as an "act of righteousness" (*dikaiōma;* see on 5:16) that has as its effect (literally from the Greek) "an acquittal that consists in life." The language is very compressed. Paul has in mind not only the lifting of a death penalty but a "liberation" (redemption) that is entry into a whole new form of life, a sharing in Christ's resurrection life (see 6:1-11). It is as though a death row inmate had not only had his sentence commuted but was given a complete pardon and allowed to begin life over again on a whole new basis.

Finally, in 5:19, Paul defines Jesus' "righteous act" in terms of obedience to God: "For as by one man's disobedience many were made sinners, so by one's man's obedience many will be made righteous." This line shows us what Paul means by the "faith of Jesus." It is his obedient response to God in his life and above all in his death. This is the "faith that makes righteous." Paul's language is precise. By Jesus' action, many "will be established as righteous." That is, his action provides the basis for the possibility for them also to be righteous. Just as Adam's action established a framework of sin that twisted even goodness into rebellion, Jesus' action creates a new set of possibilities for humans to live in "right relationship" with God. The key to understanding Paul's point here is the passage in Phil 2:6-11 that depicts Jesus as the suffering servant, "obedient to death, even death on the cross" (see, e.g., C. H. Talbert, "The Problem of Pre-Existence in Philippians 2:6-11," *Journal of Biblical Literature* 86 [1967]: 141-53; G. Howard, "Phil 2:6-11 and the Human Christ," *Catholic Biblical Quarterly* 40 [1978]: 368-87). This is what Paul means by "the obedience of faith" that he proclaims to the Gentiles (1:5; 16:26).

Once more in 5:20, Paul makes an allusive remark concerning the law: "Law came in to increase the trespass, but where sin increased, grace abounded all the more." We must, for the moment, place this comment with the others (including 5:12) that have been accumulating on this point and put them off until the next chapter, when we can finally deal with the question, What *is* the problem of the law, anyway? For now, we note that its effect, according to Paul, is to "increase the trespass," but that also, in light of the gift now given, the eventual result is that "grace abounded even more"–indeed, the Greek could be rendered, "superabounded." By so asserting, Paul has planted the seed of the problem we must deal with in the next section: if sin makes for more grace, why not keep sinning, so that there is still more grace (see also 3:8). But before approaching that problem, he concludes this section much as he began it, with a solemn assertion that pulls these separate elements of *synkrisis* together into a final comparison: "So that, as sin reigned in death, grace might also reign through righteousness to eternal life through Jesus Christ our Lord" (5:21).

Summary

Chapter 5 is the heart of Paul's argument concerning how God's righteousness revealed itself by making humans righteous by free gift. After this, Paul must deal with questions that his argument logically raises. As we have seen, this chapter is also the christological core of Romans, as Paul explicates in terms of "obedience" what he means by the "faith of Christ" and shows that "the righteous will live by his faith" must be understood in terms of the resurrection life which Jesus the righteous one entered through his obedient faith and which has been shared with believers by "the love of God poured into [their] hearts by the Holy Spirit" (5:5).

In this part of his argument, we have learned the true depth of Paul's apprehension of Christ. As Son of God, Jesus was not, for Paul, simply another human teacher, nor was his death that of all mortal flesh, nor his resurrection another resuscitation after a "near death" experience. Jesus was rather, for Paul, the start of a new humanity; his death was a vicarious offering in behalf of all humans, and his resurrection meant the outpouring of God's Holy Spirit. The "life" Paul speaks of here is not simply the continuation or slight improvement of mortal human existence, it means a share in the transformative power that lies at the source of all reality.

The resurrection of Jesus is, then, truly a new creation, the start of a new age for humanity: "If anyone is in Christ there is a new creation; the old has passed away, behold, the new is come" (2 Cor 5:17). For Paul, this is not mere metaphor but literal reality: "all this is from God" (2 Cor 5:18). How do we learn all this? By Paul's bold move—comparing Jesus not to Abraham or Moses but to Adam, the first of the "old humanity" that had sold its freedom into slavery and degradation. By the power of resurrection, the one who "gave his life for all" can now give *God's life* for all, making him the *New Adam*, firstfruits of God's new creation (1 Cor 15:23).

Because of Christ, "many will be established" in righteousness. He has opened up the possibility for others to respond to God as he has, so that God now justifies "those who share the faith of Jesus" (3:26). The tone of chapter 5 is entirely positive and celebratory. The gift is real; it has been given and has been received. Now Paul must turn to the hard questions the gift itself poses (chapters 6-11) and then to the manner of life it demands (chapters 12-15). But all of that follows and builds on this reality: "we have peace with God through our Lord Jesus Christ" (5:1).

ANSWERING OBJECTIONS:
GRACE, SIN, AND LAW

Romans 6:1-7:25

The use of questions, either posed by the imaginary interlocutor or, as here, by the author himself, adds to the vivid dialogical character of the diatribe. More importantly, such questions enable the writer to clarify obscure points and amplify difficult ones. Already in 3:1-9 and in 3:27-31, as we have seen, Paul raised a number of hard questions, to which he then responded mainly by means of a brusque disclaimer ("By no means!"), or a cryptic slogan. Now, after having developed his positive thesis fully, he is in a position to take up those same questions at leisure.

The questions are neither idle nor random. They are the sorts of issues that a careful reader/listener of Paul to this point ought to have in mind and ready at the lips. We will, in the present chapter, investigate the questions found in Romans 6-7. In chapter 8, we will find Paul once more in a positive expository mode, much like that in chapter 5. We will then take up the final and most difficult set of questions posed in chapters 9-11.

Grace and Sin (6:1-14)

The first question was asked earlier in 3:8, "Why not do evil that good may come?" and is now framed as, "Are we to continue in sin so that grace may abound?" (6:1). That such a question could arise precisely from Paul's emphasis in chapter 5—the more sin, the more grace—is shown by Paul's admission in 3:8, "as some people slanderously charge us with saying." Paul obviously is not indulging in what has sometimes been called—in discussions of novelists such as Graham Greene and François Mauriac—the "mystique of sin," that is, a fascination with sinfulness as an oblique way of celebrating the mystery of divine mercy. He responds to what he considers a canard, and his answer is important above all for showing how he regards sin and grace not

94

as formal categories but as real conditions. It is noteworthy also for the role played by baptism in his argument, making it clear that, for Paul, baptism was not a mere ritual of initiation but a powerful participation in the death and resurrection of Jesus (see R. Schnackenburg, *Baptism in the Theology of St. Paul* [New York: Herder & Herder, 1964] 105-70). The key to the first part of Paul's response is his appeal to his readers' own experience: "Do you not know that all of us who have been baptized into Christ Jesus were baptized into his death?" (6:3). The question, "Do you not know . . ." invariably points to some element of shared tradition (Rom 11:2; 1 Cor 3:16; 5:6; 6:2-3, 9, 15, 16, 19; 9:13, 24) that reader *should* know about. And if they really knew it, they would not raise this objection!

As in an embarrassingly large number of cases, however, what Paul and his readers presumably knew, we must guess at on the basis of slender evidence. That baptism was the distinctive Christian ritual of initiation is clear enough (see Matt 28:19; Acts 2:38, 41; 8:12; 10:48; 1 Cor 1:16; Gal 3:27; Heb 6:2; 1 Pet 3:21). We know that it was carried out "in the name of Jesus" (Acts 10:48), or "in the name of the father and of the son and of the holy spirit" (Matt 28:19); that it involved washing with water (1 Cor 6:11; Eph 5:28), the putting off of old and putting on of new clothing (Gal 3:27; Col 3:8-10; Eph 4:22-25; 1 Pet 2:1), the relativization of social status (1 Cor 12:13; Gal 3:28; Col 3:11); that it was associated with the gift of the Holy Spirit (Acts 2:38; 1 Cor 12:13); and that it involved a close identification with Christ (1 Cor 12:12-13, 27; Gal 3:27-28).

The evidence that baptism was associated specifically with the death and resurrection of Jesus, however, is—apart from the present passage, of course—scant, especially if we must disregard the entirely obscure reference to being "baptized for the dead" in 1 Cor 15:29. That leaves only the implication of Jesus' question to his followers in Mark 10:38-39, "Can you be baptized with the baptism I am to be baptized with?" which clearly points to his approaching death, and the section of Col 2:12-3:11 that bears so much resemblance to Rom 6:1-14. There Paul says explicitly, "You were buried with him in baptism, in which you were also raised with him through faith in the working of God who raised him from the dead" (2:12). Despite the relatively meager evidence, we must consider that Paul would not evoke this understanding of baptism from two communities (Colossians and Romans) that he himself had not founded, unless it had been part of their tradition. We may confidently assume, then, that the understanding of baptism as an entry into the death and resurrection of Jesus was wider than the Pauline circle and not an invention of Pauline theology (for another view, see H. D. Betz, "Transforming a Ritual: Paul's Interpretation of Baptism in Romans 6," in *Paul in His Hellenistic Context*, ed. T. Engberg-Pedersen [Minneapolis: Fortress, 1995] 84-118).

It has sometimes been supposed that the conception of baptism here reflects the early influence of "mystery religions" on Christianity, perhaps as it moved out of Palestine into the presumably more hellenized areas of the diaspora, the stage at which the "Jesus Movement" became the "Christ Cult" (see, e.g., W. Bousset, *Kyrios Christos: A History of the Belief in Christ from the Beginnings of Christianity to Irenaeus*, trans. J. Steely [Nashville: Abingdon, 1970]). It is certainly the case that the understanding here *is* cultic, but there is no reason to presume that its presence in Christianity is the result of some "foreign" implantation. So to think would be to misunderstand the way "participation" is a feature common to all group ritual.

The ritual of the Jewish Day of Atonement (Yom Kippur), for example, presumed a "participation" or "identification" between the people of Israel and the goat that was banished to the wilderness bearing their sins (Lev 16:20–22). Likewise, the celebration of Passover in every age has made its celebrants into participants contemporary with those who had been led out of Egypt (Exod 12:14–20; see also the *Passover Haggadah*). It is in just such a context that Paul can say of the Passover generation itself, "all were baptized into Moses in the cloud and in the sea" (1 Cor 10:2). Such language does not require the influence of the Greek or Roman mysteries—indeed, in the few fragments we have from such liturgies we find little evidence of this sort of language. All it requires is the religious sensibility of virtually all ages, which perceives ritual in terms of the transfer of transforming power through words and gestures that participate in a reality larger than that of the humans who are acting and speaking.

Whatever its roots, Paul's understanding of baptism is startlingly realistic; he does not think of ritual in terms of an arbitrary set of signs, but rather as a *symbol* that participates in that which it signifies. The word "cat" or a poster saying "Stop" are merely signs, an arbitrary set of markings that have significance within a system of language and social practices. In contrast, a loaf of bread has been for many cultures, a *symbol* of fellowship, no matter what word is used for either the wheat product itself or the fellowship. The reason is that bread gathers diverse elements together in its making, and in its eating gathers diverse members together, literally "inhabiting" them simultaneously. Bread symbolizes fellowship because sharing is what fellowship is.

In similar fashion, Paul regards the ritual of baptism as such a symbol, an event that activates within the community the experience of Jesus' death and resurrection. The ritual probably included immersion in water (see the accounts of Jesus' baptism in Matt 3:16 and Mark 1:10, where Jesus comes "up out of the water"). This action symbolizes the death of Jesus: "all of us who have been baptized into Christ Jesus have been baptized into his death" (6:3). Specifically, the *immersion* into the waters seems to have been the enactment of being *buried* with the crucified messiah (see 1 Cor 15:4): "we were buried therefore with him by baptism into death" (Rom 6:4). Paul does not here explicitly connect the coming up out of the water with the resurrection of Jesus, although that would be the logical correlation, and one made by Col 2:12: "You were buried with him in baptism, in which you were also raised with him through faith in the working of God, who raised him from the dead." The ritual of baptism, we see, is a ritual of initiation that *imprints* in believers a certain identity, namely, the paschal reality of the crucified and raised messiah.

This realistic apprehension of baptism is pertinent to Paul's main point here, which is that the gift of God in Christ Jesus is not remote from them. It has happened to and in them, with their baptism. We would not, I think, be far wrong if we connected to this baptismal ritual as well Paul's earlier statement that "the love of God has been poured into our hearts through the Holy Spirit" (5:5). By baptism, Christians "put on" a new identity (probably symbolized by the taking off of their old and putting on of new clothing—Gal 3:27; Col 3:8–10; Eph 4:22–25), which is that of Christ himself. Paul will later echo this in 13:14, "Put on the Lord Jesus." But what is of greatest importance is the aspect of Jesus' identity that they have "put on," namely, his obedient death and his sharing in God's new life. This becomes the *essential* pattern of Christian existence.

Paul's first response to the question of "continuing in sin," therefore, is to appeal to the *reality* of what they had experienced. The gift they had received was for this purpose: "so that as Christ was raised from the dead by the glory of the Father, so we too might walk in newness of life" (6:4). Paul could not be clearer in his conviction that the life of believers is one that, through the gift of the Holy Spirit, shares in the resurrection power of Christ: "I have been crucified with Christ; it is no longer I who live but Christ who lives in me" (Gal 2:20). The present passage in Romans shows that what Paul stated in Galatians was not simply the expression of a personal mysticism but rather his sober estimate of the new creation in which Christians now participate (2 Cor 5:17).

The reading here stands in tension with one tradition of interpretation that goes back especially to Martin Luther, which so emphasizes the juridic character of justification and the fact that it is *extra nos* ("outside of us, accomplished by God") that it tends to diminish the transformative aspect of righteousness as Paul presents it. For Luther, humans remain *simul justi et peccatores*, at once justified and sinners. They are not fundamentally touched in their freedom. They remain "in the flesh and under the power of sin," but despite that, and because of Christ's saving death, God "regards them as righteous" (see, e.g., Luther's *Lectures on Romans* [Glosses, on 7:16]). However religiously powerful this reading has been, it simply does not adequately encompass all of Paul's position as stated in this letter. Christians, he says, are to "walk in the newness of life" precisely because they have been given the power of new life (5:17, 21). So for Paul it is patent that "if we have been implanted into the likeness of his death, we will likewise be of his resurrection" (6:5).

Paul again appeals to what he assumes is shared knowledge in 6:6, namely, that their "old self was crucified with us." Paul must mean that as *they* were engrafted into the death of Christ, so this "old self" (literally, "old man," probably with reference to the "Adamic" self) must have been crucified, for he continues, "so that the body of sin might be destroyed and we no longer be enslaved to sin. For the one who has died is vindicated (or: justified/ freed) from sin" (6:6-7). What changes then is the entire identity of the person and the entire direction taken by the person's freedom.

The argument is lined up chiastically in 6:7-10: (a) persons who die are free of sin (6:7); (b) if they die with Christ they will live with him (6:8); (b') when Christ died, sin no longer ruled him (6:9); (a') the one who dies, dies to sin once for all; the one who lives, live for God (6:10). Elements a and a' connect sin and death, while elements b and b' connect their death and life with Christ's. The conclusion is spelled out in 6:11: "Thus you also are reckoning yourselves as dead with regard to sin, but alive to God," with the final phrase providing the logical link for the entire set, "in Christ Jesus" (6:11). Through their baptism "in Christ," we learn, they have passed from a way of living defined by the reign of sin and death, into one defined by the "newness of life" (6:4) that comes from God in a "new creation" (2 Cor 5:17; Gal 6:15).

If they are in a "new world," then their behavior should follow accordingly. But although they share in God's life through the gift of the Holy Spirit, they still inhabit mortal bodies and live within the structures of the world. They need therefore to learn how to translate this new "christic" identity into a consistent and coherent mode of behavior. Before taking up individual deeds, Paul thinks in terms of overall orientation, which for him is always a matter of *obedience*. In 6:12-14, he exhorts his readers to a new form of obedience in terms of the disposition of themselves (see B. Byrne, "Living out the Righteousness of God: The Contribution of Rom 6:1-8:13 to an Understanding of Paul's Ethical Presuppositions," *Catholic Biblical Quarterly* 43 [1981]: 557-81).

Formerly, they had lived under the rule of death and sin (5:14). Now, in this new life, they must not let "sin rule in your mortal bodies, so that you obey its passions." The reader will recall, I hope, how Paul described those under the reign of sin who were "handed over in the passions of their hearts in uncleanness and the dishonoring of their own bodies" (1:24). Now they are to be like those raised to an entirely new way of living, "presenting their members" not as instruments of wickedness for sin but to God as instruments of righteousness (6:13).

Paul states confidently, "sin will not rule over you" (16:14). The power of this new life is effective. They can act upon it confidently. But then he adds, still once more, an apparently gratuitous comment about the law: "for you are not under the law but under grace." We shall see shortly what Paul is getting at in this sort of statement. Briefly, he means that the law can tell us what to do but cannot empower us to do it, whereas God's gift (*charis*) is a transforming love that empowers a new way of living. This, finally, is why the question, "Why not sin so there will be more grace?" is nonsensical to Paul. Sin, as he has defined it, represents a closure to the gift. To accept the gift of God means to be in the realm of faith. There are only these two options. Although in hindsight Paul can praise God for having brought a still greater gift out of the depths of human sinfulness, to suppose that one could continue "in sin" would be to show that the gift had never been received, and to demonstrate that it had never really been accepted in faith.

Freedom and Slavery (6:15–23)

The next rhetorical question, "Should we continue to sin because we are not under the law but under grace?" (6:15), is triggered by Paul's aside concerning the law in the previous verse. He responds indignantly, "Of course not!" This question, like that in 6:1, reveals a misunderstanding of the realities of which Paul speaks. *Sin* is not a matter of breaking laws, but is a disease of the human spirit. As Paul has shown, sin can "reign" over persons even when there is no law spelling out what God wants (5:13–14), for sin is essentially a rebellion against God, a turning away of the heart in disobedience. In the same way, *grace* is given not by the law, as Paul has shown (3:21–24; 5:15) but through the personal empowerment of human freedom through the Holy Spirit. The question, then, is strictly impertinent—the law is not a major player in the fundamental drama of human relatedness to God. This drama is about the deepest responses of the human heart.

It may be the mention of the law, however, that leads Paul to cast this next discussion in terms of slavery and freedom, for such were the issues in his previous lengthy discussion of the law in Galatians. There he identified law with a form of slavery (Gal 3:28; 4:1, 7–9, 24–25; 5:1), from which Christians were free (Gal 2:4; 3:28; 4:22–31; 5:1, 13). Paul's constant theme of obedience and disobedience is therefore now spelled out in terms of slavery and freedom. Oddly enough, this part of his argument, which probably seemed to Paul to represent the sheerest common sense, will appear to many present-day readers as one of the least convincing parts of the letter.

The reason is the different sorts of presuppositions readers today have concerning freedom and slavery. Some effort is required, then, both to clarify present-day assumptions and to contrast them with those in Paul's world, so that even if his argument does not win assent it can at least earn understanding.

People in the present-day Western world are heirs of the Enlightenment and see the world in two ways that are fundamentally different from the view of Paul and others in the first-century Mediterranean world. The two ways, in fact, are interrelated. The first is that the present outlook places an absolute value on freedom. Slavery is regarded as an abomination, unacceptable in any circumstances. To be a slave is to be regarded as less than human. Slavery, furthermore, is defined in social and economic terms as being deprived of the "rights of freedom." Slavery is not something that one would ever "freely choose." It is entirely a result and sign of oppression.

Freedom, in turn, is defined largely in negative terms as the absence of constraint, having the ability to choose one thing rather than another, to move and speak and write "freely," that is, as one chooses. Our sense of freedom is highly individualistic. We think it essential for human dignity to have the "right of self-determination." This, in turn, affects our view of the state as a necessary evil, and as having authority only by the consent of the governed.

These values attached to slavery and freedom are connected to a view of the human place in the world that also derives from the Enlightenment. Our sense of powers in the world other than or higher than that of humans is greatly diminished. Not only the religious sense of the presence of God, but also the awareness of other forces for good and evil in the world, is generally regarded as the province of the paranormal, that is, slightly crazy. What ancient cultures thought of as spiritual people and shamans, we are likely to think of as sickos and schizoids. The world of the Enlightenment is a rational system of laws to which all natural powers are subject, and which are all potentially open to a human understanding that can win mastery over them. God, insofar as there is a God, is far away in heaven and has confined himself in obedience to these same rational and predictable laws. Humans on earth are defined in terms of individual freedom of choice. From such a perspective, Paul's language in this section must seem strange indeed.

The world Paul inhabited saw things very differently. Paul and his contemporaries lived, first of all, in a more richly furnished universe. In polytheism, the presence of the divine pervaded every aspect of life: humans were constantly in the position of responding to personal forces greater than themselves, which governed rivers, seas, mountains, ships, armies, love-making, farming (see R. M. Ogilvie, *The Romans and their Gods in the Age of Augustus* [New York: W. W. Norton, 1959]). Even in Judaism, belief in intermediate spiritual beings between God and humans was widespread; God governed the world through "guardian angels" of nations and peoples (see J. Danielou, *The Theology of Jewish Christianity*, trans. J. A. Baker [London: Darton, Longman & Todd, 1964]). Since these spiritual beings were, for the most part, superior to humans in their intelligence and power, they were also in a position of real if subordinate authority over them. Some such spirits were also inimical to the rule of God and operated in something of a counterkingdom, sponsors of the evil that kept humans in alienation from God.

The hierarchical arrangement of the universe corresponded, in turn, to the hierarchical structure of society, in which someone was always subject to someone else. In Paul's world, one was always "obedient" to someone and "bound" to some authority which one "served." The only question was *which* higher power did one serve. Was it ultimate or not? Service to the most ultimate power meant, logically, freedom with respect to the lesser authorities. On the social plane, being a slave of Caesar meant freedom with respect to other authorities. Thus, if "sin is ruling" the world, slavery to sin meant freedom with regard to whatever sin suppresses, in this case, the truth about God.

Freedom in this view is defined not so much in terms of freedom of choice as in terms of the degree of authority/value/power offered by the one served. Freedom of spirit mattered more than freedom of choice. Thus, philosophers called the freedom to engage in vice no freedom at all, but a kind of bondage. Persons so obsessed with pleasure or possessions or power that they are driven to the compulsive indulgence of such passions are obviously controlled by their addictions and are not free in any meaningful sense. In contrast, a person might be the slave of the emperor, or merely the house servant of a merchant, yet because of virtue and self-control might be regarded as fully human and genuinely free. Such, then, is the cultural context for Paul's discussion in this section, which makes intelligible his opening query, "Do you not know that if you yield yourselves to anyone as obedient slaves, you are slaves of the one you obey?" Of course they know this! It is a commonplace of the Greco-Roman social and religious world.

The point Paul strives to make is that the human response to reality takes place at the level of profound commitments moving in one direction or another. "Freedom" is not a series of random acts performed willy-nilly without logic or order, but is a form of service to allegiances that are more or less adequate to the human spirit, more or less ennobling or degrading of the self. Paul thanks God (6:17) that although they were once slaves of sin, they have "become obedient from the heart to the standard of teaching (*didaskalia*) to which you were committed." The phrase "standard of teaching" seems odd in this discussion, although it seems to mean basically the Christian's commitment to the gospel and the pattern of life inscribed by the experience of baptism. We observe that in 16:17, Paul warns against those who create dissensions "in opposition to the doctrine (*didaskalia*) you have been taught." In the present passage it must mean to live in sin, against the "pattern" they had learned in Christ. Note that Paul says that they "have been committed/dedicated" to this pattern of teaching. One result of this commitment/allegiance is that they have been freed from one bondage (that of sin) for another, so that they can be "slaves of righteousness" (6:18). Paul apparently recognizes the paradoxical and shocking character of this language even for his contemporaries, for he adds, "I am speaking in human terms, because of your natural limitations" (RSV; literally, "because of the weakness of your flesh"). What he means, I think, is that the metaphor of slavery is not adequate to the relationship of which he speaks, but he needs language sufficiently powerful for them to realize what a fundamental shift has taken place in their condition, and therefore in their allegiance (obedience).

Their specific actions, here described as "presenting [their] members" (see also 6:13), should follow from this change in status and shift in loyalty: "just as you once yielded your members to impurity and to greater and greater iniquity [see 1:24–28], so now yield your members to righteousness for sanctification" (6:19). The exhortation is very similar to 6:12, with the differences being twofold. First, Paul spoke there about "the reign of sin," whereas here he approaches the metaphor from the side of the one showing obedience to a ruler. Second, he earlier stopped with, "make your members instruments of righteousness," whereas here he adds, "to righteousness for sanctification." This additional element of sanctification will be picked up by Paul's final set of contrasts, where he makes the obvious point that when they were slaves of sin they had been "free from" righteousness—but all they got for that false freedom was a result of which they are now ashamed [compare "I am not ashamed" 1:16; "our hope does not shame" 5:5], and which leads to death (6:22). In contrast, by being "free from sin" they have become "slaves of God"–like Paul (1:1)!–with quite a different result: "the fruit that is sanctification, and the end result that is eternal life" (6:22).

In this section, Paul has introduced the language of sanctification, or holiness. It plays a larger role in some of his other letters, from which we can gain some sense of its importance for Paul, an importance that is assumed rather than developed in Romans. Before launching this discussion, I should point out, for present-day readers who do not know Greek, that the English terms "sanctification," "sanctify," and "saint," all translate the same Greek words that can also be translated as "holiness," "holy," and "holy ones" (viz., *hagiasmos, hagiazō, hagios*). So, in 6:22, the translation, "the fruit that is holiness" would be equally accurate and appropriate.

The idea of holiness or sanctification is deeply rooted in Paul's Jewish heritage, in which holiness was considered to be the defining characteristic of God and therefore also the human requirement for approaching God. In Lev 19:1, the Lord says to Moses, "Say to all the congregation of the people of Israel, 'You shall be holy, for I the Lord your God am holy.'" The basic idea of holiness is easy enough. It simply denotes "otherness" or "difference." To be holy means to be different, to be set aside from other things. The holiness of God meant first of all, then, that God is utterly different from the world. For God's people to "be holy as I am holy," must mean, then, that they were to be different *within* the world as God was different *from* the world. Their "otherness" from other people signaled their commitment to a God who was "other" from everything! The entire behavior code of ancient Israel works from that premise, which makes intelligible some ritual practices that might otherwise appear odd or arbitrary, such as the observance of the sabbath, or the cutting of the corners of the hair, or circumcision, or separating meat and dairy products. The point, you see, at least to a considerable extent, was *simply to be different*, and the odder the practice, the more obviously "holy" it was.

Paul carries the ideal of holiness to his Christian communities: "this is the will of God, your sanctification" (1 Thess 4:3). They had been sanctified (1 Cor 1:2), but were also "called to be holy ones" (1 Cor 1:2) made completely holy (1 Thess 5:23). Indeed, Paul's most common appellation for the community is "the saints" or "holy ones" (see 1 Cor 6:2; 2 Cor 1:1; Eph 1:1), which he uses in contrast to "the world" (that is, those not in the community; see 1 Cor 5:9). But what is the basis for "differentness" in his communities? Two things are certain, though not entirely spelled out. The first is that holiness is connected to Jesus. The scandalously executed criminal has been made by God "our wisdom, our righteousness, and sanctification, and redemption" (1 Cor 1:30). The second is that holiness is rooted in the gift of the Holy Spirit that comes from the raised messiah Jesus (see 1 Thess 4:8).

In Romans, Paul has spoken of Jesus as "being Son of God in power through the spirit of holiness" (1:4). He writes to those who are "called to be holy ones (saints)" (1:7). He has declared that God's love has been poured into our hearts through the Holy Spirit which has been given to us (5:5). Now he says that having been put into right relationship with God, their continuing obedience–the "presenting of their members"–to God is to lead to a community identity progressively marked by the "differentness" demanded by the shape of the gift given by God. In chapter 8, Paul will show that this transformation is the work of the Holy Spirit among them. The goal is to be "holy in root and branch" (11:16), a "holy and acceptable sacrifice" offered to God (12:1), so that "the offering of the Gentiles may be acceptable, sanctified by the Holy Spirit" (15:16).

Paul ended 6:22 by stating that the goal (*telos*) of sanctification was "eternal life" (*zōē aiōnios*). This expression also needs some attention. He had earlier referred to those who "in patience and well-doing seek for glory and honor and immortality," to whom, in response, God gives "eternal life" (2:7). In 5:21, he triumphantly concluded his exposition: "grace may also reign through righteousness to eternal life through Jesus Christ our Lord." The expression "eternal life" is so familiar to present-day readers of the New Testament that it may come as a shock to realize that it is virtually absent from the LXX translation of Torah. Its most emphatic appearance is in the Maccabean literature, where it is associated with the future life awaiting those who have given their lives in martyrdom (2 Macc 7:9-36; 4 Macc 15:3). The New Testament, in sharp contrast, uses the phrase frequently with reference to the future life (see Matt 19:16, 29; 25:46; Mark 10:17; Luke 10:25; 18:18, 30; John 3:15, 16, 36; 4:14, 36; 5:24, 39; 6:27, 40, 47, 54, 68; 10:28; 12:25, 50; 17:2-3; Acts 13:46-48; 1 John 1:2; 2:25; 3:15; 5:11, 13, 20; Jude 21). Outside Romans, Paul uses the expression "eternal life" in Gal 6:8; 1 Tim 1:16; 6:12; Titus 1:2; 3:7. There can be little question then, that, like other early Christians, Paul conceived the *telos* of a life of holiness to be sharing in the very life of God after human death. He concludes his response to the question of 6:15 with this sharpest of contrasts (which has adorned countless billboards in the southern United States), "the wages of sin is death, but the free gift of God is eternal life in Christ Jesus our Lord" (6:23). Although the specific Greek term is different, Paul's use of *opsōnia*, which in ordinary usage refers to payment for labor (see Luke 3:14; 1 Cor 9:7; 2 Cor 11:8), deliberately picks up the note of "reward to the laborer" in 4:4. The point of the contrast here is simple and builds on the entire preceding argument. What do people get as payment for serving sin? Death. What have they been given as a free gift in Jesus? Eternal life. The lesson? Serve God, not sin.

The Problem of the Law (7:1-25)

No part of Romans has been the object of so much scrutiny or the source of so much misunderstanding as Paul's discussion of the law in 7:1-25. The reason for both is not hard to figure out. For the first time in the letter, Paul uses the first person pronoun *ego* explicitly and frequently (7:9, 10, 14, 17, 20, 24, 25). Is this not an obvious invitation to read what he has to say as coming from his personal experience? Furthermore, in 7:13-24, he describes a situation of deep inner dividedness, a split consciousness, in which one part of a person wants to do good, but another part chooses evil. Finally, the precipitant for this struggle is God's law (*nomos*), specifically in the commandment (*entolē*) "Do not covet" (7:7), which uses the Greek verb *epithymein*, which can easily be read in terms of "having passionate desires" (see 1:24). These four factors (Paul, conflict, law, desire) have provided interpreters through the ages with a field day of speculation concerning Paul, the author.

Two lines of interpretation have resulted. The first uses Romans 7 as the clue to Paul's pre-conversion life and subsequent attitude toward the law. In the eyes of some hostile critics, Paul is seen as a neurotic personality at best, whose inability to keep the law was due to his inability to control his passions. His pent-up frustrations led him to a fury of resentment at those followers of Jesus who were free of such tension. When his violent persecution against them failed, he came over to their side, taking revenge on his past by rejecting the law that had tormented him (see, e.g., F. Nietzsche, *The AntiChrist, an Attempted Criticism of Christianity;* and G. B. Shaw, "Preface on the Prospects of Christianity," both excerpted in W. A. Meeks, *The Writings of St. Paul* [New York: W. W. Norton, 1972] 291-96, 296-302). A somewhat milder version sees Paul as a romantic figure whose emotional impulses make him incapable of remaining within the "classic form" of a religion of law such as Judaism (see L. Baeck, "Romantic Religion," excerpted in Meeks, *Writings of St. Paul,* 334-49).

Such a reading of Romans 7, however, makes it stand in contradiction to the evidence offered by Paul's other letters. Even 1 Tim 1:15, which refers to Paul as "the greatest of sinners" and describes his life as one of "blaspheming and persecuting and insulting" Christ, does not connect any of the attitudes to his uncontrollable passions or troubles with the law. And in other (unarguably Pauline) passages, Paul shows himself as fully confident concerning his position with regard to keeping the law. In Gal 1:14, he declares, "I advanced in Judaism beyond any of my own age and among my people, so zealous was I for the traditions of my fathers." He gives no sign here of a tortured conscience; indeed, his "zeal for the traditions" suggests a single-minded devotion. In Phil 3:6, Paul again describes himself before his conversion: "as to zeal, a persecutor of the church, as to righteousness under the law, blameless." Now these are directly autobiographical, confessional statements. They reveal no problem with the law and no history of disordered passions, before Paul's call to be an apostle. Such statements make it unlikely in the highest degree, indeed virtually impossible, for Paul here in Romans 7, without any warning, to start speaking about his former life as a Jew in the manner suggested.

The second line of interpretation has also read the chapter as autobiographical, but now as reporting on Paul's *continuing* struggles with passion and law. This way of reading Romans is deeply indebted to Augustine, who read Paul in the context of his own long struggle with sexual passion.

Augustine had experienced an *intellectual* conversion to Christianity, but found his desire (in Latin, *concupiscentia*) continuing to battle against "the law of his mind." For Augustine, such internal dividedness could only be overcome by the overwhelming and personal gift of God's grace, but even when the grace was given, the struggle continued in the Christian's life. He therefore explicitly read Romans 7 as being about Paul's life after his baptism (see Augustine, *On Marriage and Concupiscence* 28–36; *Against Two Letters of the Pelagians* 14–24). This tradition of reading continues in Martin Luther, for whom, as we have seen, righteousness is attributed externally to humans in virtue of the death of Christ, but humans remain captive to the power of sin. In his *scholia* on Romans 7, Luther declares, "for this passage on to the end of the chapter, the apostle is speaking in his own person and as a spiritual man, and by no means merely in the person of a carnal man" (*Lectures on Romans* [Scholia on 7:7]). The Lutheran perspective remains a powerful influence especially in Protestant theological interpretations of Paul (see, e.g., R. Bultmann, "Romans 7 and the Anthropology of Paul," in *Existence and Faith,* ed. and trans. S. Ogden [New York: Meridian Books, 1960] 147–57).

In order properly to answer this powerful tradition of interpretation, we need to return to the first part of chapter 7. Before Paul begins his explicit discussion of the law in 7:7–25, he provides a transitional argument in 7:1–6, which seldom receives the attention it deserves. One reason the passage is not taken more seriously is that it is very difficult to follow. Paul attempts an analogy to the laws of marriage, but, as later with his venture into horticulture in chapter 11, it is less than completely successful. His assertion in 7:4, however, indicates what he was getting at: "you have died to the law through the body of Christ, so that you may belong to another, to him who has been raised from the dead in order that we may bear fruit for God." This statement makes clear that Paul is continuing the death/life, slavery/freedom, obedience/disobedience themes that he began in 6:1–23: those incorporated into Christ are under a new "rule" and live with a new life.

It is in light of this statement that 7:1–3 must be read. Paul declares that a law is valid only during a person's life, and he tries to use the example of marriage to illustrate the legal point (see J. A. Little, "Paul's Use of Analogy: A Structural Analysis of Rom 7:1-6," *Catholic Biblical Quarterly* 46 [1984]: 82–90). At the heart of the analogy is the assumption that the law may dictate a set of obligations but does not itself constitute the relationship: she may be called an adulteress if she "lives with another man while her husband is alive," for such is the legal definition. But the legal obligations owed the husband cannot keep her from loving another or make her love him. His analogy limps, because he gets the relations confused. In the parallel, a woman is free to marry another if her husband dies (7:3). But in the present case, it is the baptized person who has "died with Christ." No matter. What Paul wants to show is that with a death, the law becomes invalid, as well as the obligations it demands. For him, the experience of death and new life, first with Christ and then for those grafted onto him in baptism, establishes a new relationship with God, not mediated by law. In effect, "now we are discharged from the law, dead to that which held us captive, so that we are not under the old written code, but in the new life of the Spirit" (7:6). The contrast is the same one that Paul draws in 2 Cor 3:7–18. We will soon pick up Paul's explicit problem-posing statement on the law in 7:5. But for now, we need to assert, against the previous history of interpretation, that Paul's statements on the law in chapter 7 are written first of all not as autobiography but as part of his argument concerning God's righteousness. And, just as important, his comments are written not from the perspective of one struggling under the law but from the perspective of one who serves God freely "in the new life of the spirit."

Only in recent years—and not without struggle—has the earlier tradition of interpretation been reversed. The most important step came with the recognition of how Augustine and later theological interpreters imposed on Paul a difficulty with keeping the law that he explicitly denied having. It is to K. Stendahl's great credit that he was able to make this case so convincingly (see "The Apostle Paul and the Introspective Conscience of the West," in *Paul among Jews and Gentiles* [Philadelphia: Fortress, 1976] 78-96), and helped prepare the way for studies of Paul that would deal with his understanding of the law in more neutral and nuanced fashion (see, e.g., E. P. Sanders, *Paul and Palestinian Judaism: A Comparison of Patterns of Religion* [Philadelphia: Fortress, 1977]).

The next important step toward a more adequate reading of Romans 7 came with the recognition that, if Paul was not speaking autobiographically, then there must be some rhetorical motivation for this "first-person discourse." There are two similar speeches in 1 Corinthians that throw helpful light on Romans 7. In 1 Corinthians 9, Paul's first-person discourse is clearly and obviously self-referential: he speaks out of and about his own experience. But in 1 Corinthians 13, the so-called "hymn of love," the first person discourse is obviously intended to be illustrative and exemplary. A look at the actual statements he makes supports this conclusion. Paul neither claims to have all the qualities listed in 13:1-3, nor to entirely lack *agapē!* Likewise, his "when I was a child, I spoke as a child" (13:11) can scarcely be taken as specific self-revelation; it is first-person speech used to make a point vividly and personally. The first-person discourse is less a window giving access to Paul's personality than it is a mirror for the reader's reflection and self-examination.

Something similar is going on here. Paul's "speech in character" is typical of the diatribe, where a position will suddenly be adopted and "spoken out of." Thus, in Epictetus's discourse on the Ideal Cynic, we find him mouthing the speech of the would-be philosopher, "I wear a rough cloak even as it is, and I shall have one then; I have a hard bed even now, and so I shall then; I shall take to myself a wallet and staff, and I shall begin to walk around and beg from those I meet, and revile them" (3.22.10). Such personification enables an author to bring a logical position vibrantly to life, by "performing" it. The ancient rhetorical designation for such "speech-in-character" was *prosōpopoiia* ("making a mask"), and it fits what Paul is doing here very well (see S. K. Stowers, "Romans 7:7-25 as a Speech-in-Character (*prosōpopoiia*)," in *Paul in His Hellenistic Context,* ed. T. Engberg-Pedersen [Minneapolis: Fortress, 1995] 180-202). Paul's argument is still rigorously logical. The only difference is that here, where the personal dilemma of humans under sin needs most to be personalized, Paul uses the "fictive I" to accomplish that task (see S. Stowers, *A Rereading of Romans: Justice, Jews, and Gentiles* [New Haven: Yale University Press, 1994] 264-72).

Paul has been building toward this discussion for a long time. He has dropped a number of comments about the law as *obiter dicta*, but has developed none of them. Even in 1 Corinthians, where a debate over Torah was scarcely an issue, Paul concludes his argument concerning the future triumph of God with the comment, "the sting of death is sin, and the power of sin is the law" (1 Cor 15:56). But he did not say why or how. Likewise, in Gal 3:19, after showing how the promise was given and was received by faith long before the law was revealed on Sinai, Paul asks, "Why the law? It was added because of transgressions." Above all in Romans, however, he has heightened the suspense concerning this issue by touching on it time after time with provocative remarks hinting at some collusion between sin and the law, but he has provided no follow-through. In 3:20, he said, "through the law comes knowledge of sin," and in 4:15, "for the law brings wrath, but where there is no law there is no transgression." In 5:13, he declared that "sin was in the world before the law was given, but sin is not counted where there is no law," and in 5:20, "law came in to increase the trespass." In 6:14, he said, "sin will have no dominion over you since you are not under the law but grace."

Finally, in 7:5, precisely in the middle of his statement concerning the present condition of baptized persons—that they are not serving the written code but in the new life of the Spirit (7:6)—Paul declares, "while we were living in the flesh, our sinful passions, aroused by the law, were at work in our members to bear fruit for death." In this climactic statement, the law appears virtually as an agent in the execution of the "will of the flesh." Therefore, Paul's question is all too pertinent and finally must be confronted directly:

"What shall we say then? That the Law is sin?" (7:7). He responds vigorously, "By no means!" Proving it will be more ticklish.

In this case, before following Paul's statements sequentially, we should take the time to consider why this problem is so pronounced in Paul and not elsewhere in the New Testament. Among all the members of the nascent messianic movement, Paul's position was the most peculiar. It was not, as we have seen, that he could not keep the law. He claims just the opposite. It is, rather, that as a devout Pharisee, Paul's perception of the law was so elevated and his expectations of it so absolute. He saw Torah as the adequate frame for God's self-expression, having all the attributes he listed in Rom 2:17-20. Before his experience of the risen Lord, furthermore, Paul considered that "perfection in the law" was not only possible but that he had accomplished it (Phil 3:6).

Such convictions undoubtedly underlay his attempt, as one "zealous for the law," to suppress the Christians by persecution (Gal 1:13). The claims made by these followers of Jesus—that he was alive and among them in the Spirit—appeared flatly to contradict Torah. According to the norms of Torah, Jesus' life had been that of a sinner, and his death cursed by God (Deut 21:23). So long as Paul thought of Jesus as a dead man and a failed messiah, he had no difficulty with the law at all; in fact, his persecution of the church was precisely a defense of the law to which he was so devoted. Nor could there be any ambiguity in this position, since Torah was unequivocal about the fate of hanged men.

Paul's problems with the law began with his experience of Jesus as risen Lord. His encounter with Jesus (1 Cor 9:1; 15:8) created a condition that sociologists call "cognitive dissonance," a state of mental tension in which two deeply held convictions appear to oppose each other, or deeply held convictions are challenged by undeniable experiences. A homely (though tragic example) would be the "cognitive dissonance" created by parental physical abuse: on one side are the conviction that one's parents are loving; on the other side are the injuries resulting from beating. Meeting Jesus not as a failed and dead messiah but as a powerful and commanding Lord, Paul was placed in an impossible dilemma. Either Torah was absolute and Jesus was a fake, or God was truly at work in Jesus, and the law could not be the absolute and adequate frame for God's activity that he had considered it to be. If he were to follow his experience—and given the immediacy and power of that experience, what choice did he have?—then the claims for Torah would need to be reexamined.

The fruits of that reexamination are what we find in Paul's scattered statements and finally here in more organized fashion. Only Paul among the first generation believers saw the need for resolving the "problem of the law" in such dialectical fashion, for only he truly *saw the problem*. He alone combined in his own person the two horns of the dilemma: the framework of Scripture as absolute, meaning the exclusion of Jesus as messiah and the persecution of his followers, or Jesus as messiah and Lord and Scripture no longer the norm he had thought. It is from the perspective of one who has "gone with his experience" and taken his stand on the gift of God in Jesus (5:1) that Paul now engages the issue. Chapter 7 does not report on Paul's early life experience. It is, rather, his coolly reasoned appraisal of a problem only his *subsequent* experience brought to light.

We should note from the start that Paul by no means considers the law itself to be the problem. In fact, he will declare in 8:3 that those who walk in the Spirit have "the just requirement of the law fulfilled in us." The law comes from God (even if through mediators; see Gal 3:19) and therefore must be good. He declares explicitly in 7:12 that the commandment is good, and it reveals God's will for humans (7:7). As God's word, furthermore, the law is spiritual (7:14). In summary, "the law is holy, and the commandment is holy and just and good" (7:12). As *revelation* from God, therefore, the law is entirely a blessing.

Then what is the complaint? Why does Paul think of the law as potentiating sin (5:20)? Because the law can *identify* sin but cannot *prevent* it. The commandments reveal wrongdoing to be, precisely, sin. They show that wickedness is not merely immorality but the breaking of the most profound of all relationships, that between God and humans. It is the law that transforms "lawlessness" into "transgression" (7:7, 9, 13). An example ("for our human frailty") may help. Suppose that a child, out of curiosity, boredom, mischief, feels an irresistible urge to tease the family cat. Can't seem to stop doing it. But only when the child's parent tells her, "Don't tease the cat," does the deed become the transgression of a commandment. Now if the child teases the cat, it is not only wrong but disobedient: "the law brings knowledge of sin" (3:20). The distinction is all-important. Perhaps a vague stirring of conscience tells a four-year-old that splashing paint on furniture is a "perversion of nature." But if a parent says, "Do not paint," the splashing is not only "wrong," but "sin," the deliberate rejection of the expressed will of the powerful and originate one!

Here we come to an important dimension of the problem as Paul sees it. Because the commandment of God identifies sin but cannot prevent it, the effect is that sin is potentiated. Another analogy: suppose I experience a mild but nonspecific tickling between my shoulder blades. My teacher warns me, "Don't scratch in class, young man!" The commandment not only does nothing to take away the itch, it actually makes it worse, by isolating and diagnosing what until then had only been a latent symptom.

So also are the commandments of Torah only *verbal* in character. They cannot empower new behavior in a person or heal the dangerous and self-destructive impulses within them. Paul says, in this characterization, "I am in the flesh, sold under sin" (7:14), to show the other side of the situation, the way the power of sin (7:8, 9, 11) can continue to drive human action despite the conscious knowledge that such action now offends God. The problem with the law, therefore, is its inadequacy to the task, its powerlessness to actually change the heart.

But this brings us to another aspect of the law's problematic status. The deeper difficulty is not the law's inadequacy but the *claims* that it makes for itself, or the claims that humans can make on its basis. The key passage is Gal 3:12, a quotation from Lev 18:5; Paul says, "but the law does not rest on faith, for 'he who does them shall live by them.'" The text from Leviticus claims straightforwardly that the performance of the commands will give "life." But this promise, Paul says, is a false one, and deeply deceptive. Life of every sort, sheer existence itself, cannot be secured by any human performance but is given, moment by moment, as gift from God. If this is the case with sheer human existence, how much more is it for a share in God's life, "eternal life"? If it were possible for me to secure life by keeping the commandments, then it would be possible to control God's gift by my performance.

This promise has been shown to be false, Paul knows, by the experience of Jesus' death and resurrection. Here is one whose death went against the law, yet *God gave him life*, and so much of it that this life could be poured out on others ("the first Adam became a living being, the second Adam became life-giving Spirit"). Life was superabundantly given outside and against the law. The claims of the law to provide life through observance are seen now, from the perspective of this experience, to be both false and deceptive, for those who put their reliance on those claims would be in a self-deceived and self-destructive posture. Paul alludes to the law's promise in 7:10, "the very commandment which promised life proved to be death to me." If these claims are made the basis of one's ultimate trust, then they can actually kill: "Sin, finding the opportunity in the law, killed me" (7:11). In the same way, a critically ill patient, having received a doctor's diagnosis and even a script for medicine, is not helped. What is needed is the medicine. The problem with the law is that it is a prescription but not power.

The fundamental tension, therefore, is between the perception of the good, made available by revelation through Torah, and the lack of the ability to do it, because of the self-aggrandizing power of sin. But Paul's perception goes even farther. The tension is present *even when the commandments are observed*. This point is essential to Paul's argument as a whole, even though it becomes explicit only in 9:32–10:4. The Jews could reject obedience to God's action in the crucified and raised messiah precisely on the grounds of the observance of Torah, because they could (as Paul in fact did) regard Torah as the absolute and adequate norm for *God's* action as well as their own. For Paul, the statement "I serve the law of God with my mind, but with my flesh I serve the law of sin" (7:21) applies even when the law is kept—if the power of sin is still operative in human freedom. It is not just the case of someone addicted saying, "I know I should stop drinking but I can't stop"; it's also the virtuous person who gives alms and basks in the confirmation that action gives of being in right relationship with God.

Imagine two children. The first focuses on the parent as the source of life and the loving giver of gifts, feels trust in the parent, and responds flexibly to the parent's initiatives. Although such faithful responsiveness actually "fulfills" all the rules laid down by the parent, the relationship is not defined by those rules, for there are dozens of exchanges that take place every day that no rule can capture. This child does not rebel against the rules, but the rules are not the focus; the loving exchange of gifts is the focus. The second child out of some anxiety seeks to secure "the right relationship" with a parent on the basis of punctiliously observing every one of the parent's commands—no less and no more. The child seeks to make the relationship fit entirely within the frame of law: "Tell me what you want and I will do it." The child clearly misses the entire point of such a relationship, which, to be alive, must be flexible and responsive on both sides. The "keeping of the law" in this case is a rigid form of self-protection and extortion: "you must reward me because I did everything you said perfectly." By insisting on keeping everything a matter of rules, it suppresses the chance of spontaneous life occurring outside its self-imposed boundaries. If we supply "the flesh" for the child's anxiety, and "sin" for the child's compulsive need to keep control, we have some sense of Paul's perception.

We gain thereby some sense of how Paul can see his fellow Jews' "zeal for Torah" as "not enlightened" because being ignorant of the righteousness that comes from God, and seeking to establish their own, they did not submit to God's righteousness" (10:2–3). This is to anticipate. But it is important to realize that Paul feels as much pity and perplexity about his kinsmen as we feel for the confused and hostile child who in effect rejects every parental gift by insisting that every exchange be in terms of wages. Once one is locked in that frame, only some power from the outside can break its vicious hold, some gift that can create the capacity for freedom from fear and compulsion (7:24), that can enable a gift to be received with the simple trust that Paul calls "faith." For Paul, of course, that gift has been given, and he gives thanks in return (7:25).

Having now sketched some of the main components in Paul's position, we will try to follow his points sequentially, for his treatment is, if less clear than the analysis, far livelier and more engaging. We begin by reminding ourselves of Paul's starting point. Those to whom he is writing "serve not the old written code but in the new life of the Spirit" (7:6), because they "belong to the one who has been raised from the dead in order that we might bear fruit for God" (7:4). It is how "when we were living in the flesh, our sinful passions, aroused by the law, were at work in our members to bear fruit for death" (7:5) that requires the explanation.

Paul begins, in 7:7–11, by outlining the paradoxical character of law. The commandment reveals God's will by exposing what is forbidden (7:7), yet cannot keep the human person from doing it. Paul's choice of the commandment "You shall not covet" as an example is brilliant, for it fits his point precisely. Some commandments, for example, "you shall not kill" or "you shall not steal," are self-limiting, and one can easily tell when they have been done or not. In contrast, the command "you shall not covet" cuts to the secret places of the human heart and not simply to actions in the external world.

As I mentioned above, although the term *epithymein/epithymia* tended to have in Hellenistic moral teaching a strongly sexual connotation, since "sexual desire" is so obvious a form of passion (Plato, *Phaedo* 83B; *Phaedrus* 232B), it actually denotes "desire/coveting" in the broadest sense. It is the "I want to have" passion. The texts to which Paul alludes (Exod 20:17 and Deut 5:21) specify a number of objects of such "wanting." Only the first is sexual, "coveting your neighbor's wife." Also included are the neighbor's house and field and male slaves and female slaves and oxen and ass, "or anything that is your neighbor's." The "desiring disease" is not specifically sexual. It applies to all craving. Paul's choice is brilliant because this "disease of desire" fits perfectly what I have called the idolatrous impulse that lies at the heart of sin. Coveting is that need to have, or possess, to acquire, in order to secure being and worth.

Coveting manifests itself in every form of acquisitiveness (*pleonexia,* "craving more"), which Paul associates with idolatry in 1:29, and which in Col 3:5, he designates simply as "idolatry." It is this unquenchable thirst for being, this (to return to the earlier metaphor) *itch* that drives human freedom to secure itself through some form of having, whether of pleasure or possessions or power. And, as the commandment itself shows, it is a drive that seeks to have at the expense of "the neighbor." Paul acknowledges, "I would not have known what it is to covet" if the law had not spelled it out this way (7:7). The commandment identified the itch for what it is and established scratching it as an offense against God's will. Paradoxically, however, such knowledge actually strengthened the impulse: "when the commandment came, sin revived, and I died." And, as we have seen, since the commandment actually promised life yet could not give it, the law actually colluded with sin and "killed me." It is at this precise point that Paul proclaims that the "law is holy, and the commandment is holy and just and good" (7:12). By so doing, he has set up the fundamental tension between verbal directive and effective power.

The next part of his argument makes this clear. It was not "the good law" that brought humans death (7:13). It was, rather, sin that used what was itself good to work death, "in order that sin might be shown to be sin, and through the commandment might become sinful beyond measure." Sin is not the breaking of the rule, but the distortion of a relationship. The rule reveals sin to be what it is, because even when the rule is kept, the relationship can be distorted. I can, for example, avoid "coveting" everything on that list provided by Torah, but that list cannot relieve the itch of the craving disease. I can still *covet*, let us say, God's favor and seek to possess it, precisely by being able to claim not to covet the things on God's list. This disease of freedom is infinitely adaptable.

Paul supplies the reason: "we know that the law is spiritual, but I am fleshly, sold under sin" (7:14). Note that Paul's imagery of "being sold" fits the overall metaphor of the rule of sin as one that enslaves, and from which God's gift must "redeem" humans (3:24). But this human alienation is due to "fleshliness" (*sarkikōs*), a dimension of the idolatrous impulse that Paul now makes explicit and thematic for the first time, though he has anticipated it in several places (see 2:28; 4:1; 6:19; 7:5). He will now begin to work out the anthropological difference between "life according to the flesh" (what might be called the weakened human capacity for freedom under the impulse of idolatry and the rule of sin) and "life according to the Spirit" (which comes from the empowerment given by God). His point here is simply that the "spiritual" character of the law (the fact it comes from God) does not supply the "spiritual power" to the person damaged by slavery to sin.

The rest of the chapter says the same thing in various ways. The goodness of the law can draw the mind's assent (7:16, 19, 22, 25), but so long as human freedom is weakened by "the flesh," it cannot translate that intellectual recognition into effective action: "I do not the good that I want, but the evil I do not want is what I do" (7:19). This inadequacy is due to the effective "rule of sin," which exploits the weakness of the flesh to turn even the desire to serve God into a distortion of that relationship: "I delight in the law of God in my inmost self, but I see in my members another law at war with the law of my mind and making me captive to the law of sin which dwells in my members" (7:23).

Paul has brilliantly exposed the inability of *any* law to mediate personal relationships. The power of idolatry (that begins in the refusal to acknowledge one's being as gift from God) and sin (that is a conscious hardening of idolatry in the face of God's gift) establish humans in a condition of enmity. It is at least straightforward. But the revelation of law as the chance to know

God and "do his will" (2:17) introduces *dividedness*. The mind recognizes the goodness, but the heart still acts out of hostility. In such a situation, even the external keeping of the law (such as Paul could claim in his past life) is compatible with self-aggrandizement and is an act of hostile self-assertion over against God. In his personification of the person sold under sin, Paul recognizes the depth of the problem: "I myself serve the law of God with my mind, but with my flesh I serve the law of sin" (7:25). Inhabiting this "fictive I," he cries out, "Wretched man that I am, who will save me from this body of death?" (7:24).

Readers stopping at this point might think that Paul is doing more than performing, is in fact expressing his own despair. But Paul immediately follows his dramatic outcry with a statement that can be read two ways, though each points in the same direction. Some manuscripts take 7:24b as Paul's own answer to his question, "Who can save me," with "the grace of God through our Lord Jesus Christ." Other manuscripts (probably to be preferred), have "thanks be to God through our Lord Jesus Christ." Both responses are, in fact, correct: it is God's gift and thanks to God that the dismal dividedness described by Paul no longer exists for those who have accepted the gift with faith. The gift has been given (5:15). The power has been poured out (5:5). It is that reality–the power of the Holy Spirit to transform the human spirit–to which Paul turns next.

LIFE IN THE SPIRIT

Romans 8:1-39

We know that in its original form this letter was not divided into chapters and verses. But the chapter divisions (which go back to Stephanus in the sixteenth century) are often insightful. Although chapter 8, for example, continues the line of argument begun in chapters 6 and 7 by responding to the question, "Should we continue in sin because we are not under the law but grace?" (6:15), it also has a definite character of its own. Chapter 8 most closely resembles chapter 5, where Paul also took the time to expound more fully the nature of the gift that God had given in Christ, with its consequences. Chapter 8 has the same quality of calm exposition, moving by way of positive affirmation rather than tense dialectic yet building slowly in a rhetorical crescendo unsurpassed in ancient religious literature.

In fact, the theme of chapter 8 is actually a continuation of 5:5: Paul there asserted that God's gift did not shame but offered secure grounds for hope because "the love of God has been poured out into our hearts through the Holy Spirit which has been given to us." Now Paul develops the role of the Holy Spirit in Christian experience, by contrasting its power and its direction to the way of life lived "according to the flesh." The term "flesh" (*sarx*) appears ten times in this chapter, more frequently than in any other part of the letter, and the word "spirit" (*pneuma*) occurs nineteen times in this chapter, more than all its other occurrences in the letter, combined.

The Holy Spirit and the Power of New Life

It may be helpful, before picking up Paul's exposition, to remind ourselves of the role played by the Holy Spirit in the earliest Christian movement. One of the most distinctive elements in the birth of this religion was its claim to an *experience of power*, whether the term used is "authority" (*exousia*; see

116

John 1:12; 1 Cor 8:9; 9:1, 4; 2 Cor 10:8; 13:10; 2 Thess 3:9) or "energy" (*energeia*; see Gal 3:5; 5:6; Phil 3:20-21; Col 1:29; 1 Cor 12:6; 1 Thess 2:13; Phlm 6; Heb 4:12), or simply "power" (*dynamis*; see Rom 1:16; 15:13, 19; 1 Cor 1:18; 6:14; 2 Cor 6:7; 13:4; Gal 3:5; Eph 3:20; Col 1:29; 1 Thess 1:5; 2 Thess 1:11; 2 Tim 1:7; Heb 2:4; 2 Pet 1:16). Such power enabled believers to "work signs and wonders" (Acts 4:30; 5:12; 14:3; Rom 15:9; 2 Cor 12:12; Heb 2:4) such as healings, prophecies, spiritual utterances, and the proclamation of the good news (Rom 1:16; 1 Cor 1:18; 2:5; 2 Cor 4:7; 1 Thess 1:5; 2 Tim 1:8). The power also worked for the transformation of those receiving it (Gal 3:5; 1 Cor 2:16; 2 Cor 3:18; Eph 4:23; Col 3:10; 1 Pet 1:22). The first Christians insisted that this power was not their own. It was not attached to their economic or military or social or intellectual prowess. Rather, it came to them as a gift from another to whom it properly belonged (Rom 1:4; 16:25; 1 Cor 1:24; 5:4; 12:3; 2 Cor 1:4; 6:7; 12:9; Eph 3:16, 20; Phil 3:10, 21; Heb 5:7).

To a remarkable extent, such statements about *power* are correlated to statements about *the resurrection of Jesus* and the *Holy Spirit*. The narrative accounts of John 20:20-23; Luke 24:47-48; Acts 2:1-4, 17-33 show how the Holy Spirit is connected to and derived from the risen Lord Jesus and brings with it the experience of power, so that the possession of the Holy Spirit appears as the experiential correlative to the confession that "Jesus is Lord" (see 1 Cor 12:3). Throughout the New Testament, the term "Holy Spirit" functions more or less equivalently to "the presence and power of Jesus" in the community of his followers. To be baptized in the name of Jesus means to receive the Holy Spirit (Acts 2:38; see Matt 28:19). It was the "Holy Spirit" that worked the "signs and wonders" done "in the name of Jesus" (see Gal 3:3-5; Acts 4:8; 1 Thess 1:5; 2 Tim 1:6), and the Holy Spirit that works for the transformation of the heart (1 Cor 2:12; Titus 3:5).

The Holy Spirit is therefore not an impersonal force, but the life-giving presence and power of the risen Lord among his followers: "Because you are sons [children], God has sent the Spirit of his son into our hearts, crying, 'Abba, Father'" (Gal 4:6). And again, in 2 Cor 3:17-18: "Now the Lord is Spirit, and where the Spirit of the Lord is, there is freedom. And we all, with unveiled faces, beholding the glory of the Lord, are being changed into his likeness from one degree of glory to another; for this comes from the Lord who is Spirit."

The connection between the Holy Spirit and the risen Jesus is stated also in 1 Cor 2:12, where Paul declares, "we have received, not the spirit of the world, but the Spirit which is from God," and concludes, "we have the mind of Christ" (1 Cor 2:16). We remember also the text quoted here several times to the effect that "the first man became a living being, the last Adam became a life-giving Spirit" (1 Cor 15:45). For Paul, participation in the Holy

Spirit and being part of "the body of Christ" are intrinsically connected: "By one Spirit we were all baptized into one body—Jews or Greeks, slaves or free—and all were made to drink of the one Spirit . . . now you are the body of Christ" (1 Cor 12:13, 27).

This explicit correlation between the resurrection of Jesus and his powerful presence in the community through the Holy Spirit is not exclusively Pauline (see also 1 Pet 1:2; 3:18; 4:6; Heb 2:4; 4:12; 6:4; 1 John 3:24; 4:13; 5:8; Jude 19, 20; Rev 2:7; 4:2; 19:10; and L. T. Johnson, *The Writings of the New Testament: An Interpretation* [Philadelphia: Fortress, 1986] 94, 106–8). But the connection is particularly strong in Paul, for whom the gift of the Spirit is both the source of new life and the guide to behavior: "If we live by the Spirit let us also walk by the Spirit" (Gal 5:16, 25). It is no surprise, then, when Paul turns to explicate more fully the meaning of "being under grace" that "comes by gift from God through our Lord Jesus Christ" (7:24), that he should do so by means of expounding the role of the Holy Spirit.

What the Spirit Accomplished (8:1–4)

Paul's use of "now" in 8:1 signals a turning point, as it did also in 3:26; 5:19; and 6:19-21, a contrast between the situation prior to the act of God in Christ, and the present: "There is now no condemnation for those who are in Christ Jesus." The judgment leading to condemnation following Adam's sin (see 5:16, 18) is not applied to those belonging to Christ. And Paul supplies the reason: "The law of the Spirit of life in Christ Jesus has set me [other manuscripts read "you" or "us"] free from the law of sin and death" (8:2). Sometimes one wishes Paul were just a little less vivid and paradoxical in his diction. As in 3:27, he can't seem to restrain himself from using "law" (*nomos*) in punning fashion. As in that earlier passage as well, the term *nomos* here means less "law" than principle, or perhaps even a power. It is simply unfortunate that, when we are trying so hard to sort out Paul's terms with some precision, he delights in confounding us by crossing the categories!

But this is simply a distraction. The main point could not be more clear. A corner has been turned, a change has occurred. God has freed us (see 6:18, 20, 22). All of Paul's language about redemption (3:24), expiation (3:25), and reconciliation (5:10) comes down at last to this human experience of freedom. His statement also makes clear what freedom is from. Paul joins in one compressed phrase law/sin/death, for it was his business in 7:13-25 to show the destructive synergy of these realities and how they worked to enslave humans. In this statement of "freedom from," we are reminded first of Paul's statement in Gal 5:1, "For freedom Christ has freed you; do not submit again to the yoke of slavery," meaning there the law.

Paul also notes in 8:2 the source of this freedom. It comes from "the principle/power (*nomos*) of the Spirit of life in Christ Jesus." Once more, his language is remarkably compressed, but we can detect in it the combination of "the gift of Christ Jesus"/"the Holy Spirit"/and "eternal life," which Paul has been building since chapter 5 (see 5:5, 10, 15, 17, 21; 6:4, 22, 23; 7:6) as the basis of true human freedom.

Now Paul spells out the meaning of this freedom in terms of a new power or capacity: "For God has done what the law, weakened by the flesh, could not do; sending his own son in the likeness of sinful flesh and for sin, he condemned sin in the flesh, so that the just requirement of the law might be fulfilled in us, who walk not according to the flesh but according to the Spirit" (8:3–4). In the last chapter, we saw that the difficulty with the law was not that it was wrong in what it prescribed but that it was powerless to enable humans to do what was right, because they were "weakened by the flesh." The reign of sin disabled humans from choosing even that which their own minds agreed was good—a precise diagnosis of impulse, addiction, spiritual slavery.

But now, Paul declares, God has acted to free humans in the most dramatic of all gestures. God "sent his own son in the likeness of sinful flesh and for sin." The final phrase could mean also "as a sin offering," which would strengthen the reading of 3:24–25 as a sacrificial act. In this solemn passage, Paul employs the language of *exchange* that is so characteristic of him. We have noted earlier his fondness for expressing the reality of God's gift in terms of a paradoxical exchange: God in Christ becoming foolishness to make humans wise, poverty to make them rich, weakness to make them strong, sin to make them righteous, dying so that they could live. Here, Paul says that God's son took on the "form of sinful flesh." For a discussion of this, see F. M. Gillmann, "Another Look at Romans 8:3: 'In the Likeness of Sinful Flesh,'" *Catholic Biblical Quarterly* 49 (1987): 597–604. We are reminded of Phil 2:7, which speaks of Jesus, though being in the form of God, nevertheless taking on the form of a slave and being found "in the likeness of humans." Paul's language here also resembles that in Gal 4:2: "When the time had fully come, God sent forth his son . . . born under the law to redeem those who were under the law." Through his son, God takes on the human condition in order to rescue it. The Greek puts special emphasis on "his own son"—a nuance that will be picked up in 8:32 by Paul's allusion to the sacrifice of Abraham's "only son."

In this compelling statement of God's act of liberation, perhaps the most startling element is the *purpose* for which liberation has taken place. They were "freed from the law of death." Fair enough. But why? "So that the just requirement of the law might be fulfilled in us, who walk not according to the flesh but according to the Spirit." The change brought about is one that affects humans in their freedom. They are now empowered to live in a new way. But the new spiritual capacity expresses itself in fulfilling the "just requirement of the law." This is an important clarification to Paul's discussion of the law in chapter 7. Now humans are given the "spiritual power" to fulfill the "spiritual law" (7:14). We will see in 12:2 that Paul will speak of their ability to "test what is the will of God," just as in 2:18, those who have the law are able to "test what ought to be done." The freedom given by the Holy Spirit, in other words, leads not to an abandonment of God's will as revealed in Torah but to the fulfillment of its righteous requirement.

Life in the Spirit (8:5-11)

The sort of contrast Paul laid out in 6:15-23 between obedience to God and obedience to sin is now recast in terms of the power of new life given to those who are in Christ. Now Paul speaks of those who are "according to the Spirit" or "according to the flesh." The Greek construction "according to" (*kata* + accusative) means here "according to the measure of," or "on the basis of." For the element of human freedom, Paul introduces the language of *phronēsis/phronēma*, which is similar to "obedience" in the way Paul uses it: a person's *phronēma* is his or her desire/will/ intention. The RSV's translation of "set the mind on" is accurate.

In 8:5-8, Paul draws three contrasts between distinct modes of behavior. It is significant that Paul focuses not on a specific act as "right or wrong" but rather on what might be called an orientation of freedom, a characteristic direction taken by a person toward or away from God. The passage gives deeper insight into the anthropological dimensions of what Paul means by sin and faith; before they are expressed in discrete acts, they are dispositions of the spirit (see L. Monden, *Sin, Liberty and Law*, trans. J. Donceel [New York: Sheed & Ward, 1965]). The first contrast, then, states what should be obvious: "those who live acording to the flesh set their minds on the things of the flesh, but those who live according to the spirit set their minds on the things of the spirit" (8:5). We recognize here the same sort of moral contrast made in Gal 5:17: "the desires of the flesh are against those of the spirit, and the desires of the spirit are against those of the flesh." The only thing we need to remind ourselves here is that Paul is not talking about "flesh" as "body" and "spirit" as the human "mind." The things of the flesh are not necessarily physical things, but all the ways of measuring reality according to the idolatrous impulse, as a closed system removed from God's claim. In contrast, the things of the spirit are not ideas but the claims of the Holy Spirit on human existence, and "setting one's mind" on such things is to be open in faith to the movements of that Holy Spirit.

The next contrast in 8:7 simply repeats the result of each orientation, one ending in death (see 1:32; 5:12, 14, 17, 21; 6:9, 16, 21, 23), the other in "life and peace." The term "peace" (*eirēnē*) recalls Paul's statement about the reward due those who seek to please God (2:10), and the present condition of humans vis-à-vis God because of the righteous death of Jesus (5:1). The term "life," we have seen, is virtual shorthand for that goal of human freedom which is sharing in the fullness of God's presence (see 2:7; 5:10, 17, 18, 21; 6:4, 22, 23; 8:2).

The reason why the different orientations lead to such disparate ends lies in how they relate the human person to God. Paul states this in 8:7-8 in terms of the one whose mind is set on the things of the flesh: it is incapable of submitting itself to God's law; it cannot please God. It is, indeed, "enmity toward God." Part of this description points to the lack of power that Paul has been stressing as the condition of the flesh. But the term *echthra* ("enmity") is much harsher, reminding us of 5:10 but finding its closest parallel in Jas 4:4, which puts a similar sentiment in different form: "Do you not know that friendship with the world is enmity with God? Therefore whoever wishes to be a friend of the world establishes himself as an enemy of God." Such a perception is not far from Paul's in the present passage. Sin is more than mere inadequacy or failure; it is the choice of being in opposition to God. As in our discussion of "God's wrath" in 1:18-32, we must remember that these concepts are not psychological but religious. What Paul speaks of here is not a matter of "hostile feelings" toward God, but rather a matter of shaping one's life according to choices that are, in fact, closed and opposed to God's activity in the world.

Paul now turns away from that sad condition and will not return to it again in the letter. He reminds his readers of their present situation: "You however are not in the flesh but in the Spirit, if indeed the Spirit of God dwells in you; if anyone does not have the Spirit of Christ, this one does not belong to him" (8:9). Paul's language about the Spirit is remarkably personal. We notice first that he can simply equate "Spirit of God" and "Spirit of Christ." These are the sorts of functional equations that led to later christological development. In terms of a close reading of the Greek, the present case might be rendered, the Spirit "from" God that is also the Spirit "of" Christ among believers. But such distinctions are not necessary; more significant is the power of life that Paul identifies as communicating God's gift in Christ and establishing humans in right relationship.

Paul also sees the presence of the Spirit to human freedom as intimate and interior. It is not a force that is manifested only in external "signs and wonders." Rather, it "indwells" the human person and community of believers. The closest parallel to this language in the New Testament is once more the Letter of Jas 4:5, which speaks of "the Spirit God made to dwell" in humans. The Spirit also makes possible an identification between the believer and Christ. If they have the Spirit of Christ, they "are his," or "belong to him." Paul goes on, "but if Christ is in you" (the language could hardly be more intimate), "even though the body is dead on account of sin, the Spirit is life on account of righteousness." I have provided a very literal translation. The RSV translation of the last phrase, "your spirits are alive," might give the impression of a body/soul dualism that is not present in the Greek. Paul is not stating the superiority of the human spirit to the human body. Rather, he recognizes that whereas human life is mortal and continues within a world where sin and death are realities, the *Spirit of God* represents "life" and "righteousness."

Such righteousness, as 8:11 now shows, finds its future in a life shared with God: "If the Spirit of the One who raised Jesus from the dead dwells in you," [again, notice the inwardness of this reality!], "the One who raised Christ from the dead will give life also to your mortal bodies, through the indwelling Spirit that is within you." Paul's point, I think, is both simple and powerful. The transforming Spirit that God has given to humans is the pledge and portent of future life in the resurrection (see 2 Cor 4:16–5:5). The resurrection, as Paul argued in 1 Cor 15:35–44, is not to be of the soul only but of "physical bodies," that is, the human body in which, as he states it in 2 Cor 5:4, "what is mortal may be swallowed up in life." The present passage brings home once again the extrordinarily close connection Paul draws between the resurrection of Jesus, the gift of the Spirit, the transformation of the human spirit, and the resurrection of humans to eternal life, all of this being "the gift of God in Christ Jesus."

The Gift of Adoption (8:12–17)

God's action in the death and resurrection of Jesus had achieved a "liberation" or "redemption" made effective by God's power being given them by the Holy Spirit. It follows, then, that those in this new allegiance owe nothing to their former condition of slavery. Paul makes this point emphatically with a very strong transition—"therefore indeed," we might translate it. They are not to be "debtors" of the flesh by living according to its measure (8:12). The term *opheiletai* is particularly striking here, for it designates those who are "under an obligation." Paul designated himself in 1:16 as "under an obligation to the Jew and Greek," and in 15:27 will declare that Gentile churches are "under an obligation" to the Jerusalem church. The meaning here, then, is that those living by the Spirit are no longer under any obligation to the flesh. Indeed, Paul continues, "if you live according to the flesh you will die, but if in the Spirit you put the deeds of the body to death, you will live" (8:13). Some manuscripts, understandably, have "deeds of the flesh" rather than "deeds of the body," and even if Paul did not say that, he surely meant it. The problem is not the body, but that "attitude of the flesh" that lives as though God had no claim on human existence. The point of the summary transition is to reaffirm, "we have said good-bye to all that."

In 8:14-17, Paul describes a still more intimate relationship with God brought about by the Spirit: "All who are led by the Spirit of God are sons of God." Paul's discussion here is close to that in Gal 3:23-4:7. There Paul had spoken of the situation of those under the law as one of slavery: "but when the time had fully come, God sent forth his son . . . so that we might receive adoption as sons. And because we are sons, God has sent the Spirit of his son into our hearts, crying, 'Abba! Father!' So, through God, you are no longer a slave but a son, and if a son, then an heir" (Gal 4:4-7).

In a more gender-conscious age such as our own, we could legitimately desire that Paul's language were rendered more inclusively as "children of God," and "child of God." And for most purposes, such a translation is both acceptable and right, for Paul clearly means that all those adopted have equal status as "children of God." When trying to capture the nuances of Paul's argument, however, the exclusive language of "sonship" remains desirable, and will—I hope with the readers' understanding—be used here.

There are three reasons why this usage is preferable. First, Paul's imagery builds on the specific imagery of Jesus (a male) as "God's son" and the "Spirit of adoption" that enables them likewise to be "sons." Second, this imagery is intrinsically connected to the ancient patriarchal system, in which males are the heirs of property. In the analogy, therefore, it is necessary to be a male to be an heir. Third, Paul's actual application of this language is gender-inclusive: "*all* led by the Spirit are sons of God." Such a status is not, for Paul, restricted to males. In order to deal with the specifics of Paul's language, therefore, male language will be used, recognizing that the *significance* (for Paul and us) is that "all humans led by the Spirit are children of God."

Both the negative and positive sides of Paul's declaration in 8:15 deserve attention. In 1 Cor 2:12, he made a similar distinction: "We have not received the spirit of the world, but the Spirit which is of God." The disjunction in Romans, however, is particularly appropriate to the argument made in this letter. They have not, says Paul, "received a spirit of slavery leading again into fear." The theme of slavery, we have seen, is connected to sin (6:6, 16, 17, 19, 20, 22). But this is the first time in Romans that Paul has used the term "fear" (*phobos*) in such a negative way. He declared in 3:18 that sinners "do not have the fear of God before their eyes" (quoting LXX Ps 33:2), but such "fear" in the biblical tradition signifies healthy reverence and obedience to God (Prov 1:7; Sir 1:11). What does he mean by a "spirit of slavery leading again to fear"? At the risk of overinterpreting, I suggest that this characterization fits Paul's description of idolatry in Rom 1:18-31. In discussing that passage, I speculated that it is the deep fear of contingency, anxiety at the threat of nonexistence, that, once the gift of God's creation is rejected, drives the compulsive need to construct one's own life and worth. I confess that my analysis of that passage was affected by my understanding of this one, where Paul presents the opposite "operative spirit." If the Spirit they now receive "frees them from slavery and fear," then, I suggest, fear can legitimately be taken as the root of the slavery that Paul describes as idolatry.

Now they have received, in place of the spirit of fear and slavery, "a spirit of adoption." The term *huiothesia* is, etymologically, "to have the place of a son," that is, to be adopted. Its legal sense is well attested on inscriptions, but it never appears in the LXX. In the New Testament, it is used only by Paul (Rom 8:15, 23; 9:4; Gal 4:5; Eph 1:5) and represents his distinctive way of connecting Jesus to his followers. Paul sets up a parallelism: as Jews are "sons of Abraham" by descent "according to the flesh," Christians are "sons of God" according to the "spirit of adoption," namely, the "Spirit of Christ" dwelling in them (8:9), since Christ is "God's own son" (8:32). It is "in" or "by" this Spirit, says Paul, that "we cry out, 'Abba! Father'!" (8:15).

As in the case of Gal 4:6, Paul may well be echoing the shout of believers as they emerge from the waters at their baptism (see W. A. Meeks, *The First Urban Christians: The Social World of the Apostle Paul* [New Haven: Yale University Press, 1983] 152). Certainly, such cultic exclamations were found elsewhere in the ancient world (see Euripides, *Bacchae* 68; 140; Ovid, *Metamorphoses* 3.528-45). What is most fascinating about the actual cry is not the term "Father," for that would follow from their status as adopted sons, but the use of the Aramaic term *abba*. The expression has not been attested for Jewish prayer in that period. It is not a solemn designation, but just the opposite: *abba* is what little Jewish children called their "daddy." It is a familial, familiar, and affectionate term, suggesting great intimacy and trust. More remarkably, the only time (apart from this passage and the parallel in Gal 4:6) that we find this expression elsewhere in the New Testament is in the mouth of Jesus, in his prayer to God before his death (see Mark 14:36).

For Paul to employ, without any warning, this *Aramaic* expression in a letter to a Greek-speaking community that he himself did not found or instruct, implies that he considered this (baptismal?) tradition to be sufficiently common that he could so casually allude to it. The fact that the expression was maintained in Aramaic also supports the position that the cry went back to the earliest days of the Palestinian church and in all likelihood to the personal prayer of Jesus himself (see J. Jeremias, *The Central Message of the New Tes-*

tament [Philadelphia: Fortress, 1965] 9–30). We can safely conclude that Paul considered the baptized to be incorporated into the identity of Jesus so thoroughly, internally, and intimately, that they could address God in the same familiar (and not frightened) fashion as Jesus himself, the truly free human being (see L. T. Johnson, *Faith's Freedom: A Classic Spirituality for Contemporary Christians* [Minneapolis: Fortress, 1990] 183–85). Paul's next verse follows naturally from this. If it is "in the Spirit" that they can cry out to God in such a manner, then, quite literally, "the Spirit itself co-testifies with our spirit that we are children of God" (8:16).

The legal corollary of adoption is picked up by 8:17: "if we are sons, then also heirs, heirs of God, fellow inheritors of Christ." These brief conclusions echo Paul's remarks about Abraham. In 4:13–14, he asserted that the promise to Abraham (that his descendents would inherit the world) happened not by law "but through the righteousness of faith." Now the results of the "faith of Christ"—namely, the gift of the Holy Spirit—enable those whom God adopts in Christ to be *heirs*.

The language of "inheritance" (*klēronomia*) is extensive in the New Testament (see Acts 7:5; 20:32; Gal 3:18, 29; 4:1, 7, 30; 5:21; 1 Cor 6:9–10; 15:50; Titus 3:7; Eph 1:14, 18; 5:5; Heb 1:2; 6:17; 9:15; 11:7–8; Jas 2:5; 1 Pet 1:4; Rev 21:7), not least because the issue posed by the Gentile mission was precisely how this messianic movement might stake a claim to the heritage of Israel from which it had originated. The solution offered throughout the New Testament, not least in Paul, was by way of redefining the nature of the "inheritance," identifying it not with the possession of the *land* but specifically with the *gift of the Holy Spirit* (see, e.g., Acts 3:37–42). Once this slight (!) adjustment is made, then it follows that everyone who has the Holy Spirit is also an heir of the promise made to Abraham. There is no need to elaborate, I think, on the obvious objection that other Jews would have to this redefinition, which had the effect of "localizing" and relativizing their own claims to be heirs of Abraham. It was fine with the Christians if they continued to claim to be heirs of Abraham "according to the flesh," for the Christians' redefinition of terms had now made that claim religiously irrelevant. Without accepting the gift of God in Christ and receiving the "Spirit of Christ," they could not claim to be "sons of God according to the Spirit" in the way the messianists could. As with Paul's use of Adam, we see in this redefined "inheritance" language what a radically new beginning Paul sees occurring in the resurrection of Jesus.

Paul attaches a rider to the affirmation in 8:17: "if indeed we suffer with him in order that we might be glorified with him." The statement provides a transition to the next "work of the Spirit" in human freedom, the deepest possible imprinting in the freedom of believers with the identity of the crucified and raised messiah. The balanced statement finds a partial parallel in

2 Tim 2:11: "If we have died with him, we will also live with him." The state-ment in Romans, however, connects not simply to the pattern of death and resurrection, but specifically to the experience of *suffering*. We find here perhaps the deepest paradox of the Christian conviction: that the Spirit of power that gives new life to humans finds its most proper expression not in ecstatic speech or healings but in weakness, *sharing the suffering* of the messiah (see L. T. Johnson, *The Real Jesus: The Misguided Quest for the Historical Jesus and the Truth of the Traditional Gospels* [San Francisco: HarperSanFrancisco, 1996]). It is this aspect of the Spirit's work among believers that Paul now develops.

The Spirit in Suffering and Hope (8:18–27)

In a section of his exposition that is extremely important for understanding the later argument in chapters 9–11, Paul deals here with the acute problem presented by the gap between appearances and reality. The appearances suggest that Christians are no better off than most folk: they remain mortal, subject to passions, and are often implicated in evil. And the ways they are different are not encouraging: because of their peculiar beliefs and behav-iors, they are persecuted and suffer. How, then, can they claim to have been touched by the all-powerful God and transferred to a realm where they are free and fully enfranchised "children of God"?

Paul addresses this problem in the most explicitly eschatological section of Romans. He makes a fundamental distinction between what is visible now and what will be manifest later, between the "already" of God's power at work, and the "not yet" of its future realization. Paul insists, as we have seen, that the essential gift has been given. God's triumph is real and defin-itive in the resurrection of Jesus and the outpouring of the Holy Spirit into the hearts of believers. This experience is the basis for speaking of a "new creation" and a "new Adam." Yet it is also the case that the structures of the world and of sinful systems have not disappeared, and full freedom has not yet come to the "mortal bodies" of believers. They may be in the process of becoming holy, but they have not yet attained that "glory" which is full shar-ing in God's eternal life.

Essential for Paul, however, is that the realization in the future will be based and built on the reality of the present. What is yet to be revealed of God's triumph is on a continuum with the believers' realized experience. It is on the basis of the gift already given that the gift fully displayed will be accomplished, on the firmament of a renewed humanity that the new cre-ation will become visible. But, since that future realization cannot be seen, it must be a matter of *hope*.

Paul must take up, then, "the sufferings of the now time." The phrase "now time" reminds us of 3:26 and 8:1, but the key word in 8:18 is the verb "I reckon" (*logizomai*). It is Paul's perception or calculation (and that of his readers) concerning the present reality that is decisive. We see that here again he appeals to shared knowledge in 8:22 ("for we know"), a knowledge that persists despite having to do with "what cannot be seen" (8:24-25). This perception is a sort of "expectation" (8:25) that Paul thinks of as cognate with an "expectation" of all creation (8:19); the "now time" can both be contrasted to the future and be seen as its preparation.

He begins by declaring that he does not consider "the sufferings of the present time to be worthy of the glory that is to be revealed in us" (preferable to the RSV's "to us"). The contrast is very similar to that drawn in 2 Cor 4:16-17: "we do not lose heart. Though our outer nature is wasting away, our inner nature is being renewed every day. For this slight momentary affliction is preparing us for an eternal weight of glory beyond all comparison." The parallel is particularly instructive since it contains the same elements as the present passage: present suffering, transformation toward the future, and an expectation out of proportion to the present appearance. The expression "weight of glory" is especially felicitous, for it captures some of the etymological richness of the Hebrew *kābôd* and points us toward the sense of "presence and power" that Paul attaches to the term *doxa* in this letter (see 1:23; 3:7, 23; 4:20; 5:2; 6:4).

In this passage, Paul makes the point of comparison the "coming glory." It is not yet manifested, but it is to be revealed "in us." I prefer the translation "in us" because the next line picks up precisely that connection. But what are the "sufferings of the now time" of which Paul speaks? He may have in mind the experience of "affliction" from the outside by means of persecution (see, e.g., Rom 5:3; 12:12; and 8:35). But he may also mean simply the "suffering together with Christ" that is a corollary of the commitment to the obedience of faith such as Jesus had, a suffering that is not always inflicted from without, but can accompany the very life of faith according to the pattern of Jesus' life for others (see, e.g., 2 Cor 1:5-7; Col 1:24; and especially Phil 3:10).

Paul thinks of these sufferings as a participation in the birth pangs of a new creation (8:19-23). Using a rare word (*apokaradokia*, otherwise only in Phil 1:20), Paul pictures creation itself as "eagerly awaiting the revelation of the sons of God." The specifically *natal* dimensions of this image will be developed in 8:22. For now, we see that Paul connects "the coming glory that will be revealed in us" to a cosmic expectation. Having made the connection, he then shifts to a consideration of creation's situation. He says, "creation was subjected to futility, not by its own choice, but on account of the one who subjected it, upon the hope that creation itself will be freed from the slavery of corruption, unto the liberty that belongs to the glory of the children of God" (8:20–21).

When Paul speaks of "creation" he means everything that was created by God. But who has done the subjecting here? The reference to "futility" is an obvious allusion back to his description of idolatry. There we saw that humans "became foolish in their designs and senseless in their hearts" (1:23). The combination here of foolishness, glory, and corruptible, it seems to me, strengthens the literary cross-reference. The most straightforward way to read "not by its own choice but on account of the one who subjected it" is as a reference to humans who distorted creation and "brought it into subjection" by their idolatry. The RSV translation, "by the will of him who subjected it in hope," makes it appear that *God* is the one who subjected creation to futility. But the translation over-reads "on account of him" by translating it as "by the will of him." The placement of "in hope" is, admittedly, awkward, but it is so if God is the subject as much as it is if humans are the subject.

To make God the subject is to miss not only the literary cross-reference but also the logic of the present argument. Paul is trying to show that, just as the fate of creation was tied to the disposition of human freedom for bad (so that human sin also corrupted God's creation), so is it tied to human freedom for good: as humans are liberated by the Spirit of God to share in the presence and power of God (= God's glory), so will creation itself share in that same liberation. But this is, as Paul notes by connecting the two clauses so awkwardly, entirely a matter of *hope*, that is, a conviction based less on visible evidence than on trust in an unseen presence and power.

As creation "awaits the revelation of sons," it goes through the suffering of birthing mothers. In a remarkable image, Paul declares that "all of creation is groaning together and is in birth-labor together until now" (8:22). The image wonderfully combines Paul's perception of the present as one of both suffering and hope. The birth of a child is the perfect image for this combination (see John 16:21–22). And if what is being born is really a "new humanity," then "all of creation" needs to be involved. But how can Paul confidently assert that "we know this"? He must be referring to the shared world of Torah, where (especially in the prophets) the image of a mother birthing was used either as an expression of hopefulness (Isa 26:17; 66:7), or of eschatological tribulation (Isa 13:8; LXX Jer 6:24; 8:21; 13:21; 22:43; 27:43; see also D. T. Tsumura, "An OT Background to Rom 8:22," *New Testament Studies* 40 [1994]: 620–21). It is an image also attributed to Jesus in his prediction of the woes to come: "these things will be the beginning of the birth-pangs" (Matt 24:8; Mark 13:8). Paul himself refers to the suddenness of the expected parousia of the Lord as the unexpected onset of labor-pains (1 Thess 5:3). Finally, Paul uses the image in Gal 4:19 for his *own* laboring to bring his communities to birth as believers. He can assume, therefore, that this image is one that "we know."

In a striking extension of the imagery, Paul asserts "not only that, but we ourselves, who have the firstfruits of the Spirit, groan inwardly as we wait for adoption, the redemption of our bodies" (8:23). Those who are being born are also the ones giving birth! And their suffering—expressed by their "groaning"—is also part of the suffering that is the birth pangs of the new creation. Once more we see the "already" and "not yet" so characteristic of Paul. Here, the "not yet" is emphasized: the fullness of their adoption will not be accomplished until their bodies also are redeemed. Paul means here the future resurrection of believers (see 1 Thess 4:13–17; 1 Cor 15:51–57; 2 Cor 5:1–5). Before that time, the "already" is not one of manifest glory, but rather of a share in the suffering of the messiah and of creation itself.

But, to swing back to the "already," they *do* have "the firstfruits of the Spirit." The expression *aparchē* is used in the LXX for the first part of a harvest or herd that is offered to God as a representation of the whole. In the LXX, the term always has this literal sense (see LXX Exod 22:29; Lev 2:12; Deut 12:16), except in LXX Ps 77:51 and 105:36, where it refers to the firstborn children of Egypt who are killed in place of the Israelite firstborn sons. In the New Testament, by contrast, the expression is used metaphorically (see Jas 1:18; Rev 14:4) and is a favorite of Paul, who uses it in other letters with reference to one of his churches (2 Thess 2:13), or first converts of an area (1 Cor 16:15; Rom 16:5), or of Jewish members of the Christian movement (Rom 11:16). The usage that comes closest to the one here is 1 Cor 15:20, where Paul refers to the resurrection of Jesus as "the firstfruits of those who have fallen asleep," signifying that Jesus' resurrection was the first of many to follow, and he continues by affirming that "in Christ all shall be made alive," (15:22) in sequence, namely, "Christ the firstfruits, then at his coming those who belong to Christ" (15:23).

The close connection in Paul's thinking between the resurrection of Jesus and the gift of the Holy Spirit is indicated here once more by his referring to the Holy Spirit itself as "firstfruits" that will eventually lead to the redemption of our bodies. Such a conclusion indicates how Paul understands the Holy Spirit as a kind of indwelling power that can grow to new proportions. Another passage containing the same sort of present/future tension is 2 Cor 5:1–5. In a discussion of how "we sigh with anxiety" as we wait for "what is mortal to be swallowed up by life," Paul touches on the ground of his hope: "He who has prepared us for this very thing is God, who has given us the Spirit as a guarantee (*arrabōn*)" (2 Cor 5:5).

Now Paul picks up this note of "hope" that he sounded in 8:20 and hammers it five times in two verses (8:24–25). Paul emphasizes that it is this quality of hope that bridges the present and the future, by perceiving possibility in "what is not seen" and enabling life to go forward on that basis. His remarks here echo two earlier passages in the letter that his first readers would certainly have caught. When Paul insists that "hope in what is seen is not hope," he recalls his own description of Abraham, who "hoped against hope" (4:18). Abraham saw how old he and Sarah were, and how humanly impossible was the promise that he should become the father of many nations. But his hope enabled him to perceive a possibility from God that goes beyond human possibility. His faith was in God, "who gives life to the dead and calls into existence things that do not exist" (4:17). By implication, this is also the "faith of Jesus," who "gave himself for us" in trust that God would vindicate him. Paul's readers have good reasons for "hoping in what is not seen." When Paul says that "we are expecting through endurance (*hypomonē*)," he also echoes 5:1-5: "endurance produces character and character produces hope and hope does not disappoint us, because God's love has been poured into our hearts through the Holy Spirit, which has been given to us" (5:5). The ground of hope is the gift of the Holy Spirit, the transforming power from God that enables Christians to see new life coming to birth where the eyes of others see only disaster, resurrection where others see only death.

Paul adds one other mode of the Spirit's presence that supports hope. "Likewise," he says, "the Spirit helps us in our weakness. For we do not know how to pray as we should, but the Spirit itself intercedes with groanings without words" (8:26). What more compelling evidence of a personal and powerful presence could there be, than that the Spirit should actually pray with and for those whose weakness inhibits them? Paul's description of the Spirit's activity here reminds us of the Johannine designation of the Holy Spirit as a *paraklētos*, or advocate, who makes intercession in behalf of believers (see John 14:16, 26; 15:26; 16:7; 1 John 2:1). It is not clear what Paul specifically means by "groaning without words." One can easily see this as part of the image of childbirth, referring to the agonizing shouts and groans that often accompany birth pangs. Another possibility supported by the context is the shout "in the Spirit" of "Abba! Father!" that Paul mentions in 8:15. With that unintelligible (to a Greek) utterance, the Spirit would "be co-testifying with our spirit" that we are children of God. A third possibility is the role assigned the Holy Spirit in early Christian prayer, above all that called glossolalia, or "speaking in tongues," which Paul himself defines in terms of a gift of the Spirit for prayer that is unintelligible to listeners (1 Cor 14:2-33; see L. T. Johnson, "Gift of Tongues," in *The Anchor Bible Dictionary* [New York: Doubleday, 1992] 6:596-600).

The unintelligibility to humans does not affect the efficacy of the prayer, says Paul, for God understands: "The one who searches the hearts knows what is the mind of the Spirit, that it intercedes for the saints according to

God" (8:27). My translation is more literal than the RSV. Paul is here suggesting an intimacy of communication between God and the Spirit speaking for humans, such as he states in 1 Cor 2:10-11: "The Spirit searches everything, even the depths of God. For who knows a person's thoughts except the spirit of the person within? So also no one comprehends the thoughts of God except the Spirit of God." In the present case, Paul envisages this same kind of communication in reverse. It is not "the Spirit searching out God" but God "searching out [same word in Greek] the hearts" of humans. It is not the Spirit who knows God's thoughts but God who knows the Spirit's intention (*phronēma*), that it "intercedes according to God." The concept is obviously the same in both passages. The presence of the Holy Spirit (or the Spirit of Christ) "dwelling in" the human heart (8:9) enables a deep communication with God that surpasses and even bypasses normal human communication. It is difficult to overstate the degree of intimacy between the divine and human freedom that Paul here presents.

God's Loving Purpose (8:28–39)

Paul has been preparing for the final and most difficult set of questions that face his thesis, those dealing with the destiny of Israel. In 8:18-27, he asserted that God is at work through the Spirit even when appearances seem to deny God's presence and power. Now, in 8:28-30, he makes a series of assertions concerning God's overarching plan for humanity.

The best way to categorize these comments in the context of the ancient world is as statements in defense of providence (*pronoia*). In the ancient world as in our own, skeptics challenged God's control of events, and in particular God's ability to bring good results out of patently bad circumstances. Pious pagan philosophers wrote in defense of God's providence (Plutarch, *On the Delays in the Divine Vengeance* [*Mor.* 548B-568A]; Seneca, *On Providence*; Epictetus, *Discourse* 1.16). In Judaism, the stakes were even higher. It was not just the "divine system" of many gods that could be brought into question by events, for the system of polytheism had as one of its advantages a certain built-in self-correction, since blame could be spread around as liberally as could blessing. In Judaism, there was one single source of all reality, a personal God whose will disposed of events. A defense of this God in the face of evil or tragic occurrences is a more daunting task. Before Paul engages the hard question of God's fidelity in chapters 9-11, therefore, he begins with his own and his readers' sense of certainty given by their experience of God in Christ.

Paul begins with a transitional statement, which once more appeals to a shared understanding: "we know that for those who love God he works all things together for good" (8:28). It is a statement whose precise meaning is obscure in any case but has also become dangerously distorted by being used out of context. For some Christians the verse has become a kind of pious slogan used to mollify grief or assuage anger in the face of hard experience, having the bromidal effect of, "Don't worry, God will make everything turn out all right."

In fact, Paul does not claim that absolutely everything works out fine for every person, whether they "love God" (one of the few times he uses this traditional designation for the pious; see 1 Cor 2:9; Jas 1:12; 2:5) or not. His statement is both more embracing and tentative. First, he does not say that God "makes everything" turn out right. Rather, it is that "God works with all things"—it is the big picture that Paul has in mind, not the incidental details of lost coins or school exams. Second, God works with them "toward good" (*eis agathon*). "Good" here stands as the goal toward which all things move rather than a quality that inheres in everything that happens. The precise import of Paul's declaration is given by his next statement, which begins, *because:* it is in the light of what we have learned about God thus far that gives us the conviction to make such a sweeping and affirmative statement. Here it has to do with "being called according to his purpose." The *good* that God is working toward, then, is that of salvation or, in other words, of belonging to God's people and eventually sharing in God's life. The topic, therefore, is that of God's "purpose" (*prothesis*, 8:28).

In order to speak meaningfully about God's purpose or "will," it is necessary to posit that what humans experience *a posteriori*, God has known and chosen *a priori*, even though temporal statements are in the strictest sense inappropriate for God. All such language is "from the bottom up," defining God in terms of the human perception of movement, change, and causality, trying to describe the eternal in terms of the temporal. What for humans is "before and after" can be in the sight of God, simultaneous. Boethius (in *The Consolation of Philosophy*) has a wonderful analogy. The human looking down on ants sees their "future" unfolding "ahead" of them, simply because the field of vision given by human height enables them to grasp in a single vision what the ant may take a day to encounter. Even such analogies, of course, falter. But they remind us that discourse about "God's purpose/will" must always remain a matter of human guesswork.

In any case, Paul begins with God's knowing and choosing of humans "ahead of time" (see 11:2; 1 Pet 1:20). "Those whom he foreknew, he also set apart beforehand" (*proorizein*). Such "designation" or "setting apart" is a mode of election; the term Paul uses here is cognate with the one he used in 1:1 for his own "being set apart" to be an apostle and for Jesus' being "set apart as Son of God" by resurrection. The selection in this case is more inclusive: "to be co-formed to the image of his son, so that he might be the first-born of many brothers." It would be difficult to find a more succinct expression of God's entire purpose, according to Paul: that humans be shaped according to the identity of Jesus. Paul's language is unusually dense and needs to be looked at more closely.

By using the language of "image" (*eikōn*), Paul returns to the contrast between Christ and Adam. In Gen 1:26, Adam is made "according to our image" (*eikōn*; see Wis 2:13). And in 1 Cor 11:7, Paul refers to a man as "the image and glory of God." But in Rom 1:23, when depicting Gentile sin, Paul says, "they exchanged the glory of the immortal God for images resembling mortal humans," a perfect way of stating that the gods of idolatry are projections of human self-image. As a result of idolatry and sin, the image of God in humans is obviously damaged. For Paul, Jesus is the new "primal person" who restores that image of God, as the beginning of a new humanity.

In 2 Cor 4:4, Paul speaks of "the gospel of the glory of Christ who is the image (*eikōn*) of God." Likewise in Col 1:15, Christ is referred to as "the image (*eikōn*) of the invisible God." In the present passage, then, Paul proposes that the work of the Spirit is to trans-form humans into a con-form-ity (*symmorphos*) to the image of Christ, who is the template of a new human-ity. As he says in 1 Cor 15:49: "Just as we have borne the image of the man of dust, we shall also bear the image (*eikōn*) of the man of heaven." And in 2 Cor 3:18, Paul attributes this work explicitly to the Holy Spirit as an agent of present transformation: "We all, with unveiled face, beholding the glory of the Lord, are being changed (*metamorphoumetha*) into this image (*eikōn*) from one degree of glory to another; for this comes from the Lord, who is Spirit" (see also Phil 3:21). The end result of this reshaping of humans according to the image of Jesus is that there will be a new people, indeed a new humanity, in which Jesus is the "eldest son among many brothers" (8:29; see Col 1:15, 18).

Paul summarizes God's work in another *sorites* or *climax* (see on 5:3–5). The last term in each phrase becomes the first in the next: "those whom he selected before hand (*proorizein*, see 8:29), he also called (see 1:6–7); those whom he called, these he also made righteous (see 3:24, 26, 30; 5:1, 9; 6:7); those whom he made righteous, these he has also given glory (see 2:10; 5:2; 6:4; 8:18, 21). Into this rhetorical figure, Paul manages to compress his argument concerning what God has done for humans through Christ. He will shortly return to these affirmations and deal with the question whether God's "selecting ahead of time" and his "calling" are truly reliable—a question inescapably posed by the situation of Paul's fellow Jews. But for now, Paul's summary stands and prepares for his magnificent peroration.

Romans 8:31–39 is rightly regarded as one of the most stunning pieces of rhetorical art in the New Testament. The first five verses build to an almost unbearable tension by means of a series of some eight questions (the exact number depends on punctuation!). The tension is resolved in 8:37–39 by two final and triumphant assertions. Paul's opening question follows the style of the diatribe, "What therefore shall we say to these things" (or "in response to these things"; see 3:3, 5, 9; 4:1; 6:1, 15; 7:7). The questions themselves, however, have the feel of a judicial closing argument. Paul, who has been presenting the defense of "God's righteousness," now sums up.

His first question says it all in one stroke: "If God is for us, who is against us?" (8:31). If the source of all that exists has demonstrated such extraordinary care for the most wayward of creatures, how can there be any significant opposition left? And, lest we have missed the entire argument to this point, Paul reminds us: "He who did not spare his only son but gave him up for all of us, will he not give us all things with him?" (8:32). We recognize at once the "how much more" style of argument we found in 5:6–11. In the words, "did not spare his only son," scholars rightly perceive an echo of Abraham's offering of his son Isaac on the altar. The LXX text of Gen 22:16 reads, "because you did this deed and did not spare your beloved son on my behalf, I will surely bless you." In a remarkable turnabout, Paul pictures God's faithfulness to his creatures in the terms of Abraham's faithfulness to God (see N. A. Dahl, "The Atonement: Adequate Reward for the Akedah?" in *The Crucified Messiah* [Minneapolis: Augsburg, 1974] 146–60). Paul's argument in chapter 4 is also echoed in the expression "handed him over for us all." We saw in 4:25, that Christ was "handed over for our sins and raised for our righteousness." Having demonstrated his love in such extravagant fashion, Paul asks, Will not God "gift us" (*charizesthai*) with all things with him?

The real basis for confidence and exaltation is the very character of the God who has been shown to humans in Jesus Christ. Thus, Paul's next question: "Who will bring a charge against the elect of God? Is it God, the one who justifies?" The phrase "elect of God" can also be translated "God's chosen ones" and picks up the language of the LXX for the people God chose to be God's own (see, e.g., LXX Deut 4:7; Ps 32:12; 46:4). That early Christians saw themselves as "elect" or "chosen" from within the larger population of the Jewish nation to be God's special people is well attested in the New Testament literature (see 1 Thess 1:4; 1 Cor 1:27–28; Eph 1:4; Jas 2:5; Col 3:12; 2 Pet 1:10), so that it becomes, like the designation "holy ones," virtually a description of the community (see Mark 13:20; Rom 16:13; 2 Tim 2:10; Titus 1:1; 1 Pet 1:1; 2:4; 2 John 1). Functionally, it is equivalent to being "called" as in 8:30 (see Rev 17:14). But if God is the one who has chosen them and justified them, then God is not going to "bring a charge against/accuse" them (for the term, compare Acts 19:38; 23:28).

The forensic context is continued by the next set of questions: "Who will condemn? Is it Christ Jesus, who died, and more than that, was raised [some manuscripts add "from the dead"], and who is at the right hand of God, and who intercedes for us?" (8:33–34). The first question is answered in its posing, if one has read the letter. But the elaborate character of the second question (which is the answer to the first) is itself noteworthy, because it introduces aspects of Paul's understanding of Jesus previously untouched in the argument. This is now the seventh mention of Jesus' death (see 3:25; 4:25; 5:6, 8; 6:9–10; 8:34) and the fifth of his resurrection (4:24–25; 6:4, 9; 8:11), so that is no surprise, although we are reminded of how central and almost exclusive a focus Paul keeps on this part of the Jesus story.

Two aspects of the resurrection of Jesus, however, emerge here for the first time in Romans. Paul says that Jesus is "at the right hand of God," clearly an allusion to LXX Ps 109:1, a verse that played a critical role in early Christian reflection on the resurrection of Jesus (see Matt 22:44; Mark 12:36; 16:19; Luke 20:42; Acts 2:34; 5:31; 7:55–56; Heb 1:3, 13; 8:1; 10:12; 12:2; 1 Pet 3:22; Rev 5:1) but is otherwise used by Paul only in Col 3:1 and Eph 1:20 (both disputed letters), although the imagery of the psalm is present as well in 1 Cor 15:27.

The second new dimension of Paul's Christology is his characterization of the risen Jesus as "making intercession on your behalf." Paul uses the same word for "intercession" (*entynchanesthai*) that he did for the prayer made by the Holy Spirit in 8:26, underscoring again the coalescence of identity and function between the risen Lord and the Holy Spirit. In that place, I mentioned that the image of the Holy Spirit making intercession was close to the Johannine image of the *paraklētos*. One meaning of that term in Greek is "advocate," or "defense lawyer," and it would not be far wrong to suppose that this is what Paul is getting at in the present forensic context. The picture of Jesus at the right hand of God making intercession for humans is similar to that in 1 John 2:1: "If anyone sins, we have an advocate with the father, Jesus Christ the righteous one, and he is the expiation for our sins." The priestly Christology of Hebrews is likewise similar at this point: "For Christ has entered, not into a sanctuary made with hands, a copy of the true one, but into heaven itself, now to appear in the presence of God in our behalf" (Heb 9:24). If Jesus acts as advocate on the side of sinners, says Paul, he will not turn around and condemn them!

Paul's next question is whether any person or circumstance can "separate us from the love of Christ" (8:35). The genitive construction in this case is surely subjective. The point is *not* the attitude of humans toward Christ but his steadfast loyalty toward those who are his "brothers and sisters" (8:29). Having eliminated God and Christ himself as agents of separation, Paul turns rhetorically to any other contenders, making use of what has come to be called a *peristasis* catalogue, a listing of circumstances (particularly perilous ones) that go to demonstrate how virtue is proved through testing (compare 1 Cor 4:10-13; 2 Cor 4:8-10; 11:23-29; see J. Fitzgerald, *Cracks in an Earthen Vessel: An Examination of the Catalogues of Hardships in the Corinthian Correspondence* [SBLDS 99; Atlanta: Scholars Press, 1988]).

It is noteworthy that every item on the list represents an *external* testing rather than interior temptation. The first two items, "affliction and distress" (*thlipsis* and *stenochōria*) have appeared twice before in the letter. In 2:9, Paul referred to the "afflictions and distress" that would befall every human who did evil, but in 5:3 he makes "afflictions" one of the things over which those made righteous can "boast." The point is one made repeatedly by philosophers such as Epictetus. External circumstances do not determine a person's destiny, but it is the person's free decision as to what such circumstances signify that defines the self; circumstances can be experienced quite differently depending on the perspective (see Epictetus, *Discourses* 3.5.8-11; 4.1.89).

Like affliction, persecution was a circumstance frequently experienced by the first Christians (see Matt 13:21; Mark 4:17; 10:30; Acts 8:1; 2 Thess 1:4), and by Paul in particular (Acts 13:50; 2 Cor 12:10; 2 Tim 3:11). Famine (*limos*) is found in descriptions of eschatological woes (Matt 24:7; Mark 13:8; Luke 21:11; Rev 6:8; 18:8) but also in Paul's list of personal sufferings in 2 Cor 11:27. Nakedness (*gymnotēs*) is a sign of great poverty and need (Jas 2:15; Rev 3:17; Matt 25:36-44), but also a sign of humiliation and shame (Mark 14:51-52; Acts 19:16; 2 Cor 5:3; Heb 4:13; Rev 3:18); it also is listed by Paul as one of the things he experienced as a servant of Christ, in 2 Cor 11:27. Danger or peril (*kindynos*) plays an especially prominent role in Paul's list of hardships in 2 Cor 11:26: "danger from rivers, danger from robbers, danger from my own people, danger from Gentiles, danger in the wilderness, danger at sea, danger from false brethren." Finally, the sword (*machaira*) is not only a symbol of power and authority in a militaristic culture (Rom 13:4; Eph 6:17; Heb 4:12; Rev 6:4) and a symbol of conflict and division (Matt 10:34), but was also for the early Christians the very real instrument involved in their suffering and that of their Lord Jesus (see Matt 26:47, 55; Mark 14:43, 48; Luke 21:24; 22:52; Acts 12:2; Rev 13:10). In short, Paul's listing of circumstances is neither vague nor hypothetical. These are the specific sorts of circumstances that his readers have either experienced or will experience. They are circumstances under which anyone's commitment to a crucified messiah might be shaken. And they are circumstances that all have a life-threatening capacity.

In light of this, we can see why Paul concludes the list with a verbatim citation from LXX Ps 43:23: "For your sake we are being killed all the day long; we are reckoned as sheep for the slaughter." The choice of verses is hardly accidental. Three things leap to the attention of the reader. First, the psalm verses suggest that such life-threatening experiences ("we are being killed all the day long") are the result of an allegiance to Christ ("for your sake"). Just as Jesus died "for them," so is their present hard experience "on account of him," because they preach and act in the name of a crucified messiah. Paul once more signals the imprinting of the pattern of the dying and rising Lord on Christian identity. Second, the combination of the term "reckon" (*logizesthai*) and "sheep for the slaughter" echo the Isaian suffering servant passage, where "we reckoned him" occurs in Isa 53:4, and "as a sheep for the slaughter" occurs in Isa 53:7. We shall see later how important this connection will be, but for now simply note that the effect is once more to join the experience of Jesus and his followers. Third, the use of the verb "reckon" is also effective within Paul's overall argument. Beginning with the use of "reckon" in Gen 15:6 (see 4:3), Paul has spoken of a number of "reckonings" from the side of humans and of God (see 2:3, 26; 3:28; 4:4-6, 23-24; 6:11). Most pertinently, in contrast to the perception of opponents that Paul and his associates should be "reckoned as sheep for the slaughter," Paul began this section by affirming, "I reckon that the sufferings of the present time are not worth comparing with the glory that is to be revealed in us" (8:18).

Based on *that* sort of reckoning, Paul concludes his peroration first with a flat statement of fact: "But in all these things, we are more than conquering through the one who loves us" (8:37). The "love of Christ" is not only incapable of being severed by such circumstances; it is actually the means of triumphing over them. On the basis of such experience, then, Paul solemnly states his conviction (*pepeismai*) that "no created thing can separate us from the love of God that is in Christ Jesus our Lord" (8:39). Once more he uses a dramatically crafted list to lead up to this conclusion, this time made up of contrasting pairs. In contrast to the earlier set of circumstances, these are all "ultimate" or "cosmic" realities.

The contrast between "life and death" is obvious and is built into the entire argument of Romans to this point; Paul will return to its significance in 14:8-9. It is through the "death and life" of Jesus that God's love has been shown to be triumphant. The next pair of terms is translated by the RSV as "angels and principalities." The terms could be used for earthly "messengers and rulers" (see, e.g., 2 Cor 12:7; Titus 3:1; Luke 12:11), but the entire context suggests here that Paul has in mind specifically spiritual forces (for "angel," see 1 Cor 4:9; 6:3; 15:24; 2 Cor 11:14; Gal 1:8; 3:19; for "principalities," see Eph 1:21; 3:10; 6:12; Col 1:16; 2:10).

The next set of elements could be seen as neatly representing the poles of the time/space axis: "neither things present nor things to come, nor height nor depth," but Paul inserts into the list "powers" (*dynameis*; see Eph 1:21), leaving us uncertain as to whether he may have in mind spiritual representatives of these cosmic realities as well. The clear point to all this listing is that nothing conjurable by the human imagination can cut off those to whom God has chosen to show love.

Precisely these ringing affirmations, however, draw Paul inexorably to the most difficult question of all. If God's election is reliable and God's love unswerving, why are some Jews (of all people surely "God's people") appearing now to be the exception?

GOD'S PLAN FOR THE SALVATION
OF JEW AND GENTILE

Romans 9:1–11:36

T he logic of Paul's own argument has brought him to this difficult place he must now negotiate. His thesis in 1:16-17 contains two elements that are potentially in tension. One element has to this point been most eloquently argued: "the good news is the power of salvation for all who have faith" (1:16). Paul has shown that "God shows no partiality" (2:11) and "makes no distinction" (3:22). If God is one and therefore the God of all, then there must be some principle by which all can respond to God, which Paul finds in the principle of faith (3:27-31). This element of the thesis can be called the element of *universality*.

Paul's thesis also declared, "to the Jew first and also to the Greek" (1:16), and with that introduced the element of *particularity*. God has worked with humans in the specific circumstances of human history, and in that history the particular placement of peoples at one point or another seemed to work for their advantage, calling into question the principle of universality (see E. M. Boring, "The Language of Universal Salvation in Paul," *Journal of Biblical Literature* 105 [1986] 269-92). Paul raised this troubling aspect first in 3:1: "Is there any advantage in being a Jew?" The question is demanded logically (if God is available to all through faith, what's the meaning of a distinction based on difference) but also experientially. In the "now time" of Paul's writing, those who were supposed to be first are now apparently not even second, but out of the game entirely. Paul's fellow Jews are not accepting Jesus as messiah. They have refused the gift of God in Christ. The dramatic and exultant claim that "nothing can separate us from the love of God in Jesus Christ our Lord" (8:39) throws into sharper relief the question of those who now seem to be separated *because* of the same Jesus. The place of Jew and Gentile in God's plan, therefore, cannot be avoided. And it is clear that Paul had no intention of not dealing with it. Already in 3:1-9, he had fired off the series of questions that he must now take up systematically. Far from being an afterthought, Romans 9-11 should be regarded as the climax of Paul's argument concerning God's righteous way of making humans righteous.

Contextualizing Romans 9-11

Before trying to follow this part of Paul's argument—the densest and most intricate part of the letter—we must consider how it should be read in its first-century context. This is all the more necessary since, like chapter 7, these chapters have been read (and misread) in the history of theological interpretation as answering questions that Paul himself was not asking. We should be clear, then, about what Romans 9-11 is *not* doing as well as what it is doing.

Paul's topic is not the eternal predestination of individual human souls to heaven or hell (see John Calvin, *Institutes of the Christian Religion* III, 21-22). It is true that Paul's *excursus* on the hardening of Pharaoh's heart leads to the impression that he is dealing with individuals. But Pharaoh is only an illustration; Paul's subject is the way God has worked in history through diverse peoples. Not their fate but their function is his preoccupation. Only a powerful and heavily tinted theological lens can find in chapters 9-11 any instruction as to what God might have in mind for individuals (but see G. B. Caird, "Predestination in Rom IX-XI," *Expository Times* 68 [1957]: 324-27). Here as throughout the letter, but even more explicitly, Paul conceives of salvation in social terms, as a matter of belonging to God's people. This is not to suggest that the future sharing of God's life by individuals was not of concern to Paul, only that nothing in these chapters addresses that concern.

Neither do these chapters pose or solve the perennial philosophical problem of reconciling divine foreknowledge and human freedom. Again, Paul's query in 9:19-24 might be taken as touching on that issue but only if pulled out of its context. Indeed, Paul, so far from solving a philosophical problem, confesses himself as engaging a theological *mystery* that far surpasses any human capacity to grasp (11:33-34). Using Paul's language in Romans 9-11 to discourse about how humans can be free if God's grace determines them, or how God can be all-powerful if humans are free, is to misuse it. Paul is not a philosopher for whom words and ideas are valuable above all when they are clear and distinct. He is a religious person for whom existential truth is of greater value than logical consistency. So he can assert, at once and without embarrassment, that humans are free because otherwise God could not be judge (3:5-6), and that "God has consigned all people to disobedience that he may have mercy upon all" (11:32).

What Paul does engage in this part of the letter is the consequence of his argument that the good news reveals God's salvation for all who have faith (1:16), and how his "making humans right" also demonstrates his own "righteousness" (3:26). He has shown in Jesus' obedient faith a model for Gentiles of a response to God apart from the law (3:21–26), and has shown in the example of Abraham how that same response of faith is witnessed to by the law (3:21) and is available also to those who are circumcised (4:13, 16). The fundamental issue of God's truthfulness (*alētheia* = fidelity/loyalty) is, however, raised by the disaffection of those circumcised Jews who do *not* accept this revelation. As Paul put it in 3:3, "Does their faithlessness nullify the faithfulness of God?" There he answered, "By no means!" but now he must demonstrate it, by showing in detail that "it is not as though God's word had failed" (9:6). In order to engage this issue, Paul must not only refer to present experience but take on as well the entire repertoire of texts in Torah, in order to show that God's way of acting in the "now time" is not radically discontinuous with Torah but is rather paradoxically and dialectically continuous with it, that although the gift of Christ is "apart from law" it is "witnessed to by Law and Prophets" (3:21; see J. Munck, *Christ and Israel: An Interpretation of Romans 9–11* [Philadelphia: Fortress, 1967]).

Paul's argument here is definitely *midrashic*, moving entirely by means of rereading some thirty separate texts from Torah in light of present circumstances (see J. W. Aageson, "Scripture and Structure in the Development of the Argument of Romans 9–11," *Catholic Biblical Quarterly* 48 [1986]: 265–89). These circumstances, as we have said, are his own standpoint of messianic confession ("Jesus is Lord," 10:9) and his fellow Jews' rejection of that confession in the name of fidelity to Torah. In order to make sense of God's word in the present, he needs to come to a new understanding of that word in the past. For those committed to the proposition that God has a "will" or "plan" (*prothesis*, 8:28), such a move is both required and instinctive.

Paul's instinct was one shared by many fellow Jews of his age. The Hellenistic period was a tumultuous one for Judaism, exposing it to new cultural influences and political realities, forcing the issue of how much Judaism could adapt itself to such new experiences and still remain itself. Although Judaism appeared to outside observers in the Mediterranean world as a remarkably unified phenomenon, it was in the first century actually severely divided from within, because of different answers to this question, and therefore competing versions of what "authentic Judaism" should look like. To a large extent, being a Jew in the first century meant to take part in a debate over the meaning of Torah, with each sect and group finding in the tradition the basis of its own claims to uniquely represent the people to the exclusion of the claims of others.

A favorite technique for grounding claims in Torah was rereading the biblical history, finding in the events and words of the past precedent for the convictions marking off one Jewish group from another and support for their claims to uniqueness. Each such rereading began from a set of experiences or convictions in the present that were regarded as fundamental and nonnegotiable. As a result, each rereading also "discovered" texts to be important that other groups had not considered at all and "reread" from this new perspective texts that others would agree were important but would understand in a completely different fashion. Sometimes it even meant altering the ancient texts themselves in order to help them say even more clearly what they were "supposed" to say.

A full survey of such rereadings of Torah is not possible here, nor is it necessary. But a few examples can be mentioned. The various *targums*, for example, which "translated" the classical Hebrew texts into the Aramaic that most Palestinian Jews spoke, shaded the texts according to later perceptions. Jacob's blessing of his sons in Genesis 49, for example, becomes, in *Targum Pseudo-Jonathan*, a passage filled with messianic expectation that did not appear in the original Hebrew. In Qumran literature, we find at least three separate retellings of the biblical story from the perspective of the Dead Sea sectarians, who thought they alone were authentic representatives of God's people. The *Genesis Apocryphon* is a lightly retouched version of the Genesis story; the book of *Jubilees* (possibly written outside the Qumran sect but with views fully compatible with it) recounts early Israelite history from the perspective of distinctive cultic and calendric concerns; and the *Damascus Document* recounts the story of the people as one pointing directly to the Qumran community itself. From within the developing Pharisaic/scribal movement, moreover, an equally tendentious version of the biblical history can be found in Sirach's encomium of past heroes (Sir 44:1–50:21). Jewish writers seeking to make points against Hellenistic tendencies rehearsed aspects of the biblical story in order to make their apologetic points (see Wisdom of Solomon 13–19; Pseudo-Philo, *Biblical Antiquities*; and the fragments of Eupolemus and Artapanus).

Indeed, it would have been astonishing for a splinter group of Judaism such as the first Christians not to have engaged in a similar exercise. In fact, the New Testament contains three such sustained rereadings of the biblical history. Pieces of the story are retold in Acts 13, but it is in the speech attributed to Stephen in Acts 7 that we find the most elaborate narrative retelling of the biblical story, told from the perspective of belief in Jesus as the "prophet like Moses." The Letter to the Hebrews 11:1–29 is much closer to the encomiastic tradition of Sirach, but, once more, its distinctive point of departure is Jesus, "the pioneer and perfecter of faith" (12:3), in the light of whom all the past history of Israel is read in terms of faith.

Paul's argument in Romans 9–11 is the most intensely dialectical of the three and reflects his own peculiar position as a committed Pharisee who has become a proclaimer of a crucified messiah to Gentiles. As we read through his passionate presentation, we become aware of certain assumptions that he does not make entirely explicit. The first is the most important. God is the primary actor in the drama: "from him, through him, to him are all things" (11:36). To an extent incomprehensible to present-day readers, Paul assumes God's activity in everything that happens: "since the creation of the world his invisible nature, namely, his eternal power and deity, have been clearly perceived in the things that have been made" (1:20). If this is so for "things made," in nature, how much more can God's activity be presumed in human history. The second assumption, then, is that God's activity is effective and is directed to the good of humans. If Paul can state, "God works together with all things toward the good for those who love him" (8:28), this must apply also to those who are properly called "lovers of God," namely, the Jews. Paul's third assumption is that humans can respond to God's self-revelation in history by means of obedience or disobedience (faith or faithlessness/sin). The "plan of God" involves the delicate interplay of human freedoms to reach its goal. Paul's fourth assumption is that God *is* in fact faithful to his word, his promises, his commitments, and that God never gives up even on those who reject him. Finally, Paul's fifth assumption is that history has a dialectical character, that is, the drama of God and humans goes through alternating moments of yes and no, now to the advantage of this people, now to the advantage of that, but each having its own function for the working out of God's mysterious will.

Paul's Perspective (9:1–5)

The transition from Paul's triumphant peroration in 8:31–39 is dramatic. He approaches the most difficult topic in his letter with an obvious reluctance and trepidation. He must begin with a statement of his own position vis-à-vis his fellow Jews, "my brothers, my kinsmen according to the flesh," precisely because the import of his argument concerning God's righteousness seems to have completely relativized (if not nullified) the place of the Jews in God's plan for the world. If it is now possible for one who calls himself a Jew to actually ask, "What advantage is there to being a Jew?" (3:1), his answer must be preceded by a clear statement of his personal allegiance to the people. That Paul does make such a statement so explicitly and with such emotional force is of first importance for those readers (ancient and modern) who consider him the first "Jewish anti-Semite." But that he should have had to make the statement at all, and with such defensiveness, shows how his argument has placed him in a delicate position with his fellow Jews.

He begins, then, with a threefold statement that is tantamount to an oath: "I am telling the truth in Christ. I am not lying. My conscience bears me witness in the Holy Spirit" (9:1). In three other places in his letters, Paul finds it necessary to assert his truthfulness. In 1 Tim 2:7 (a disputed letter), the statement "I am speaking the truth, I am not lying" appears to be a formality, since there seems to be no reason to challenge the content of his statement. But in 2 Cor 11:31, his assertion "I am not lying" appears in a context where his veracity in word and behavior has very much been called into question, and where his list of hardships endured for Christ might well have stretched credulity, so it is accompanied by the added warrant, "The God and Father of the Lord Jesus Christ, He who is blessed forever, knows that I do not lie." In Gal 1:20, again in a situation where he is reporting facts that might be disputed by others, Paul invokes the divine witness: "in what I am writing to you, before God, I am not lying." It is clear that Paul's speech here betrays his awareness that his position can very well be regarded as that of a renegade to his own people, whose word cannot be trusted. His double protestation of truthfulness is therefore accompanied by the witness of his conscience in the Holy Spirit. The reader who has been paying attention will catch the echoes of 2:15 and 8:16.

What does Paul assert with such protestations of sincerity? "That I have great sorrow and unceasing anguish in my heart" (9:2). These are powerful negative emotions, all the starker for Paul's not yet having supplied any reason for feeling them. The emotion of sorrow or grief (*lypē*) responds to the pain of loss or disappointment (see 1 Macc 6:4; 4 Macc 1:23; John 16:20; 2 Cor 2:2-5; 1 Thess 4:13), that of anguish (*odynē*) has a broader range of meaning (see, e.g., LXX Ps 40:3; Sir 27:29). The two terms appear together in LXX Isa 35:10. Paul expresses, then, a sense of personal loss and desolation. He says, furthermore, that these feelings are "unceasing." His emotional response is neither superficial nor transitory but remains with him as a chronic condition.

It is only at this point that the reader following in sequence comes to the realization that Paul's anguish is caused by the situation of his fellow Jews. He declares, "For I could wish that I myself were accursed and cut off from Christ for the sake of my brethren, my kinsmen by race" (9:3). The designation is literally, "kinsmen according to the flesh," which recalls 4:1 and locates Paul within that extended family that traced itself back to Abraham (see 2 Cor 11:22; Gal 1:13-14; Phil 3:4-5). But now Paul not only claims a part in this heritage; he asserts a role within it as great as that played by Moses. His being willing to be "cut off by curse from Christ for their sake," unmistakably alludes to the gesture made by Moses in Exod 32:32. The Israelites had rebelled against the Lord while Moses was on the mountain. He came down, smashed the golden calf, and shattered the tablets of the law. He ordered the rebellious Israelites to be killed (Exod 32:15-28). But then Moses entreated the Lord, "Alas, this people have sinned a great sin; they have made for themselves gods of gold. But now, if thou wilt forgive their sin—and if not, blot me, I pray thee, out of the book which thou hast written."

Paul's statement is remarkable on several counts. First, it reveals something of Paul's self-understanding as an apostle. Paul compares Jesus not to Moses the lawgiver but to Adam the first human. Paul himself plays the role of Moses in this "new covenant." The same comparison is made elaborately in 2 Cor 3:17-18 (see H. Marks, "Pauline Typology and Revisionary Criticism," *Journal of the American Academy of Religion* 52 [1984]: 71-92). Second, his gesture is all the more stunning because of the series of affirmations he had just completed in 8:31-39, that nothing "will be able to separate us from the love of God in Christ Jesus our Lord" (8:39). Now Paul asserts his willingness to be "accursed from Christ" (the term *anathēma* suggests both separation and being put under a curse, being used to translate the Hebrew *ḥerem*; see LXX Lev 27:28; Josh 6:16; 7:1). Third, the statement suggests an intimate identification with Jesus himself. In the eyes of some Jews—and apparently Paul himself before his call—Jesus was "cursed by God" (Deut 21:23; Gal 3:13). Now, as Christ "became a curse for us" (Gal 3:13), so Paul is willing to bear a curse "for the sake of" his people.

Paul follows this declaration with a series of assertions bearing on the distinctive character of his "kinsmen according to the flesh." He begins with the designation "Israelite," which derives from Isaac's son Jacob after his night of struggle with the angel, "for you have striven with men and with God and have prevailed" (Gen 32:28). For Paul, the term Israelite has a special significance, connected to his understanding of *Israel* as a religious people (see below). Thus, Paul uses *Ioudaios* (literally a resident of Judea = "Jew") as an ethnic category distinct from "Gentile" (see Rom 1:16; 2:9, 10, 17, 28, 29; 3:1, 9, 29, and especially 9:24). But the term "Israelite" appears to connote a special commitment to the *religious* heritage of this people. Of his rivals in 2 Cor 11:22, he asks, "Are they Israelites? So am I!" And he makes the same claim in Rom 11:1, "For I myself am an Israelite." It is, then, not simply as "Jews," but as Jews who affirm the religious heritage of Torah, that Paul can make the following claims concerning them. "From them" or, perhaps better, "theirs" are "the sonship, the glory, the covenants, the giving of law, the cult, and the promises." Theirs also are "the fathers" (that is, the patriarchs) (9:4-5).

There are two noteworthy textual variants in 9:4. Some scribes considered the plural of "covenants" and "promises" to be erroneous and so changed them to the singular. Since the manuscripts evidence is mixed and the plural remains the harder reading, it will be the version read here. The listing indicates ways in which God had gifted this people with different modes of presence and access. It differs from the list in 2:17 above all because there the "one who calls himself a Jew" boasted about *himself* with reference to other people because of God and Torah. The present list is better regarded as the continuation of the one begun and not finished in 3:2. There, in response to the question "What advantage has the Jew?" Paul responded, "To begin with they were entrusted with the oracles of God." That category can stand also as the beginning of the present listing, since all the other ways of specifying the relationship of God with this people are found in these "oracles," that is, the texts of Torah.

It was Israel first of all who was told, "you are the sons of the Lord your God" (Deut 14:1), and "out of Egypt I called my son" (Hos 11:1). It was with Israel in the wilderness that "the glory of the Lord" appeared and remained in the cloud (Exod 16:10). The Lord remembered the covenant he had made with this people through Abraham (Gen 17:9; Exod 2:24), and through Moses made a full covenant with all the people (Exod 19:5). Through Moses also the law was given that expresses both the will and the wisdom of God (Deut 4:5-6; 31:9-26). To this people also was given the cult (*latreia*) as an elaborate system of feasts and sacrifices and observances that made themselves and their actions holy, dedicated to the Lord who so showed them how to act (Lev 16:1-23:43). The Lord God's history with this people could be punctuated by the making and keeping of promises, the verbal expression of fidelity and trust between persons (see Gen 12:2-3; 15:4-6; 22:15-18; Exod 3:9-12).

It must be said, however, that with "promises," Paul touches on an element that is exposed by the New Testament as latent in Torah but not really explicit within it. The language of "promise," in fact, is virtually absent from the LXX. In the New Testament, and above all in Paul himself, the "fulfillment of promise" becomes a primary focus for reading the story (see, e.g., Acts 1:4; 2:33, 39; 7:17; 13:23, 32; 26:6; 2 Cor 1:20; Gal 3:14, 16, 17, 18, 21, 22, 29; 4:23, 28; Eph 1:13; 2:12; 3:6; 6:2; 1 Tim 4:8; 2 Tim 1:1; Heb 4:1; 6:12; Jas 1:12). Paul has already in this letter distinguished the inheritance that comes by promise from the covenant of law (4:13, 14, 16, 20), and he will shortly make a similar distinction in 9:8-9. I point this out as an indication of how a listing that appears as entirely straightforward and neutral contains as one of its elements a feature that the "rereading" itself has discovered.

The final two elements in the list are distinctive. First, they concern people rather than verbal or social institutions. Second, they point to the beginning and end-point of the people's story. The "fathers" are the ones to whom the promises were given (see Rom 4:11, 12, 16, 17, 18; 9:10; 11:28; 15:8). For Paul, in turn, "the messiah according to the flesh" represents the fulfillment of those promises: "Now the promises were made to Abraham and his seed . . . which is Christ" (Gal 3:16). Paul will state shortly, "messiah is the end (*telos*) of Torah" (Rom 10:4). These two points (fathers and messiah) are joined by Paul in 15:8: "Christ became a servant to the circumcised in order to show God's truthfulness, in order to confirm the promises given to the fathers."

The last phrase in 9:5 is notoriously difficult to figure out. The Greek is capable of being read in two ways. It can be read as, "The messiah, the one who is over all God, blessed forever, Amen." Although this is a possible reading, it is unlikely for two reasons. First, the title *ho theos* ("God") is in the New Testament jealously reserved for "God the father." Apart from the present (disputed) passage, the only other places where *ho theos* could possibly refer to Christ is John 1:18 (also textually disputed), John 20:28, and (by allusion) Heb 1:8. Please understand that the issue is not whether Paul conceived of Christ as in some fashion divine. I think he did, as his language about his being "son of God" and "in the form of God" (Phil 2:5) and "the image of God" (Col 1:15) suggest, as well as his assigning to Christ divine functions (e.g., 1 Cor 8:6). The issue is only whether he uses *theos* of Christ in this place, and his linguistic practice elsewhere supports the position that its use here would be unlikely. The second reason is that the attribution of the title *theos* to Christ here would disrupt the logic of the passage. Before this line, Paul has been listing the gifts God has given to Israel. After this line, he declares that God's word has not failed (9:6). Clearly, God is the subject, not the messiah. With the majority of scholars, therefore, I take the alternate reading as correct: ". . . the messiah. May God who is over all things, be blessed forever. Amen." Thus, God is praised for all that God has done for Israel. Additional support for this position is offered by Paul's customary use of the blessing formulary ("blessed be God"), which always has God as the object of blessing (see 2 Cor 1:3; 11:31; Eph 1:3), as already in this letter, Rom 1:25.

Paul's list has celebrated God's extravagant generosity toward a tiny portion of the world's population, in the spirit of Deut 4:7: "What great nation is there that has a God so near to it as the Lord our God is to us?" It has also shown why this people, given "the oracles of God," plays a distinctive role in history—their combination of institutions and symbols was, indeed, unique in the ancient world. The very concept of "messiah," for example, made sense only within the symbolic world of Torah. Nowhere else in the ancient religious literature of the Mediterranean do we find such a heightened sense of a people directed by a God through loss to restoration. Messianic expectations within Judaism were, to be sure, diverse. But all such expectations were distinctive to this people and made sense only within the framework of their "oracles." This realization is one that Gentiles, who might grow overweening because they now "have" the messiah, need to remember–they are grafted onto a tree they did not plant (see 11:17-32).

It is also a realization that leads to the present problem Paul must address. If Jesus is the messiah, how can it happen that the people Israel is rejecting him? And after all the gifts bestowed on them by God, how could the people (in Paul's view) miss this one so badly? In the face of these realities, Paul must go through the story again for clues. His conviction must be the one he states immediately in 9:6, "it is not as though God's word has failed." It is surely impossible for Paul to give up Jesus as messiah in order to save Torah–to do that would be to turn his back on the gift of life itself! But it is equally impossible to give up Torah in order to have Jesus as Christ, for "Christ" is intelligible only within the story of Torah! Out of this "great and abiding sorrow and anguish," Paul turns to search the Scriptures, seeking to trace the markings of the mystery of God in his passing.

The Past: God's Way of Shaping a People (9:6-29)

Paul begins his midrashic argument by seeking a precedent for the present in the past. He is looking for the pattern of God's action with respect to forming a people for himself, and he finds it in the very first stages of the people's common story. Paul lays out his conclusion first, then presents the case: "Not all those who are out of Israel are Israel" (9:6). The distinction may be arguable for other Jews, but for Paul it is fundamental. There is a difference between all those who could claim to be "descended from Abraham" (or Jacob) and those who constitute Israel as "the people of God." Paul's move is not unprecedented. A similar sort of distinction was widespread among the various sects of Judaism who competed for the claim to being the "authentic people." Thus, the Pharisees distinguished themselves from those who were "sinners" or the "ignorant" (4 Ezra 7:17-25; *Psalms of Solomon* 2:3-18; 4:1-20), and the Qumran community saw itself as the exclusive "holy remnant" that could sanctify the land (1QS 8:6-8; 9:3-11). Paul's *way* of making that distinction, however, is his own.

He demonstrates first that Israel is a matter of election rather than birth (9:6-13). Not all those called "children of Abraham" are actually his "seed" (*sperma*), as he shows from the LXX of Gen 21:22: "In Isaac, your seed will be named." For those of us whose memory of the biblical story is less than exhaustive, a reminder may be helpful, in order to see the point as sharply as Paul is making it. Abraham had a child named Ishmael (Gen 16:15), with

Sarah's Egyptian maid, Hagar (Gen 16:1-6). But, says Paul, he was not "the seed." And he draws the lesson: "This means it is not the children of the flesh who are the children of God, but the children of the promise are reckoned as seed" (9:8). He supports this with reference to the promise concerning the birth of Isaac found in Gen 18:10, 14: "About this time I will return and Sarah will have a son."

Before moving to his second piece of evidence, we should note how Paul's reading itself *shapes* the meaning of the texts. We see, first of all, that he makes the language of "promise" explicit, although it is not found in the LXX text. We notice as well that Paul has subtly shifted from "children of Abraham" to "children of God." The shift is subtle but significant. If Abraham's "seed"—as opposed to all his children by biological descent alone (as through Hagar)—comes about through God's promise and *power*, then they are not simply "Abraham's seed" but quite literally "God's children." By this semantic shift, Paul makes his readers see the development of Israel as a specifically *religious* reality, one owed to God's presence and power from the start.

Paul's next example concerns "Israel" himself, that is, Jacob. It will be recalled that Isaac's wife Rebecca was also barren. It was in response to Isaac's prayer that God enabled her to conceive (Gen 25:21). She conceived twins, but during her pregnancy "the children struggled within her" (Gen 25:22). She inquired of the Lord, who told her that the children were two nations, two peoples, that one was stronger than the other and (as Paul quotes it) "the elder will serve the younger" (Gen 25:23; Rom 9:12). Paul seizes on this story. It shows, he says, that election for God's purposes has nothing to do with human morality; neither child had done anything good or bad. The role to be played by the people Israel descended from Isaac, therefore, was not based on its virtue or on Esau's vice, but "in order that God's purpose might remain a matter of election" (9:11). He repeats for emphasis, "not on the basis of deeds, but on the basis of the one calling," it was told to her that Esau would serve Jacob. Paul concludes this episode with a citation from the prophet Malachi: "I loved Jacob but I hated Esau" (1:2).

Before moving forward, we should note again what Paul is arguing here. It is not the individual, historical *person* "Esau" that God "hated." The prophet Malachi himself makes clear that he refers to the Edomite nation, traditionally thought to be descended from Esau (Gen 25:24-26:30). Nor is it a matter of God "loving" Jacob personally. The fate of these historical individuals is not the point. The point is how *they represent the historical function of the peoples of the earth.* God's "loving" Jacob is the election of the people Israel to play a certain historical role, without reference to the salvation or blessedness of Jacob the person. Therefore, it is not a matter of "deeds" or "doing good or evil" (which, according to Paul, very much determine a person's destiny), but of God's selection of a "people" to play a certain role in history.

Paul himself seems to recognize, however, that his meaning might be misconstrued. In 9:14–21, therefore, we find something of a clarifying excursus. It begins with one of the diatribal questions we have so often encountered, "What then shall we say?" used to set up a logical rather than a real objection to what has been proposed. Paul asks, "Is there injustice on God's part?" The question was already posed somewhat differently in 3:5, "If our wickedness serves to show the justice of God, what shall we say? That God is unjust to inflict wrath on us?" He there answered, "By no means, for then how could God judge the world?" In the present passage he responds again with "By no means!" It is unthinkable that wickedness (*adikia*) be associated with God (see Deut 32:4). But this time Paul's development of the point proceeds not with the showing of wrath but with the showing of mercy. Quoting Exod 33:19 from the LXX, he says, "For I will have mercy on whom I have mercy, and I will have compassion on whom I have compassion" (there is little difference in Greek between *eleein*, "to show mercy," and *oiktirmōn*, "to have compassion").

In these two responses, we find an anticipation of Paul's conclusion in 11:29–32. It is also noteworthy that the statement from God to Moses takes place in the exodus story very shortly after the passage in Exod 32:32, where Moses offered to give himself up for the sake of the people. Now Moses asks that he "might see thy glory" (Exod 33:19). The Lord's response is that Moses will be able to observe all God's goodness passing before him, but "no one shall see my face and live" (Exod 33:20). The statement about "showing mercy" appears in this context: "I will proclaim my name, 'the lord,' and I will be gracious to whom I am gracious and show mercy on whom I show mercy" (Exod 33:19). An implied conclusion that the reader might draw is that humans can observe God's loving action "as it passes by" but cannot grasp the knowledge of God "face to face."

Once more in 9:16–18, Paul clarifies just whose "will" is at work in the shaping of history. Picking up from 9:15, he says, "therefore it is not from the one who wills or the one who runs, but from the will of God." The reverse side of the mercy shown to Moses (and therefore the Israelites) is shown to Pharaoh (and therefore the Egyptians). Paul points out, "Scripture says to Pharaoh that 'I have raised you up for the very purpose of showing my power in you, so that my name may be proclaimed in all the earth.'" This citation does not match either the Hebrew text of Exod 9:16 or the LXX, and Paul may be adapting it to his own purposes. Especially significant is that the LXX and Hebrew have "for this reason you have been preserved/kept alive. . . ." Paul's version emphasizes that God's *choice* of Pharaoh (i.e., Egypt) is for a certain purpose in history, namely, to demonstrate God's power. How?

By showing how God could overcome even the greatest of human empires. In the case of Egypt, God's method was the plagues and the "hardening of Pharaoh's heart" (Exod 4:21), which finally made the liberation of Israel from Egypt possible. Paul concludes: "therefore he has mercy on whomever he wills, and he hardens the heart of whomever he wills" (9:18).

The imaginary interlocutor is not content with this and pushes Paul further: How can God continue to blame humans if everything is in God's control? "Who is able to oppose his will?" (9:19). The objection has a surface plausibility, which is why it continues to tease the imagination. If God does whatever God wants anyway, why should humans have or take any responsibility? Paul's response, it must be admitted, does not satisfy the sort of mind that would raise such a question. At first, in fact, it looks as though he is avoiding the question altogether by an *ad hominem* attack: "But who are you, O Human being, to be the one who is arguing with God?" Only when we pause over this response do we recognize it as more than an avoidance, as something that cuts to the core issue of "God's righteousness."

The use of the verb *antapokrinesthai* ("argue") echoes the use of the same term in Job 16:9 and prepares for the next line, which is a mixed citation/allusion to Isa 29:16 and Job 9:12: "Does the thing made speak to the maker, 'Why have you made me this way?'" Both passages in Torah emphasize the distance between God and creature, and the ludicrousness of humans railing against their maker. Isaiah 29:16 reads, "You turn things upside down! Shall the potter be regarded as the clay, that the thing made should say of its maker, 'he did not make me' or the thing formed of the one who formed it, 'he has no understanding'?" The full citation is important, here, for it asserts not only the derivation and dependence of the creature on the creator but also the inability of anyone not having "maker's knowledge" to know the entire plan within which each piece might fit. The creature is not in the position to state of the creator, "he has no understanding," because the creature is never in the position of observing the plan whole, much less grasping it.

The context of Job 9:12 is likewise one that states the distance between God and humans: "How can a human being be just before God? If one wished to contend with him, one could not answer him once in a thousand times" (Job 9:1). In Job 9:12, the actual text of the LXX reads, "If he [God] alters something, who will turn it back? Or who will say to him, 'what have you done?'" Paul has altered this slightly but significantly: "Why have you *made me in this way*?" It is not simply God's actions but specifically God's way with humans and the roles that they play that Paul says cannot be challenged.

It is just at this point that we need to make an imaginative leap in order to align ourselves with Paul's perspective. The reason the interlocutor's objections seem so logical to us is that we tend to hold the same point of view. It is the outlook shaped by human philosophy concerning "justice" (*dikaiosynē*)–the same word, we remember that is also translated "righteousness." In Plato's *Republic* or in Aristotle's *Politics*, the concept of justice is important as a key to the ordering of society and the individuals within it. A great deal of thought was given to what "justice" meant–how it involved an appropriate distribution of goods, for example, and a reciprocity of rights and responsibilities. In other words, it is assumed that "justice" is, while difficult to achieve on the political level, nevertheless perfectly possible to understand on the theoretical level. It is measured by human intelligence, which is fitted to precisely this task. It can be tested by reliable criteria, such as equality or proportionality. From this perspective, a king who was arbitrary in decision making, let us say, would be held to account and judged as a tyrant, making it entirely appropriate to challenge his rule.

Paul's perspective, in contrast, is that not of the philosopher but of the religious person. He begins with the assumption not that reality is a static system that can be analyzed and grasped by human intelligence but that reality is a gift given at every moment by one who, creating out of what does not exist, can surprise at every moment. The creature is not a free agent who can now stand as a critic. The creature is at every moment utterly dependent on the one who sustains in being. What is the ground on which to stand for a criticism? The "king" in this case is not another citizen slightly more elevated beyond his peers but still part of the *polis*. The king is the one who makes the system as he goes along!

For Paul, then, justice is not a matter of our knowing how things should work and then applying that measure to God. Justice is, rather, *learned* precisely from *what God does*! Here is the fundamental distinction between philosophy and theology. The complaint to which Paul responds, then, really *is* irrelevant, for it supposes that humans and God are on the same scale and operate as parts of the same system, so that God can be measured by a human concept of justice. Paul's response is simply that God is the maker, and therefore also the measure.

He picks up the image of the potter from the Isaiah passage and develops it further to drive home his point that the creator has complete freedom to do what he wishes with what he makes, since only the creator is in the position to know "the plan" into which all the things made find their place. It is striking that he uses the language of "right" or "authority" (*exousia*): "Has the potter no right over the clay, to make from the same lump of clay one vessel for honorable use and another for dishonorable?" (9:21; a similar analogy is found in 2 Tim 2:20). That answer to the question "Why have you made me thus?" is fine in the abstract. Obviously, potters have the right to use the clay any way they choose.

But now Paul moves from the general principle to the specific application and by so doing begins to make the transition back from the excursus to his main argument. His next statement is lengthy and anacoluthic (the end of the sentence does not connect syntactically with the beginning), and not entirely intelligible. Part of the clumsiness is due to Paul's slipping between analogy and allegory. The effect is of another rhetorical question, and the RSV's "what if" captures its "real/hypothetical" character. Now we see that it is God who is "the potter" and it is the world's peoples who are "the pots." But the more Paul tries to work out the allegory, the more awkward it becomes, and he trails off weakly, "in order to make known the richness of his mercy" (9:23), with the next verse shifting back explicitly to the issue of Jews and Gentiles. I would argue that 9:22-23 simply doesn't yield good sense, possibly because Paul's mind was moving ahead of his metaphor. He wanted to present an analogy: some pots are destroyed and some are preserved. Fine. But in his trying to apply the analogy, it ends up that God does not break any pots! God wants to show his wrath and power, but what comes through is his patience and mercy! Paul does not follow through on the merciless determinism of his primary analogue, perhaps because as he sees it, nothing in the end gets broken. This is certainly his conclusion in 11:32: "God has shut up all humans in disobedience so that he might show mercy to all."

Having asserted, if not convincingly argued, the power of God to direct history without complaint from humans, Paul returns in 9:24 to his description of how, in fact, God has shaped a people for himself. He had argued from Scripture in 9:6-12 that the Israel of the promise was not coextensive with Israel according to the flesh. Out of all the children who could trace their descent to Abraham, God chose only some to be the "seed" that would serve as his special people in history. "Israel," in other words, is smaller than the population of Jews. Now he makes a more dramatic deduction. Israel can also be *larger* than the boundaries of Jewish ethnicity: "even us whom he called not only from among the Jews but also from among the Gentiles" (9:24). For this conclusion, Paul also finds support in Torah, this time in the words of Hosea the prophet.

Actually, Paul's use of Hosea is another example of the interesting ways in which the texts of Scripture are used in this sort of midrashic argument. He introduces the citation with the words, "as also it says in Hosea"—making the present call of the Gentiles by God the point of reference for the text he will cite. He is surely aware that the people spoken of in LXX Hos 2:1, 25 were not "the nations" but rather the people of Israel itself who had fallen away and were being called back to the covenant. But Paul reads them as though they anticipated the contemporary call of the Gentiles: "the one who is not my people, my people, and the one who has not been beloved, my beloved." Paul draws this much from LXX Hos 2:25 but has also *added* (at least to the Masoretic Text [MT] and the LXX) the key word "I call." The MT and the LXX have "I will say to." The use of *kalein* ("call") makes the Hosea text work as a passage about election (see 8:30; 9:7, 11) and become a "proof text" for the call of the Gentiles in 9:24. Paul also adds to this an earlier text from LXX Hos 2:1, "and it will be in that place where it was said to them, you are not my people, there they will be called sons of the living God." In Hos 2:1, as the first part of the verse makes clear, this refers to the children of Israel. But the contrast between "not my people" and "my people" works perfectly for the call of the Gentiles, and so Paul uses it in that application. The designation "sons of the living God" is especially appropriate, after Paul's designation of his Gentile readers as "sons of God" by the Spirit in 8:14, 19, and 29.

If God can expand the people by calling in new members, he can also contract its size. Paul turns to Isaiah for the evidence that, by God's decision, the empirical Israel could be pruned and purified as an expression of God's righteousness. The cited text in 9:27–28 is an amalgam of Isa 10:22 and 28:22, but with a first line that echoes Hos 2:1: "Though the number of the sons of Israel be as the sands of the sea, only a remnant of them will be saved; the Lord will exercise his decree upon the earth with rigor and dispatch."

The manuscript evidence for this verse is mixed, with some witnesses having and others lacking the word "with righteousness" (*en dikaiosynē*) after "with rigor and dispatch." The original text of Isa 10:22 has the phrase, and it is easy to understand why some scribes would want to add it if Paul had left it out, so the "harder reading" that leaves it out is to be preferred. Nevertheless, it is hard to imagine that, even if Paul did not cite it, the presence of the phrase in the Isaian original did not help influence his choice of the text.

In any case, the text introduces the Greek word *hypoleimma* (in place of the LXX's *kataleimma*), which will recur in a slightly different form in 11:5. In the LXX, the term *kataleimma* translates the Hebrew *šĕʾērît* (that which is left, remains), and is used in some passages with reference to a portion of the people that survives some disaster (Isa 14:22, 30; 37:31; Sir 47:22). The concept of the "remnant" is hopeful in Isa 37:31–32. The remnant is the basis for the renewed life of Israel: "And the surviving remnant of the house of Judah shall again take root downward and bear fruit upward, for out of Jerusalem will go forth a remnant, and out of Zion a band of survivors." This *agricultural* sense of the remnant as a pruned-back root out of which new life can spring is important for Paul's exposition in chapter 11.

The point of the present use of the image is to show how the prophets provide a precedent for a "righteous decree of God" that, despite the great numbers of the Jews in the world, might leave only a small number as "saved" (*sōthēsetai*). Paul accentuates this sense of diminution again by a final quotation for this stage of his argument in 9:29, this time again from Isaiah, who "spoke ahead of time" (see 1:2): "If the Lord of Hosts had not left us children, we would have fared like Sodom and been made like Gomorrah" (Isa 1:9). The destruction of Sodom and Gomorrah (Gen 19:24–25) was by a "righteous decree" by which "God showed his wrath and power," which led to total destruction. The RSV translation, however, camouflages the most important word in the citation. It is not "children" who are left (in the Greek, "remnanted") but a "seed" (*sperma*). The word choice is perfect. It shows how a cut-back "remnant" also contains within itself the power for new growth, and this connects it to Paul's understanding that those who are now a "remnant by faith" (11:5) are truly the "seed of Abraham" (4:13, 16), which, as he also said in 9:7, is *not* to be equated with all those who are his "descendants according to the flesh." The choice of *sperma* is perfect, finally, because for Paul the basis of this "remnant by faith" is the true "seed of Abraham," who is the messiah Jesus, the righteous one who lives by his faith.

The Present: The Remnant by Faith (9:30–11:6)

Paul now enters the most painful part of his argument. He will try to show how God has both contracted and expanded "Israel" on the basis of Jesus the messiah (see C. K. Barrett, "Romans 9:30–10:21: Call and Responsibility of Israel" in *Essays on Paul* [Philadelphia: Westminster, 1982] 132–53).

He introduces the discussion with the (by now familiar) question, "What, then, shall we say?" but this time his answer is not theoretical or textual, but is based on the present situation as he perceives it—and as it is very much affected by his own mission: "The Gentiles who did not seek righteousness have attained it on the basis of faith, but Israel, pursuing a law of righteousness [= righteous law] did not reach the law" (9:30–31). The sentence is difficult to translate, not least because of textual variation on the vital point: some manuscripts replace "law" in the final phrase with "righteousness" or "law of righteousness." Such textual variation is a sign of scribal unease in trying to make sense of the sentence as it stands, an unease shared by any close reader. Paul's statement concerning the Gentiles is clear and conforms to his argument to this point. It is the clause dealing with the Jews that is difficult. My translation is more literal than the RSV's "seeking a righteousness based on the law," which may be correct, but plays a bit loose with the actual Greek construction. For a discussion of the problems, see C. T. Rhyne, "*nomos dikaiosynēs* and the Reading of Romans 10:4," *Catholic Biblical Quarterly* 47 (1985): 486–99.

Paul's language suggests that his fellow Jews failed to reach or attain (for *phthanein*, see 2 Cor 10:14; Phil 3:16) the very thing they pursued, the law itself. We can see why the scribes had trouble with this, for they were reading out of a theological tradition that already saw Judaism as a "religion of law" and Christianity as a "religion of faith," so it would appear intolerably paradoxical for Paul to state that the Jews missed the very thing that all of us know they at least had. Unfortunately that *is* what he is saying, and we must try to figure it out. And Paul helps. He asks, "Why is this?" and responds: "because not out of faith but as if out of works." This is undoubtedly cryptic, but a little work should enable us to get to his meaning.

He does not suggest, we notice, that his fellow Jews could not keep the law. The ability to keep the law is everywhere assumed by this letter. The difficulty, rather, is that such legal observance is not the heart of a relationship with the living God. To pursue a "righteous law" therefore would mean to observe the law *as an expression of faith*. To this, Paul opposes "as though out of works [= on the basis of works]." To pursue the law as though it were simply a matter of accomplishment, of performance (works), means for Paul to miss the essential meaning of law as a response in faith to the living God. Now, does Paul suggest that all his fellow Jews lacked faith in God? By no means. He will shortly admire their "zeal for God" (10:2). What he is saying, I think, is that at the critical moment of being offered Jesus as messiah, many of his fellow Jews failed to respond in faith. This, in fact, is his next statement: "they stumbled over the stone of stumbling. As it is written, 'Behold I am laying in Zion a stone of stumbling and a rock for tripping, and the one who has faith in him will not be put to shame.'"

This is another complex citation that combines disparate texts from the prophet Isaiah and amends them. The presence of similar combinations of texts dealing with "stones" in other New Testament writings (see 1 Pet 2:6-8; Luke 20:17-18) raises the possibility that Paul is relying on an earlier *catena* of prophetic passages already being used for apologetic purposes (see B. Lindars, *New Testament Apologetic* [London: SCM, 1961]). In Isaiah, we find two different sorts of "stone" passages. In the first (8:13-15), the Lord himself will "become a sanctuary, and a stone of offense, and a rock of stumbling to both houses of Israel." The passage instructs the prophet not to heed or walk in the way of the people; rather, "the Lord of Hosts, let him be your fear, and let him be your dread." The one who trusts the Lord, by implication, must be willing to follow where others are turned away ("offended/made to stumble"). The second Isaiah passage (28:16) has the Lord laying "in Zion for a foundation a stone, a tested stone." Here the stone itself functions as the principle of faith: "The one who believes in him will not be ashamed." Paul (or the *catena* before him) has combined the passages on the basis of the image of the *stone*, which now bears the double connotation of being precious and a source of faith for some, and a cause of stumbling and rejection by others.

Although Paul himself does not make the connection explicit, the "ideal reader" can pick up in this language of "scandal" (stumbling block) Paul's understanding of what there was about this "stone in Zion" that was difficult for Jews to accept. In 1 Cor 1:18, he speaks of the "word of the cross" as being "the power of God for those who are being saved" (compare Rom 1:16!). But to the Gentiles who seek wisdom, the cross of Jesus is perceived as foolishness—Hellenistic sages who achieved immortality or apotheosis did not die so miserably. More pertinently, to the Jews "who seek signs," the cross of Jesus is a "stumbling block" (*skandalon,* 1 Cor 1:22-23). Paul does not mean that Jews were looking for "signs and wonders," for there were plenty of those. He meant "signs of the messiah," ways of evaluating whether Jesus met the norms of Torah for the messiah. Did he obey the law himself? Did he teach such obedience to the law? Did he restore the people under Torah? Was his death the death of a righteous man, a martyr for Torah? For such Jews, says Paul, the cross is a "scandal," because according to Torah, a crucified man is "cursed by God" (Deut 21:23). It was the *death* of Jesus above all that failed to meet the "sign of a messiah." In contrast, for those who experienced after his death the power of new life coming from him, he was the stone placed in Zion and "faith in him" would not be put to shame (see Rom 1:16, "I am not ashamed of the good news"). But for those who viewed his life and death only within the strict frame of Torah, it was clear that Jesus was *not* the messiah, but a sinner and cursed by God.

In 10:1-2, Paul expresses once more his personal feelings and convictions concerning his fellow Jews, much as he had in 9:1-3. Now, however, Paul emphasizes that the desire of his heart and his prayer to God in their behalf is "for salvation." If my understanding of *sōtēria* in Romans is correct, he is praying that his fellow Jews be gathered into the people that God is now forming on the basis of faith in the messiah. This fits the statement of his thesis that the good news is "the power of God for salvation for all who have faith, Jews first, then Gentiles" (1:16). At this point in the story, it appears as though the Jews have missed entirely, although Paul will modify that perception in 11:1. Paul is also confident enough of his credentials as a Jew to "bear witness for them" (10:2): they have, he says, "zeal for God."

The term *zēlos* in this context has an entirely positive connotation. They are passionate in their commitment to God (compare John 2:17; 1 Cor 12:31; 14:1, 12). Paul himself is a Jew with the same sort of religious intensity. He had been, he tells us, exceptionally "zealous" for the ancestral traditions before his call (Gal 1:14). He knows the people of whom he speaks. What now separates Paul from his fellow Jews? He has come to a certain "recognition" that they have not. He says, "They have zeal for God but not according to recognition" (10:2). The RSV translation "enlightened" is misleading. Paul's choice of terms, I think, is careful and deliberate. In speaking of idolators in 1:28, he had said, "they did not see fit to *acknowledge God*," using the same Greek term (*epignōsis*) as here. The reader will remember, I hope, the distinction I made at that time between knowing and acknowledging, between cognition and recognition. Idolators knew there was a God, but they did not wish to acknowledge God by recognizing his claim on them. Paul is suggesting something very similar here. When God chose to gift humans in a new and unexpected fashion through a crucified messiah, those who were "zealous for Torah," could not recognize and acknowledge it.

Such is the appropriate context for evaluating Paul's next statement, which comes completely from the perspective given after the experience of Christ: "not recognizing the righteousness that is coming from God, and seeking to establish their own, they did not submit to God's righteousness" (10:3). Before turning to the grounding for this declaration, we should note that Paul is by no means suggesting that the Jews "did not know God's righteousness," as though Torah did not teach truly. The verb *agnoein* can bear the meaning "be ignorant of" (see Rom 1:13; 7:1; 11:25; 1 Cor 10:1; 12:1; 2 Cor 1:8), but it can also mean "not recognize or acknowledge" (Acts 13:27; 17:23; 1 Cor 14:38; Rom 2:4; 6:3). The latter meaning must be operative here, for the point is that, when offered Jesus as messiah, they did not "recognize" in him the "righteousness that is coming from God," and in that decision "sought to establish their own righteousness" by insisting that God had to work within the precedents set by Torah—that is, their understanding of the precedents set by Torah. That this is precisely the issue is indicated by Paul's next statement, which, we notice, is connected to the previous one by *gar* ("for"), meaning that it provides the basis for what had just been asserted. Here is the ground for stating that the Jews' zeal for God is without recognition: "For Christ is the end of the law unto righteousness for everyone who has faith" (10:4).

The second part of the statement is clear from the entire argument, for "unto righteousness for everyone who has faith" simply restates the thesis (1:16). More difficult to evaluate is what Paul means by "Christ is the *telos tou nomou*." The Greek term *telos* has the same ambiguity as the English noun "end," in that it can mean both "termination" and "goal." Both senses are probably contained in Paul's use here (see G. E. Howard, "Christ the End of the Law: The Meaning of Romans 10:4ff," *Journal of Biblical Literature* 88 [1969]: 331-37).

For those who have faith in the gift of God that is Christ Jesus, the law has *ended* as an absolute and ultimate norm for righteousness. The gift was given, after all, "apart from the law" (3:21), and as we have seen, Jesus' death appears to actually *contradict* the law. In the choice between Christ and Torah, therefore, only one norm can be ultimate, and faith in Christ demands that the way God's righteousness was revealed in the faithful death and resurrection of Jesus become the norm for understanding righteousness. In my judgment, however, Paul's main emphasis in this passage is on Christ as the *goal* of Torah. He means that Jesus messiah was what Torah was pointing to all along. He was the subject of Torah that "pre-promised the good news through the sacred writings" (see Rom 1:2). This Jesus was "witnessed to by Law and Prophets" (3:21). Not to recognize Jesus as messiah, therefore, means also not to have understood Torah itself! Thus, in 9:31, "they did not attain law (Torah)." That is why, for Paul, the refusal of Christ on the basis of defending Torah is not really a defense of Torah at all but a "seeking to establish one's own righteousness." The ultimate paradox for those who refuse Christ on the basis of Torah is that they also refuse what Paul believes to be the "intent" (*telos*) of Torah (see S. R. Bechter, "Christ the *telos* of the Law: The Goal of Romans 10:4," *Catholic Biblical Quarterly* 56 [1994]: 288–308).

That such is Paul's understanding is shown immediately by 10:5-21. He provides two daring midrashic reinterpretations of Torah from the standpoint of faith, the acceptance of God's gift of Jesus as messiah. The first is from "the law" proper, namely, Deuteronomy, and the second is from "the prophets," namely, Isaiah. Paul will read Christ back into Torah, and thus show that the good news was "pre-promised in the sacred writings through the prophets" (1:2) and was "witnessed to by Law and Prophets" (3:21). Such a collapsing of horizons (reading the past in the present and the present in the past) is found also in 1 Cor 10:1-4. Describing the generation of Israel that came out of Egypt and wandered in the wilderness, Paul says, "They all drank from the same spiritual drink. For they drank from the spiritual rock that was following, and the rock was the messiah." In the same way, Paul will "find the messiah" in texts where his fellow Jews did not see him.

He begins with a contrast between the "righteousness from the law" and the "righteousness out of faith" similar to that in Gal 3:12. As in that passage, he quotes Lev 18:5, "The person who does these [commandments] shall live by them." It is striking that this citation is introduced by the words, "Moses writes"–remember how Paul sets himself up in 9:1-2 as the counterpart of Moses. In contrast, the "righteousness that is out of faith" is virtually personified, for it "speaks." What is astonishing is that "she" speaks out of the pages of Torah itself.

In a daring maneuver, Paul uses a passage in Deut 30:12-14 that refers explicitly to the *commandment* of God and makes it into words spoken by "righteousness out of faith." Here is the original text from LXX Deut 30:11-14:

For this commandment which I command to you this day is not too hard for you, neither is it far off. It is not in the heaven, that you should say, "Who will go up for us to heaven and bring it to us, so that we may hear it and do it?" Neither is it beyond the sea, that you should say, "Who will go over the sea for us, and bring it to us, that we may hear it and do it?" But the word is very near you; it is in your mouth and in your heart, and in your hand, so that you can do it.

Paul seizes on several aspects of this passage, notably the pattern of ascent and descent (which he sharpens) and the element of proximity and interiority. He makes the passage become a speech made by "faith righteousness" through the words of Torah that can be understood only in light of the messiah and as referring to the messiah. So he lines up the elements. "Do not say in your heart (the wording here is from Deut 9:4), 'who will go up into heaven,'" now takes on a new meaning: "that is, to bring messiah down" (10:6). Paul's next phrase diverges both from the LXX and MT. Rather than "across the sea," he has "go down into the abyss." He may have been influenced by the wording of LXX Ps 106:26 or by the general association of the sea with the abyss, or he may simply have imposed this pattern because it matches that of the death and resurrection of Jesus. This is, in any case, the connection he makes: "that is to bring back messiah from the dead" (10:7). Paul also *omits* from the Deuteronomy text the references to "hearing and doing" the commandment. In effect, his rereading makes messiah replace the commandment, and faith the performance. Paul then continues, "but what does she [i.e., faith righteousness] say," and inserts the line from Deut 30:14, "The word is close to you, in your mouth and in your heart," and identifies this *word* not as the commandment, but "the word concerning faith which we are proclaiming" (10:8).

With the connective "because" in 10:9, Paul provides the basic content of the word being proclaimed. Remarkably, he makes the following verbs into the second person singular, creating the effect of an intimate appeal, "For if you [the individual reader] confess with your mouth that Jesus is Lord and believe in your heart that God has raised him from the dead, you will be saved." The distinction between "mouth" and "heart" derives from Deut 30:14. The confession "Jesus is Lord," as we know, is part of the primitive Christian tradition. We saw earlier how Paul connects this confession to being "in the Holy Spirit" (1 Cor 12:3). We also recognize in "God raising him from the dead" an echo of 4:25. This combination of faith and confession, says Paul, leads to salvation, that is, places one among the restored people that God is drawing from among the world's population. This "social" understanding of salvation is confirmed by Paul's next line: "For it is believed by the heart unto righteousness and confessed by the mouth unto salvation" (10:10). The "right relationship" with God, Paul has asserted from the beginning, consists in an internal response of the human spirit, therefore comes from "the heart" (2:29; 6:17; 8:27; 9:2). But confession with the mouth is a public and social act, and it is to this social reality that Paul now connects "salvation."

Paul repeats the conclusion of the passage from Isa 28:16 that he had quoted in 9:33, this time adding the word "all": "all who have faith in him will not be put to shame." The reason for this addition? Paul returns to his theme of the fairness and impartiality of the one God (see 3:29): "there is no distinction between Jew and Greek, for *the same God is of all people*, richly gifting all who call upon him" (10:12). The syllogism is closed by the citation of Joel 3:5 (see also Acts 2:21): "all who call on the name of the Lord will be saved" (10:13). By adding the word "all" to the Isaiah passage, Paul has created a tight argument: (a) there is one God for all, who gifts those who call on him; (b) all those who call on the name of the Lord will be saved; (c) those who have faith in the heart that God raised Jesus from the dead call him Lord; (d) those who have faith in him shall not be put to shame.

The next part of Paul's argument (10:14–21) is extremely difficult. It appears to most commentators that Paul shifts entirely to the contemporary Christian proclamation of the good news, and at first his use of the rhetorical *sorites* seems to support that suggestion. He starts with the obvious question concerning "all who call on the name of the Lord"; people don't call on the name of one they don't have faith in (11:14). Then he begins the *sorites*: "How can they have faith if they have not heard? How can they hear apart from one who has proclaimed? How can they [in turn] proclaim unless they are sent out?" But it is not entirely clear what Paul has in mind by this (perfectly logical) set of questions. Does he really have in mind the Christian mission throughout the empire? If he does, this seems an awkward interpolation into his argument concerning Christ as *telos* of Torah (10:4).

Another possibility is that Paul does not have in mind the missionaries of his own day (although they may not be excluded), but is again "collapsing the horizons" between present and past and engaging in a reading of the prophet Isaiah that will yield a "pre-promising of the good news in the sacred writings through the prophets" (1:2). Thus, the citation of Isa 52:7, "How beautiful are the feet of those proclaiming good news" has reference not to *Paul's* day, but to *Isaiah's* day. Read in this way, the question whether people had been sent out to preach touches on the issue of God's fairness to the Jews. Why should they, after all, have recognized the messiah in Jesus? In some sense, Paul answers, the good news was proclaimed already to the Jews of the past and was recorded in the prophets. Read this way, Paul's next line makes better sense: "But they did not all obey the good news" (10:16). The tense of the Greek verb here is aorist, fixing the disobedience firmly in the past. But how can this be? The next citation is from Isa 53:1: "Lord, who has believed what was heard from us?" Paul, in other words, has the *prophet* complaining about a failure to respond to good news proclaimed by the prophet himself!

Paul draws a conclusion that is either banal or provocative. He says, "therefore faith comes from hearing, and the hearing is through the word of/concerning Christ [messiah]" (10:17). Some scribes, perhaps struck by the oddness of this construction, corrected it to "the word of God"—isn't that, after all, what the prophets proclaimed? But "the word of Christ"—or, better, "the message about Messiah"—is the harder and better reading. Then what can it mean? If it means simply "Christian preaching," then Paul is again moving away from the previous point of his argument. But what if he means quite literally "the message concerning the messiah" that was preached by Isaiah?

There are two reasons for thinking that Paul may have intended precisely this. The first reason was suggested already in the introduction to the commentary. I pointed out there how analysis of Paul's citations and allusions suggests that he had read and studied the latter part of Isaiah very carefully and exploited it in the composition of this letter. If we line up those allusions and citations, we see that they cluster in particular around that part of Isaiah devoted to the servant songs:

Isaiah	49:18	(see Rom 14:11)
	50:8	(see Rom 8:33)
	51:1	(see Rom 9:31)
	51:8	(see Rom 1:17)
	52:5	(see Rom 2:24)
	52:7	(see Rom 10:15)
	52:15	(see Rom 15:21)
	54:16	(see Rom 9:22)
	59:7	(see Rom 3:15–17)
	59:20	(see Rom 11:26)

Now if Paul had been working through this section of Isaiah—as he clearly had—he could hardly have avoided the most vivid of all servant songs in Isaiah 52:13–53:12, which we know played a role in early Christian reflection on the suffering of Jesus (see Acts 8:32–33; 1 Pet 2:22–25). There is, indeed, every reason to think that Paul made allusion to Isa 53:5 in Rom 4:25, and Isa 53:12 in Rom 4:24. In Rom 5:19, moreover, the statement, "the obedience of one man will establish many as righteous" appears to be a clear allusion to LXX Isa 53:11, "the righteous one who is serving well will make many righteous." In short, the text of Isaiah suffuses this writing, and it is more than likely that Paul has already alluded to the suffering servant song in Isaiah 52–53.

The second reason is that Paul's explicit citation, "Lord, who has believed what was heard from us," comes specifically from Isa 53:1, triggering for the attentive reader an allusion to the song as a whole. If, then, Paul thinks that Isaiah already proclaimed a "message about Messiah," and that this message was about a messiah who, despite being "counted among the lawless" (Isa 53:12), was actually "bearing the sins of many and was handed over for their sins" (Isa 53:12), suffering as a righteous person who made others righteous (53:11), then those who read Torah *should* have been able to "recognize" the messiah in the death of the righteous person Jesus. Israel should have been able to see in such a rejected servant one whom God would "exalt and lift up" by resurrection (Isa 53:13), so that he could see "an abundant seed (*sperma*)" (Isa 53:10).

The effect of Paul's daring midrash on Isaiah is to secure two points. The first is that the good news was quite literally "pre-promised" in the prophets and the "message about Messiah" was already proclaimed in Torah. The second is that such a knowledge of Torah should have enabled Israel to recognize in Jesus the sort of suffering messiah that Isaiah proclaimed. The question of God's fairness to Israel is settled by this intricate and allusive argument.

Paul now moves to a rapid-fire recitation of texts from Torah that returns to the question posed in 10:14, "How can people believe if they have not heard," by asserting that the message has indeed been spread abroad, as Torah itself demonstrates. Psalm 18:1 shows how all of creation proclaims the glory of God, and the rhythm of night and day expresses God's word and knowledge of God (18:2). In the verse quoted by Paul, "their sound has gone out to all the earth and their words to the end of the world" (LXX Ps 18:5). So he can answer "Indeed they have," to the question "Have they not heard?" It is impossible, I think, to decide finally whether Paul sees this as referring to God's revelation to all through creation (see 1:18–2:16), or the "message about Messiah" through the prophets preached in synagogues all over the world (see Acts 15:21), or the Christian proclamation. The last seems to me to be the least likely, for Paul himself clearly does not think of the good news as having yet reached "the ends of the world," since that is the task to which he is dedicated and for which he is seeking funds! The allusion may simply be a loose one, serving primarily to rebut the implication that the Jews were badly dealt with because God caught them by surprise with a crucified messiah.

The translation of the next verse (10:19) is pivotal for the entire interpretation I have been presenting. The RSV renders it, "Again I ask, did Israel not understand?" But the syntax of the question (an interrogative introduced with *mē*) demands something more like this: "But I say, Israel was not ignorant, was it?" This is a better translation both because it recognizes that the syntax of the Greek demands a negative answer and because the following citations go to demonstrate again that Torah points clearly to the present situation—therefore, Israel should have known.

First, Moses declares in Deut 32:21, "I will make you jealous of one that is not a nation, and with a foolish nation I will provoke you" (10:19). In Deuteronomy, this verse occurs in the Song of Moses, which predicts the bad consequences to fall on Israel as a result of apostasy to idolatry. Paul cites the verse to show that the events of the present— the Jewish rejection of Gentile believers and what he thinks will eventually be their emulation of them—could be found predicted already in Torah. As for the Gentile inclusion in Israel, Isaiah could see that coming: "I was found by those who did not seek me; I showed myself to those who did not seek me" (Isa 65:1), even as (in the very next verse!) he could see the rejection of the good news by Israel: "All the day long, I stretched out my hands to a disobedient and contrary people" (Isa 65:2).

A pause for summary: Rom 10:5-21 serves to show how "Christ is the *telos* of Torah." By means of a midrashic appropriation of Deuteronomy 30 and Isaiah 53 (and with the help of a few other verses as well), Paul argues that the entire drama of his own time is found already in the words of Torah. The death and resurrection of the messiah, his suffering in shame for the sake of others, are already found in both Law and Prophets. But so is the pattern of disobedience of Israel to the word of God: they do not believe (10:16); they are disobedient and contrary (10:21). The clear implication is that Paul's fellow Jews should not have been scandalized by the death of Jesus but should have recognized him as the suffering messiah, and further, that God had played fair with them by limning the image of such a messiah already in the pages of Torah.

Despite the disobedience and contradictoriness of Israel (shown already by Torah), God remains faithful. As Paul had said in 3:3-4, "What if some were unfaithful? Does their faithlessness nullify the faithfulness of God? By no means! Let God be true though every person be false." So now Paul answers the question in the form of its asking, "Therefore I say, God has not rejected his people, has he? By no means!" (11:1). As in the past, God's process of election is at work to create a *remnant* out of which a greater and restored Israel can emerge. Paul's first piece of evidence that this is happening is—himself! "For I am also an Israelite, from the seed of Abraham, the tribe of Benjamin" (11:1). The point of this personal reference is that Paul, as a Jew, represents at the very least a "remnant of one," who has placed his trust in this new gift of God to the people. And if there is even one Jew who belongs to "Israel according to the Spirit," then, Paul can assert, "God has not rejected the people whom he knew beforehand" (11:2; compare 8:29).

Paul does not, however, make up the remnant of Israel by himself. There are, as he knows, other believers in Christ among the children of Israel. He can therefore advert to the case of another prophet, Elijah, who felt he was the only one faithful to the Lord, saying, "Lord, they have killed thy prophets, they have demolished thy altars, and I alone am left, and they seek my life" (1 Kgs 19:10, 14). This text must have seemed vividly pertinent to Paul. He saw some Jews involved in the killing of the Lord Jesus and "the prophets" (1 Thess 2:14-16), and seeking to kill him as well (2 Cor 11:24-26). The rejoinder to Elijah from God is therefore also a reminder to Paul that he did not stand alone, that God has others who are faithful within the people: "I have kept for myself seven thousand men who have not bent the knee to Baal" (1 Kgs 19:18). Paul's conclusion, therefore, is that God's way of diminishing his people in order to create a remnant (9:27-29) is happening again in the recent rejection of Jesus by the majority of Jews: "Thus therefore also in the now time [compare 3:26; 8:18] there has come to be a remnant (*leimma*) according to the election of grace" (11:5).

The principle by which the people is being divided is precisely "grace," that is, the new gift of God in Jesus Christ. Those who can receive this gift become part of the remnant people. Paul had repeatedly asserted that belonging to Israel was not a matter of descent but of promise (9:4), not a matter of doing good or evil but of election (9:11), not a matter of works but of call (9:11), not a matter of human exertion or effort but of God's mercy (9:16). So now, he states emphatically, "If it is by gift, it is not by works, otherwise a gift would no longer be a gift" (11:6).

My translation of this verse follows a text that is found in many but not all manuscripts. Some manuscripts (and the best critical Greek edition) have a different version of the statement. Instead of "not (*ouk*) by works," they have "no longer (*ouketi*) by works." It appears to me that this variant is more easily explained by scribes' being influenced by the presence of *ouketi* in the next phrase, and by a view of Pauline theology that thinks he wished to replace "works of the law" with "grace." But Paul has insisted that humans are able to do the works of the law, and under grace are able to fulfill the "just requirement of the law" (8:3). I think it better here to take "works" as referring simply to human effort or accomplishment (as in 9:11) and to keep the sharp disjunction reflected in the text I have translated. In any case, Paul's emphasis is on the positive rather than the negative: this remnant people is being formed on the basis of God's gift in Christ Jesus (5:15; 6:23).

The Future: Israel in God's Mysterious Plan (11:7–36)

Before moving to his vision of the future, Paul sums up: that which Israel sought, it did not obtain (11:7; see 9:31), except, as he has just shown, for a remnant: "the elect have attained." The "elect" is the community of Jewish Christians, among whom Paul can count himself. But how does he account for those who have not accepted Jesus as their messiah? Paul had already stated that their zeal for God was not according to "recognition" (10:2). Now he employs more properly prophetic language: "the rest have been hardened." The verb *poroun* means literally "to petrify or turn to rock," and serves metaphorically for "insensitivity" or "dullness." LXX Job 17:7 speaks of "my eyes [becoming] hardened from anger." In the New Testament, this word is used exclusively for disbelief or rejection. In 2 Cor 3:14, Paul says of the Jews, "their minds were hardened; for to this day, when they read the old covenant, the same veil remains unlifted, because only through Christ is it taken away." In John 12:40, the quotation from Isa 6:10 uses *poroun* for the Jews who disbelieve in Jesus. The expression "hardness of heart" is likewise attributed to Jewish nonbelievers in Mark 3:5 but is then also used of Jesus' disciples in Mark 6:52; 8:17. In Eph 4:18, on the other hand, "hardness of heart" is attributed to Gentiles.

Paul uses the term here and in 11:25 to characterize that part of the Jewish population that is "insensitive" to the messianic claims made for Jesus. Combined as it is with "zeal for God" and "lack of recognition," it appears that the "hardness" here should be understood more in terms of understanding than in terms of attitude. They "just can't see it." This visual dimension, in fact, is found in the two passages from Torah that Paul uses to support his contention that they are in fact "blind" to the work of God in Christ.

The first citation is a thoroughly mixed one, combining elements of Deut 29:3 ("God gave them/ until this day") and Isa 29:3 ("a spirit of stupor") and Isa 6:9 ("so their eyes do not see and their ears do not hear"). All three passages in their original context deal with the incapacity of Israel to perceive God's work in their midst, so that the combination of texts captures the essence of all of them. The passage from Isa 6:9 in particular plays an important role elsewhere in the New Testament for expressing the blindness of Israel in failing to respond to Jesus as messiah (see Matt 13:14; Mark 4:12; Luke 8:10; Acts 28:26).

Paul's second choice of texts is more intriguing. With only slight variation, he cites LXX Ps 68:23-24: "Let their table become a snare and a trap, a stumbling block and a recompense. Let their eyes be darkened so they cannot see, and their backs be bent forever" (11:9-10). At first glimpse, the only reason for including this text is the presence of the term "blindness." But two other features of the passage should be noted. The first is that LXX Psalm 68 is one of the psalms used most frequently for the interpretation of Jesus' passion and death (see Matt 27:34, 48; Mark 15:23, 36; Luke 23:36; John 2:17; 19:18; Acts 1:20). Furthermore, Paul explicitly quotes Ps 68:10 in Rom 15:3 with reference to the sufferings of Jesus. This citation, then, has the effect of connecting the Jews' blindness directly to the death of Jesus. The second feature follows from that, namely, how Paul has reversed the word order of the LXX, placing "stumbling block" (Greek *skandalon*) before "recompense." The effect is again to sharpen the focus on the death of Jesus as the stumbling block that the Jews cannot get over (see 9:32; 1 Cor 1:23).

The final words of Ps 68:24 seem to suggest a permanent curse to be borne by the unbelieving Jews: "May their backs be bent forever." Paul is therefore moved to pose the question concerning their blindness and hardening. Is it forever? "I ask therefore: they have not tripped so as to fall, have they? By no means!" Notice how the image of the stumbling block/scandal is deliberately carried forward by Paul. They have "tripped" but have they "fallen"? No. God is simply using their mistake to advance God's own purpose. In an instant, Paul sketches his sense of what function is being served by their "trespass" (*paraptōma*).

So Paul begins his dialectical analysis. What happens to the various peoples of the world happens in function of God's plan for humanity: "by their trespass salvation is to the Gentiles, in order to arouse them [Israel] to jealousy" (11:11). Paul says a great deal in a small space. In order to make sense of it, we need to remember the sequence "to the Jew first, then to the Gentile" in 1:16. That describes, in fact, the historical sequence: Jews believed in Christ first, then Gentiles did. But as the account in Acts vividly shows, the mission to the Gentiles came about only after, and possibly because of, the rejection of the message by the majority of Jews. Acts tells of persecution of missionaries scattered from Jerusalem to Samaria and Judea (Acts 8:1-3), and eventually to Antioch (11:19-26), from where the Gentile mission really began (13:1-3). Acts shows us as well how the missionaries continued to proclaim Jesus in synagogues and only after rejection there turned to the Gentiles (13:46-47; 18:5-6). Paul is therefore giving the most sober historical analysis when he declares that Israel's blindness gives the Gentiles a chance at "salvation," that is, inclusion in God's elect people (Acts 28:25-29). The inclusion of the Gentiles is not, however, an end in itself: Paul sees it as serving a role for the eventual restoration of Israel, which he states now very cryptically, "so as to make Israel jealous." We will return to this, below.

Now, in 11:12, Paul expresses something of his hope: "But if their trespass is wealth for the world, and their diminishment (*hēttēma*) is wealth for the Gentiles, how much more will their fullness be?" Although the specific terms of this sentence are somewhat obscure, the general sense is clear. We note again the use of "how much more" (*posō/pollō mallon*), which Paul used for the contrast between sin and grace in 5:9-10. The contrast in this case is between trespass and *hēttēma* on the one hand and wealth and fullness on the other. The exact meaning of *hēttēma* is difficult because it occurs so seldom (see only LXX Isa 31:9; 1 Cor 6:9). The RSV translates it here as "failure," but the other uses seem to support more the sense of "diminishment/loss," and that translation would provide a more suitable contrast to *plērōma* ("fullness"). Despite this uncertainty, Paul obviously sees Israel's destiny as positive and as one that will benefit all humanity, in imitation of the one whose death for transgressions led to life for many (4:25; 5:17; 6:10; 8:3–4; see T. L. Donaldson, "'Riches for the Gentiles' (Rom 11:12): Israel's Rejection and Paul's Gentile Mission," *Journal of Biblical Literature* 112 [1993]: 81–98).

At this point (11:13), Paul turns to the Gentiles, just as in 2:17 he had turned on the one "who calls himself a Jew." In that place, the purpose of the direct address was to caution the Jew against arrogance and pretentiousness because of his relationship to God and possession of Torah; Paul reminded the interlocutor that God gave the Gentiles also the ability to respond from the heart (2:17–29). The direct address here has the same purpose in reverse. Now it is arrogance on the part of Gentiles because of their relationship to God and "possession of the messiah" that must be forestalled. Paul confesses that his "glorifying" his mission to the Gentiles (see 1:5) is really in service to his kinsmen, "that I might make my fellow Jews jealous, and I might save some of them" (11:14).

This, then, is the other shoe. The Jews' failure to accept the messiah meant that the Gentiles got to hear of him. Paul therefore sees the opposite also as a possibility. The success of the Gentile mission will make his fellow Jews jealous, so that they too will want to join the people. Note again how "that I might save" simply must mean "get to join this people," since the sharing by individual Jews in God's eternal life is neither in Paul's power to grant nor on his agenda in this discussion. The notion of "stirring to jealousy" is derived from the text of LXX Deut 32:21, which he quoted in 10:19: "I will stir you to jealousy of one not a nation." Paul sees the present circumstances as following the pattern of God's work in the past. The events that appear to be against Scripture turn out to be, when read from a different angle, a revelation of the true intention of Scripture.

Those without Greek will not notice that this stirring to jealousy is actually a sort of pun. Paul had declared in 10:2 that his fellow Jews were "zealous for God." The term *zēlos* can serve both for "zeal" and for "jealousy." To be zealous for God is also in a sense to be jealous for God. So when Paul says that he will "stir them to jealousy," he is also saying that he is stirring their zeal. It is not, in other words, out of envy of the Gentiles that the Jews will turn to Christ but out of their zeal and jealous love of the God they regard as their own.

Using the same sort of rhetorical contrast as in 5:12–21, Paul imagines in

11:15 the results of such a salvation of his own people. Their "rejection" (*apobolē*) meant the reconciliation of the world (compare 2 Cor 5:19). When they are "added in" (*proslēmpsis*) there will be "life from the dead." It is possible to read this eschatologically, so that the "ingathering" of all the Jews would mean the final resurrection of the dead. But the text does not say that explicitly and perhaps should not be pushed too hard. His image may mean simply the "life after death" of Israel itself, which has been whittled down to a "stump/remnant" by the present circumstances.

Such a reading provides a better transition to the next statement: "If the first fruit is holy, then the lump is as well, and if the root is holy, the branches are as well." It must be confessed, however, that the precise point here is hard to determine. Both images propose a relationship between a part and a whole, in which the part stands for the whole. The "firstfruits" is the portion of dough in a cereal offering that is offered to God (Num 15:19–20). If this offering has been dedicated, then the remainder of the "lump" of dough can be considered dedicated as well. (We can hear Paul the Pharisee clearly in this discussion). How does the image apply? Are the believing Jews the "firstfruits" (remember how Paul uses this elsewhere for converts) that make the other believers (the Gentiles) "holy"? Or are the believing Jews the firstfruits that make the rest of the *Jews* holy? If Paul uses the images to the same end, then the first suggestion must be right, because this is the way he uses the second image. By itself, the image of the root and branches would be equally obscure, except that Paul goes on immediately to apply it to Jews and Gentiles.

In the light of 11:17–21, then, the root and branches must refer to the whole of "Israel," with the *root* (as is appropriate) signifying the remnant that is the basis for any growth that is to come. If it is "holy," then the branches to grow out of it also will be "holy." If I have followed him correctly, then, Paul means that the present believing community of Jews, including himself, is the remnant of Israel that both *represents* all of Israel and also prepares for its full restoration.

What becomes clearer in 11:17–24 is that Paul's comments have had the effect of stressing the special and irreplaceable role of Israel in God's plan. He essays a rather ambitious horticultural allegory, which is not terribly successful at the level of science but is nevertheless effective in making his point. He begins with the process: first, God cuts off some of the branches. This fits the image of pruning a tree, appropriate to the concept of "remnant/stump/root." Thus, we are to understand, some of the Jews have been "cut away" from the people because they did not believe in Jesus as messiah, leaving only the "stump/root/remnant" of Jewish-Christians. Next, God performs a transplant operation (which Paul recognizes as "against nature" in 11:24). God grafts a wild olive shoot into the place formerly held by the branches that were cut away. Allegorically, these are the Gentiles, who have been "transplanted/grafted" onto the remnant/root of Israel. As a result, this transplant "shares the richness" of the olive tree (11:17).

The Gentiles had not even sought God, yet they now get to share in all the wealth of God's people expressed by the symbolic world of Torah (9:4-5)! This is all God's doing. But what should be the Gentiles' attitude? Paul tells them, "Do not boast over the branches" (11:18). Notice once more the reversal of 2:17, where the Jew boasted over the Gentiles because of all the gifts possessed through Torah. If it was wrong for the Jews to boast over the Gentiles, Paul suggests, it is ludicrous for Gentiles to boast over Jews. As they boast, Paul suggests, they might remember that the root is bearing them, not them the root (11:18). They do not give life to the root, but draw life from it.

Paul allows the imaginary Gentile interlocutor to have a voice (11:19): "Branches were broken off so that I might be grafted in." This claim, in fact, is one made by supersessionist Christians who think that Israel is to play no more role in God's work. Their time is past, it is said; now *we* are God's people (such is the argument found, e.g., in Tertullian's *Against the Jews*). But Paul emphatically rejects such a position. He replies sardonically, "Good for you!" (compare Jas 2:19; John 4:17). Then he reminds them of the fragility of their status. The Jews were "cut off" because of faithlessness, and the Gentiles stand on the basis of faith. Paul says, "Don't think high thoughts. Be afraid" (11:20).

They should fear because their perch is a precarious one: "If God did not spare the natural branches, neither will he spare you" (11:21). The language here is remarkable, not only because the use of *kata physin* ("natural") here anticipates *para physin* ("unnatural") in 11:24, but also for the use of *pheidesthai* for "sparing." The reference to natural/unnatural draws the reader back to the attack on idolatry in 1:18-31. The Jews are "natural" to God, and the Gentiles are "unnatural." The reader is reminded forcefully of the same language used in 1:26-27. Even more strikingly, Paul's use of "spare" recalls 8:32, "God did not spare his own son." There, we recognized an allusion to Abraham's offering of Isaac in Gen 22:16. Is it too much to suppose that Paul is once more making a connection between the Jewish people (who had, we remember, the first claim to "sonship," 9:4), and the messiah himself? God did not spare them, for the sake of the Gentiles. As in 11:12, the role assigned to the people is to continue the messianic pattern found in Jesus (see R. B. Hays, *Echoes of Scripture in the Letters of Paul* [New Haven: Yale University Press, 1989] 61).

For Paul, the pattern of history shows the "mercy and severity" (*chrēstotēs, apotomia*) of God (11:22-23). What is new here is that God shows one or the other depending on the human response to God's gift.

Here is the other side of the delicate interplay between divine power and human freedom, and what distinguishes God from the blind and ruthless "fate" (*heimarmenē*) of late antiquity. If those who now enjoy God's favor reject it, they too can be cut off. And if those now cut off repent of their disbelief, they can be grafted into the tree that is natural to them once more: "God has the power to graft them in again" (11:23). Indeed, this operation is much easier than the first one (11:24)!

This set of statements says at least three things about Paul's midrashic argument in Romans 9–11. First, he remains fundamentally Jewish in his perception of the nature of God and of relationships between God and humans. God is a God of both justice and mercy. Humans are free to accept or reject the gifts of God. Sin and conversion are always possibilities; the game always remains open. Second, the possibility of such *individual* responses indicates that Paul's language about call and election was directed to populations and nations, rather than to individuals. God's overarching plan to shape a people for himself—to "save humans"—reflects his deep game-playing. At the level of the individual person, the choice is always there to join or leave a certain population. Third, we see once more in this argument Paul's perception of God as creator, who calls into being that which did not exist and raises the dead to life. There is a structural continuity between the birth of the people in the person of Isaac from "as-good-as-dead" parents, and the resurrection of Jesus from the dead, and the regeneration of the people Israel from the stump of the remnant. In every case, God's desire is for the being and life that can show God's "glory" (his presence and power).

Paul now begins to summarize his argument, by reminding his Gentile readers once more not to "get above themselves" because of their present status. They do not know it, but they are involved in a mystery (*mystērion*), which is something else altogether than a problem. A problem is something that human intelligence can eventually work out, because it stands still, is detached from personal involvement, and can be regarded as objective. Such are chess moves or crossword puzzles or broken carburetors. But a mystery is not something humans can detach themselves from and treat as objective and manipulate. Nor is it like a secret that, once told, can be utterly known and controlled. A mystery, rather, is deeply ungraspable, even when it is revealed. It resists manipulation and control. Nor can it be viewed with detachment without distortion, for mystery involves the human person's freedom.

Paul's use of *mystērion* may reflect slightly the language of the mystery religions (see C. Caragounis, *The Ephesian Mysterion* [CB 8; Lund: CWK Gleerup, 1977] 3–19) but appears to be more dependent on the LXX translation of the Hebrew *rāz*, which in Dan 2:18–47 refers to the things revealed by God to humans concerning future events. In Qumran literature, likewise, we find references to the divine *rāz* ("mystery") as the revelation of God's plan for humans (1QS 3:23; 11:19; 1QpHab 7:5, 13–14; CD 3:18; see R. E. Brown, *The Semitic Background of the Term "Mystery" in the New Testament* [Philadelphia: Fortress, 1968]). Paul's usage elsewhere fits into this framework. He and Apollos are "stewards of the mysteries of God" (1 Cor 4:1) and communicate the "mysteries of God" to that church (1 Cor 2:1) concerning the cross of Christ, which is a "mysterious wisdom" (1 Cor 2:7). Under the influence of the Holy Spirit, says Paul, people can know (1 Cor 13:2) and speak (1 Cor 14:2) mysteries. Most significantly, what will happen at the end-time is a "mystery"—"behold, I am telling you a mystery" (1 Cor 15:51)—it is something we can speak of at all only because of what God has already shown us, but cannot speak of adequately because God has not yet revealed it fully. In Paul's letter to the Colossians, the "mystery" is primarily what God has done to include the Gentiles in his people (1:26–27; 2:2; 4:3), as it is also in Ephesians (1:9; 3:3–4, 9; 6:19). The only other occurrence of "mystery" in Romans comes at the end of the letter (16:25–26); there, as here, it refers to the revelation of God's plan (hidden in the past but now made known) concerning the obedience of faith among the Gentiles.

The "mystery" that Paul now shares with his Gentile readers is that the "hardening" of Israel is only partial and temporary (11:25). It will last only until the full complement of Gentiles enters into the people (see M. A. Getty, "Paul and the Salvation of Israel: A Perspective on Rom 9–11," *Catholic Biblical Quarterly* 50 [1988]: 456–69). For Paul, the end-point of "salvation" is the restoration of Israel as God's people: "And thus all Israel will be saved" (11:26). Paul's expectation that this could happen—at the time of his writing—must have been like Abraham and Sarah contemplating their age and barrenness, like the followers of Jesus staring at the tomb on Good Friday. All the evidence was against it—is against it still! Yet Paul's faith, like Jesus' faith—and, one hopes, like Christians' faith—is not in human possibility but in "the God who brings into being that which does not exist and gives life to the dead" (4:17).

In the meantime, there is the hope offered by the Scriptures, so many of which had already been fulfilled in unexpected and paradoxical ways. The prophets spoke words not understood when spoken but glowingly fulfilled by the messiah Jesus. Might not the same happen with these texts as well? Paul's citation in 11:26–27 is one of his most mixed, being made up mostly of Isa 59:20–21 but with wording taken from other texts as well. In the LXX, Isa 59:20–21 reads, "and for *the sake of Zion* there will come the deliverer and he will turn away wickedness (*asebeia*) from Jacob. And this is my covenant with them." In this text, notice, it is "for the sake of Zion" that the deliverer comes. And what is the covenant? The Isaiah passage goes on to describe it in terms of the presence of God's words and spirit among them and their "seed" (*sperma*). Paul might have had in mind this connection to the seed and his own understanding of the covenant in terms of the Holy Spirit.

But the wording of the citation is influenced as well by LXX Ps 13:7: "Who will give *from Zion* the salvation of Israel? When the Lord turns around the captivity of his people let Judah rejoice and Israel be glad." Once more, the text speaks of a return, but this time it is one "out of Zion" who will give "salvation" (*sōtēria*). The last part of the citation also shows the influence of Isa 27:9 in the words "when I have taken away their sins." The continuation of this verse is another prophetic passage promising restoration of the people! "In that day . . . those who were lost in the land of Assyria and those who were driven out to the land of Egypt will come and worship the Lord on the holy mountain at Jerusalem" (Isa 27:13). The "holy mountain" here is equivalent to "Zion" in the other texts. In short, Paul's citation draws together texts that are linked by the theme of Zion and the restoration of God's people.

Who is the "deliverer from Zion"? Paul's use of the verb *rhyesthai* elsewhere suggests that he could have in mind God (see 2 Cor 1:10; Col 1:13; 2 Thess 3:2; Rom 7:24; 15:31), or even Jesus himself (see 1 Thess 1:10). In either case, the deliverer will reverse the effect of "sin" (see 3:9) and "wickedness" (see 1:18; 4:5; 5:6) in which Israel now paradoxically finds itself, having (like the Gentiles who did not "recognize God") refused to "recognize the righteousness that comes from God" in the crucified and raised messiah Jesus. Torah itself, declares Paul, contains the hope that God can turn this tragic condition around.

In a series of crisp affirmations (11:28–32), Paul brings his long argument to a close. The Jews who have not recognized the messiah are now "enemies" (see 5:10; 8:7). But he qualifies this immediately by "with reference to the good news" and "for your sake." In other words, their response to the gospel message has temporarily put them in opposition to God's plan. But as Paul has shown, they do not know that God's plan can use such opposition "for the Gentiles' sake." Insofar as they are the elect of God, however, the Jews remain "beloved on account of the fathers." Paul's statement relies on the same sort of understanding undergirding 8:32. In Pharisaic Judaism, the good deeds of the patriarchs were regarded as building up merit on which later generations could draw (see S. Schechter, *Aspects of Rabbinic Theology* [New York: Schocken Books, 1961] 170–98). God not only called humans but respected their response to him. So God's loyalty to this generation of Jews has much to do with earlier generations of Jews' fidelity to God. For Paul, however, such a system of *quid pro quo* is ultimately inadequate. God's loyalty is not really defined by human response so much as by

God's own nature: "For the gifts of God and the call of God are unchangeable" (11:29). If they *seem* to be changed, then we must reassess the evidence, as he does here: "For just as you were once disobedient to God but have now received mercy because of their disobedience, so they have been disobedient in order that by the mercy shown to you they also may receive mercy" (11:30–31). This is Paul's most perfect expression of his dialectical sense of history. We notice that in both cases, even though the human word to God is no, the response of God to humans is mercy: "For God has closed up all humans in disobedience in order that he might have mercy on all" (11:32).

Paul will still have more to say about God's work among Jew and Gentile in 15:1–13. But this stage of his exposition he draws to a close with a rapturous expression of wonder at God's will (11:33–36), bringing theology to its most proper articulation in the praise of God's glory. Paul's praise in this case focuses on the sheer "otherness" of God. The "depth of the richness and the wisdom and knowledge of God" is not exhausted by what God has shown of himself in the world, and is not capable of being fully grasped by any human mind. God's judgments are not the sort that can be "searched out" as the texts of Torah can be "searched out" by means of midrash, for the living God always moves ahead of and beyond scriptural precedent.

God's paths, he declares, are not "traceable." His language suggests the following of a trail. Humans pick up the scent of God's power and presence in the world and try to follow the direction God is moving, but our minds are too puny and frail even to catch up with his traces as God moves rapidly before us. This describes the "mystery" of God: even when God reveals God's self, humans cannot know God in a manner that defines or controls God or confines God to God's own precedents. In support of this, Paul quotes first from LXX Isa 40:13, "Who has known the mind of the Lord, or who has become his counselor?" The verse occurs in a context that celebrates the distance between the creator and creatures. After the verse cited by Paul, Isaiah continues, "Whom did he consult for his enlightenment, and who taught him the path of righteousness?"

For Paul, however, the "otherness" of God is not just a matter of God's inscrutability. It is a matter above all of God's being the underived source of all reality. The creature remains always dependent on the one who creates. Paul asks in 11:35, "or who has given to him and it must be repaid?" Paul seems to be making an allusion to the LXX version of Job 41:3, "Who is it that stands against me, or who will resist me and endure?" and Job 35:7, "If you are righteous what do you give to him, or what will he receive from your hand?" Both statements in Job are challenges to the human presumption of standing on the same plane with God. Paul's reference to "giving a gift that must be repaid," also echoes his conviction concerning God's impartiality (see 2:11). If God were like a human judge, then God might be fooled by appearances or might even be susceptible to a bribe. But the creator before whom all creatures are as nothing cannot be impressed by any gift given by humans. Paul's conclusion is resounding: "For from him and through him and to him are all things" (11:36). God is the source, the sustainer, and the goal of all that exists.

By so saying, Paul has brought his argument to the place it needed to reach, namely, the recognition of God's glory in creation. This is what the Gentiles failed to recognize in their turn to idolatry (1:21). This is what Abraham did in his faith and hope in the one who calls all things into being (4:20). And this is what Paul now does: "To him be the glory forever. Amen."

THE TRANSFORMATION
OF MORAL CONSCIOUSNESS

Romans 12:1–13:14

Making sense out of 12:1–13:14 is a challenge to any interpretive perspective on Romans. Those in the "Romans Debate" who think Paul's argument is generated by specific problems within the community and is directed to divisions between Jewish and Gentile believers find little comfort in these two chapters, whose contents appear to be thoroughly general and nonspecific in character. But those who think Paul's composition is motivated by his desire to share his theological vision with the Romans with an eye to financial support from them have as difficult a time figuring out why Paul should suddenly shift from the indicative to the imperative, with exhortations that, again, have little obvious connection with the grand vision preceding them in chapters 1–11 (see G. Sigma, "Romans 12:1–2 and 15:30–32 and the Occasion of the Letter to the Romans," *Catholic Biblical Quarterly* 53 [1991]: 257–73). Is this section of Romans simply an afterthought? Is it a sample of his "moral teaching" that Paul sends along to the Roman church as *captatio benevolentiae* with his theological teaching?

It is certainly better method in reading to assume that this section of Romans serves Paul's overall rhetorical purposes. Readers should assume that a writing is internally coherent until the composition itself forces a reassessment. In this case, there are four reasons for taking Romans 12–13 seriously as an integral part of Paul's overall argument.

1. He connects 12:1 to 11:36 with *oun* ("therefore"). In ancient manuscripts, there would have been no chapter or paragraph indicator between the two verses. In oral delivery, there may well have been a pause after the "Amen" in 11:36, but the very next words the audience heard would be connected to it by "therefore." The clear implication is that what Paul has said in chapters 1–11 serves as the ground for Paul's instructions.

2. We know that chapters 14–15 explicitly circle back to the issue of

Jew–Gentile relations (see especially 15:1–13). The most reasonable assumption is that chapters 12–13 provide some sort of intelligible link between chapters 1–11 and chapters 14–15.

3. The focus on specific modes of behavior in chapters 12–13 is consistent with the emphasis in Romans that God judges humans on the basis of what they do. Paul has not swerved from the fundamental principles enunciated in 2:1–10. The difference in the new situation is empowerment. Under the reign of sin, those weakened by the flesh could not "please God" by their deeds (even when those deeds did what was commanded), because of the hostility of their hearts, expressed in the self-aggrandizing selfishness characteristic of idolatry. Even though they agreed with their minds that covetousness was wrong, they were filled with covetousness, the hunger for having that is the engine of idolatry. But such fear leading to compulsion, says Paul, has been driven out by the love of God poured into their hearts through the Holy Spirit (5:5). They are now empowered to "fulfill the righteous requirement of the law" (8:3). It therefore makes sense for Paul to begin to spell out how the gift of the Spirit works in terms of practical behavior.

4. There are specific thematic links between Paul's discourse in the chapters on either side of this section and the hortatory emphasis in chapters 12–13. Most obviously, the motif of "lowly-mindedness" emerges as the antidote to the boasting and arrogance that Paul sees as characteristic of sin, and as the temptation of Gentile believers now enjoying the privileges of Israel (see, e.g., 11:18–25; 12:3, 16).

In this reading, therefore, we will try to make sense of the exhortations in chapters 12–13 as part of Paul's overall argument (see also H. E. Stoessel, "Notes on Romans 12:1–12: The Renewal of the Mind and the Internalizing of the Truth," *Interpretation* 17 [1963] 161–75). There is, however, undoubtedly a shift in the form of rhetoric. After a transitional statement in 12:1–2, the rest of chapter 12 is made up of exhortations and maxims whose internal connections are not obvious. In 13:1–7, Paul provides a more sustained instruction on obedience to civil authorities; in 13:8–10 a statement on the law of love; and in 13:11–14 an eschatological reminder. At first, everything seems chopped up, atomistic. We will see if this first impression is correct.

The Transformation of Consciousness (12:1–2)

I have already mentioned the connective *oun* ("therefore") by which Paul signals a rhetorical link between this section and the one preceding it. Two aspects of that previous section in particular should be noted. The first is that God is the source of all things and all glory should be given to God (11:36). The second is that humans confronted with the mystery of God should conduct themselves in fear and not with arrogance or boasting (11:20, 25). Paul's exhortation follows on these points. The verb *parakalein* has a range of meanings from "comfort" to "exhort." Here the hortatory sense is clearly present. Paul frequently uses "I exhort you" as a transition to the practical part of his letters (see 1 Cor 1:10; 2 Cor 2:8; 6:1; Eph 4:1; Phil 4:1; 1 Thess 4:1; Phlm 10; see C. J. Bjerkelund, *Parakalō: Form, Funktion, und Sinn der parakalō-sätze in den paulinischen Briefen* [Biblioteca Theologica Norvegica 1; Oslo: Universitetsforlaget, 1967] 156–89). The phrase "through the mercies of God," however, is oddly placed. It can modify either what the Romans are to do or Paul's exhortation. I think it basically functions here as a bridge: given the *mercy* that God has gifted you with (11:22, 31–32), how should they behave?

Paul exhorts his readers first to "present your bodies as a living sacrifice, holy and acceptable to God, which is your spiritual worship" (12:1). The language is extremely compressed and requires some unpacking if it is to be intelligible. The "presenting of bodies" reminds us forcefully of 6:13–19, where Paul called for a "presenting of your members to God as instruments of righteousness" (6:13). The language of "living sacrifice" and "spiritual worship," however, appears for the first time in this letter.

The notion that human moral actions can be thought of as analogous to, or even as a replacement for, the sacrifices of grain or animals in the temple cult, as an expression of worship, is attested elsewhere in Judaism. After the fall of the Jerusalem temple, the rabbinic tradition interpreted the study of the commandments concerning sacrifices as the religious equivalent of actually performing those sacrifices, and thus a "spiritual worship" (e.g., *b. Ber.* 5a–b, 26a; *Pesik. R.* 79a; *b. Menah.* 110a; *Aboth de Rabbi Nathan* 2). Even before the destruction of the temple, the sectarians at Qumran thought of their community as an alternative, "spiritual temple," with their own observance of the rules of the sect as a kind of spiritual sacrifice (4QFlor 1:6; 1QS 8:6–8; 9:3–11). In Philo as well, "spiritual worship" characterized the distinctive synagogal worship, which consisted in readings and prayer rather than in animal sacrifices (*Life of Moses* 2.108; *The Worse Attacks the Better* 21; *Special Laws* 1.201, 272, 287, 290).

Such transposed language is found among the New Testament writings in 1 Pet 2:5: "Like living stones be yourselves built into a spiritual house, to be a holy priesthood, to offer spiritual sacrifices acceptable to God through Jesus Christ." Paul also can think of the Christian community as just such a spiritual temple: "Do you not know that you are God's temple and that God's spirit dwells in you? If anyone destroys God's temple, God will destroy that person. For God's temple is holy, and that temple you are" (see Y. Congar, *The Mystery of the Temple* [Westminster, Md.: Newman Press, 1962]).

Clues from the immediate context of Romans, however, are more helpful in determining why Paul should use such language in this place and what he means by it. We have noted that Paul has just completed a doxology (11:36) that reverses the refusal of idolators to "give God glory" (1:21). In 1:25, Paul had spoken of their response to reality in terms of religious service: "they worshiped (*latreuein*) and served the creature rather than the creator, who is blessed forever. Amen." This *latreia* of the believers "in the Spirit" also reverses the pattern of idolatry.

Paul also spoke of his own "religious service" (*latreuein*) "with my spirit in the gospel of his son" (1:9), and again in 15:15-16 he uses similar liturgical language with regard to his mission: God had given him the grace "to be a minister of Christ Jesus to the Gentiles in the priestly service of the good news so that the offering of the Gentiles may be acceptable, sanctified by the Holy Spirit." It cannot be coincidental that these passages are so close to 12:1-2. Here he calls his Gentile readers to the sort of "spiritual worship" through the disposition of their freedom that will enable them to be the "acceptable sacrifice" that fulfills Paul's priestly work. From beginning to end, however, this is cultic language that is used to express not what is usually regarded as liturgical acts but the disposition of the self through moral behavior in the church and in society.

If the "spiritual sacrifice" of the Gentiles is not a matter of ritual but a matter of disposing their freedom, then it must move from the center of their freedom. Paul speaks next about the way in which their *minds* are to direct their hearts in terms of a threefold process:

1. They are to turn away from the measure of reality given by "this age." Paul uses this expression only here in Romans, but elsewhere "this age" functions more or less equivalently to "the world," that is, the arena of human activity outside the norms and values of the community of saints (see 1 Cor 1:20; 2:6-8; 3:18; 2 Cor 4:4). The measure of "the world" is one that operates without reference to the claim of God. His readers are not to "conform themselves" to this perception of reality. His language suggests being "fitted to a frame/ pattern" (compare 1 Cor 4:1). From everything Paul has said in the letter to this point, we would be justified in equating "this age" with "life according to the flesh."

2. In contrast to that measure, Paul's readers are to "be transformed by the renewal of the mind." This is a matter not of a new set of rules but of an internal transformation, a new form of consciousness. But whose "mind" (*nous*) are they to be conformed to? Paul's language elsewhere points in a

specific direction. In Phil 3:21, he speaks of a process of transformation effected by Christ: "He will configure our body of lowliness, transforming it to the body of his glory." In 2 Cor 3:17-18, we read, "Now the Lord is the Spirit, and where the Spirit of the Lord is, there is freedom. And we all, with unveiled faces, beholding the glory of the Lord, *are being changed into his likeness* from one degree of glory to another. This comes from the Lord, who is Spirit." Finally, in 1 Cor 2:12, Paul declares that Christians have received not the spirit of the world but the Spirit from God, and he concludes his discussion with the crisp affirmation in 2:16, "We have the mind of Christ (*nous Christou*)." In this context, and from the ways Paul will develop his exhortation, it is clear that the "new mind" to which believers are to be transformed is precisely the "mind of Christ." They are to view reality from a perspective shaped by the Holy Spirit according to the image of Christ.

3. This renewed consciousness is able to "test what is the will of God, what is good and acceptable and perfect" (12:2). In 2:18, Paul listed as one of the boasts of the Jew the ability to "test what should be done" according to the norms of Torah. Now Christians are to "test what is God's will" according to a mind shaped by Christ. The new form of consciousness leads to specific action through a process of *discernment*. In Greek philosophy, the link between knowledge of the good and the ability to put that knowledge to practical effect was the virtue of prudence (*phronēsis*), a form of practical moral reasoning. Early Christian literature speaks of "testing the Spirit" or "discernment" (see 1 Cor 3:13; 11:28; 12:10; 14:29; Gal 6:4; Eph 5:10; Phil 1:10; 1 Thess 5:21). Paul's phrasing is particularly striking here because he makes such a "testing of circumstances" an essential part of the renewal of the mind. The "will of God" might be known (*post factum* and partially) in the big picture, but "what thing" is pleasing, good, or acceptable in the here and now must be tested.

The Christian moral life that Paul here begins to sketch places an emphasis on internal transformation before external rules, and on the *process* of discerning rather than on the specific decision. These qualities will be particularly important in Paul's discussion of diversity within the community in chapter 14.

Moral Attitudes in the Community (12:3–21)

It would be astonishing, given Paul's emphasis on salvation as a social reality, if he were suddenly to describe the moral life in terms of an individual's virtues or actions. His framework here, as in all his letters, is the community as such and the sorts of attitudes needed to build up its identity. The process of "doing God's will" and "testing what is good" is as much a communal as an individual responsibility. Paul therefore calls for individual responses within a communal awareness.

His starting point in 12:3 is instructive. He had warned the Gentiles against thinking too highly of themselves and boasting over the temporarily blinded Jews (11:20, 25). Now he returns to the same point. They are not to "think above themselves" but are to think *eis to sophronein*. The Greek expression is almost impossible to translate, since it virtually summarizes what a Greek would regard as good moral character: reasonableness, self-control, moderation, prudence (see Xenophon, *Cyropaedia* 3.2.4). The ideal philosopher is one who has *sophrosyne* (Plato, *Republic* 430E). Although the term can be used specifically for moderation in pleasure, especially sexual pleasure (Aristotle, *Rhetoric* 1.9.9; Josephus, *Antiquities* 18.66), Paul uses it for a sense of "appropriateness within the community," as his next words make clear: "To each one as God has apportioned a measure of faith." What Paul calls for, in other words, is the opposite of the arrogance and self-aggrandizement that need to "have it all." What is required first within the community is a realistic sense of how God has gifted each one with faith and how that gift might be best employed within the community (see H. Moxnes, "The Quest for Honor and the Unity of the Community in Romans 12 and the Orations of Dio Chrysostom," in *Paul in His Hellenistic Context*, ed. T. Engberg-Pedersen [Minneapolis: Fortress, 1995] 203–30).

The group context for moral activity is made explicit in Paul's next statement. As in 1 Cor 12:12–31 and Eph 4:1–16, he uses the image of the body (*soma*) for the community. They are "one body in Christ" (12:4). There are four reasons why this metaphor works well for Paul. First, a body is a living entity, and this community is "alive in the Holy Spirit." Second, a body is directed by a single mind, which for this community is to be the "mind of Christ." Third, a body is complex in its composition, as is this community with its diverse ethnic backgrounds and gifts of faith. Fourth, a body is unified, which Paul desires his communities to be. He regards this unity not as a uniformity but as the cooperative operation of the diverse parts. Diversity is the prerequisite for unity. So he states, "all the members do not have the same function" (12:4), but they are all to work for the good of the whole body. As in 1 Cor 12:4–11, Paul's emphasis here is on the *diversity* of the gifts, "that differ according to the grace given us" (12:6), just as, for a first instance, it is by the "gift given to him" (12:3), that Paul instructs them this way.

He then provides a partial list of seven such *charismata* within the community (12:6–8). In contrast to the similar lists in 1 Cor 12:8–10 and Eph 4:11–12, the present one attaches qualifiers to each one, which has the effect of emphasizing the *manner* of using the gifts. Some of the gifts mentioned by Paul are common to his communities. Prophecy, for example, is mentioned in several letters (see 1 Cor 12:10; Eph 4:11; 1 Thess 5:20; 1 Tim 1:18) as a gift of speech that uses the mind and convicts the community of God's presence and power (1 Cor 14:24) and thus builds up the community (1 Cor 14:4). Here Paul says that its exercise should be "according to the measure of faith" (the term *analogia* in Greek suggests proportionality). The exercise of prophecy in the assembly, we take it, should be, at the least, an expression of faith, and in all likelihood also speech that builds up the community's faith.

The next three gifts are likewise ministries within the assembly. For each of these, Paul simply notes that they should be carried out as such, e.g., "if serving, in serving." The point seems to be that each one should do one's respective gift and not take on another. Paul uses the language of "service" (*diakonia*) in a variety of ways, as we might expect for a term so broad in its possible applications. In this letter, he uses it for his own ministry of preaching (Rom 11:13), his collection for the saints in Jerusalem (15:31) and for the work of Phoebe (16:1). A separate ministry of "deacons" appears in 1 Tim 3:8, 12, but the "gift of service" may extend beyond that office (see 1 Cor 16:15; 2 Cor 8:4; 9:1; Eph 4:12). The office of teacher (*didaskalos*) is attested in 1 Cor 12:28-29; Eph 4:11; and Jas 3:1. There is no office of "exhorter" (*parakalein*), although the practice is widely attested (1 Cor 14:31; 2 Cor 2:7; 1 Thess 5:11; 1 Tim 5:1). As with service and teaching, the exhorter is told simply to do the gift given.

The next three gifts, in contrast, have moral attitudes attached to their performance. "The one who shares" (*metadidous*) is not listed anywhere as one who practices an office or gift. The term can refer to sharing of any sort; Paul spoke in 1:11 of "sharing a spiritual gift" with the Roman church. In Eph 2:8 and 1 Thess 2:8, Paul uses it for the sharing of material as well as spiritual things, and that seems to be the sense here, particularly since the moral quality attached to it is "with generosity/ simply" used in like combination elsewhere (2 Cor 8:2; 9:11; Jas 1:5). The precise character of the next item listed is not clear. The most obvious way to read *hoi proïstamenoi* is as "those who are in authority," since that is the obvious meaning of the expression in 1 Thess 5:12; 1 Tim 3:4-5; 5:17. They should, says Paul, govern "with eagerness" (*spoudē*; see 2 Cor 7:11-12). The RSV translation, "he who gives aid, with zeal" is possible but appears to me to be overly influenced by the immediate context (acts of "giving" on either side), and by the theological bias that refuses to see any sign of local authority structure in the authentic Pauline letters (see, e.g., M. Y. MacDonald, *The Pauline Churches: A Socio-Historical Study of Institutionalization in the Pauline and Deutero-Pauline Writings* [SNTSMS 60; Cambridge: Cambridge University Press, 1988]). It is better, in my view, to take the text in its obvious sense and conclude that Paul considered "leadership" a legitimate spiritual gift that could be exercised with "eagerness" (compare 1 Cor 12:28), than to stretch the Greek term beyond recognition. That said, the third gift does again pertain to the sharing of material possessions: "the one who shows mercy, with liberality." The term *eleos* ("mercy") has had a heavy theological weight in Paul's argument. It expresses the attitude of compassion, pity, and care for another, especially the mercy God has had toward humans (Rom 9:15, 23; 11:30–31; 15:9). But it is an attitude that expresses itself in specific acts of sharing, as in God's giving his son (5:6–8). For the connection to the sharing of material possessions, see Jas 2:13–16, and for "cheerfulness" in giving, see 2 Cor 9:7.

The next part of Paul's instruction appears as *parenesis* in the technical sense, that is, as traditional moral instruction in the form of commands or maxims (see A. J. Malherbe, *Moral Exhortation: A Greco-Roman Sourcebook* [Philadelphia: Westminster, 1986] 124–29). The sentences are short and disconnected. There is little continuity of thought to be discerned. The opening line (12:9) and the closing (12:21) provide a frame that is classically parenetic: "avoid evil and pursue good." In a sense, Rom 12:9–21 is a Christian virtue list that responds to the vice list that Paul used as the climax of his attack on idolatry in 1:28–31. As with any such list, dissection of the individual items is possible but not necessarily instructive for a sense of the list's function as a whole, which is to provide a certain kind of moral impression.

We notice first that some of these instructions recommend as imperative what in earlier parts of the letter have appeared as indicatives. The most striking example is 12:9–11: "rejoicing in hope, enduring in affliction, persevering in prayer," which virtually repeats the *sorites* in 5:2–3. Likewise, the sequence "unflagging in zeal, aglow with the Spirit, serving in the Lord" picks up the thread of new life in the Spirit that shows itself in obedience to God, which Paul described in 6:4–19.

We see also that in contrast to the arrogance and boasting that were characteristic of life under sin, Paul here stresses a profound spirit of humility. They are to "outdo each other in showing honor" (12:10). Paul also picks up the warning to the Gentiles in 11:25 not to think above themselves, by exhorting, "think the same toward each other, not being haughty [literally: not thinking high things] but associating with the lowly. Do not think above yourselves" (12:16). Although he does not use the noun *tapeinophrosynē* ("lowly-mindedness") here as he does in Phil 2:3, Col 3:12, and Eph 4:2, the combination of *tapeinois* and *phronimoi* creates the same effect. Such "lowly-mindedness" was emphatically *not* a virtue for Greek philosophers, who associated it with a lack of nobility; it was to be "slave-minded" (Epictetus, *Discourses* 1.9.10; 3.24.56). Thus, such "humility" is a genuinely and distinctively "Christian" virtue that takes on its positive valence from the "mind" of one who "took the form of a slave" (Phil 2:5–11).

Having humility means placing oneself appropriately within the life of the community. Indeed, it begins with a sense of otherness, a sensitivity to what is different from oneself. The same sort of mutuality pervades the other virtues that Paul recommends. In contrast to the extreme competitiveness expressed by idolatry's vice list, living with a mind renewed according to the mind of Christ means being in solidarity with others. I have already noted that the only "competition" is to outdo each other in showing honor (12:10)! Most of all, Christians are to identify with the feelings and conditions of others: "rejoice with those who are rejoicing, weep with those who are weeping" (12:15); "love one another with fraternal affection" (12:10). Such instructions are much rarer in Greco-Roman moral instruction, where true virtue was associated with *apatheia* and lack of involvement with the cares of others; for Epictetus, such involvement makes the philosopher much too vulnerable (*Discourses* 3.22.68–76). This interconnectedness of consciousness that we call *compassion* (feeling/suffering together) is inherited from the family sense of Judaism—not, obviously, as a feeling (for the Romans and Greeks had such feelings as much as anyone) but as a moral ideal. Mutuality and commonality are not simply matters of emotion. They involve as well the real sharing of one's possessions with others. Paul exhorts them to "share in the needs of the saints and pursue hospitality" (12:12–13). In the present circumstances, Paul may have urged this with special concern, since he was at that moment involved in the "collection for the saints in Jerusalem" and expected hospitality from the Roman church! But he is also reinforcing the early Christian ideal of sharing that was radical and unequivocal (see L. T. Johnson, *Sharing Possessions: Mandate and Symbol of Faith* [Overtures to Biblical Theology; Philadelphia: Fortress, 1981]).

Most impressively in contrast to the malice and violence found in the earlier vice list (. . . envy, murder, strife, malignancy . . . heartlessness, ruthlessness . . .) are the exhortations to resist any form of retribution even against those who first do wrong to them. As the final statement in the section has it, they are not to be overcome by evil but are to overcome evil with good (12:21). Thus, they are not to "repay evil with evil" (12:17), but insofar as they are able are "to maintain peace with all people" (12:18; see 5:1). Specifically, this means not seeking revenge (12:19). Here we come to the test case for this Christian morality based in the work and character and death of Jesus the messiah. The moral code of the ancient world—that of both Judaism and Hellenism—recognized the validity of having enemies and of paying back harm done to oneself or one's loved ones. Paul does not allow it. He counters the all-too-natural desire for revenge by an appeal first to the power of God who is judge. They are to "make room for the wrath," which echoes the statement concerning "the wrath of God being revealed from heaven against all ungodliness" in 1:18. The seeking of revenge is unnecessary, says Paul, because it is in the hands of God: "Vengeance is mine, I will repay, says the Lord." Paul is quoting Deut 32:35, and in this case, his citation is closer to the Hebrew than to the LXX, which has, "In a day of vengeance I will repay." We will see shortly how Paul will also connect "the wrath" to the power of the empire.

Instead of seeking revenge, they are to provide for their enemies' needs. We are reminded of Matthew's parable of the Final Judgment (Matt 25:31–46), except that these instructions go much further. Here it is an enemy (*echthros*) whose hunger is to be relieved by the believer's feeding him, and an enemy's thirst that is slaked by the believer's giving him to drink (12:20). Paul is here drawing on the exhortation found in Prov 25:21 and includes this line, "by so doing, you will heap burning coals on his head" (12:20; see Prov 25:22). The image is certainly obscure. Does it mean that such generosity is itself a form of punishment? Does it mean that the enemy will be shamed into repentance? We simply do not know, for the image is derived from a cultural world alien to our own whose code in this case we do not know. But perhaps Paul also wants to elicit a memory of this following verse from Proverbs, which says that when a person acts that way, "God will repay you with good things" (Prov 25:22).

Submission to Civil Authorities (13:1–7)

This is another passage hard for present-day readers to grasp or appreciate, for two reasons. The first is that it reflects a view of government that is totally foreign to those living on this side of the Enlightenment, and in particular of that political child of the Enlightenment, the American Revolution. The second is that the attitudes of submission and respect here inculcated have been used to justify totalitarian and wicked regimes and, in the eyes of most late-twentieth-century readers, are dangerous attitudes to have toward any civil rule. In short, this passage carries with it the same negative associations for present-day readers as those other Pauline passages that deal with social realities no longer in practice or favor, such as the "tables of household ethics" in Col 3:18–4:1 and Eph 5:21–6:9.

In order to cut through some of these (very understandable) difficulties, it is necessary to take more than usual care with this passage, trying first to place it in its literary and cultural contexts, then clarifying its instructions, and finally assessing its hermeneutical implications (see also E. Käsemann, "Principles of Interpretation of Romans 13," in *New Testament Questions of Today* [Philadelphia: Fortress, 1969] 196–216).

The resemblance to the tables of household ethics is not accidental. This passage belongs to the same category of Hellenistic moral discourse. Since the time of Xenophon, Plato, and Aristotle, philosophers had written tractates on household management (*peri oikonomias*), seeking to define moral responsibilities within the social order (see D. L. Balch, *Let Wives Be Submissive: The Domestic Code in 1 Peter* [SBLMS 26; Chico: Scholars Press, 1981]). Throughout the Mediterranean world since the time of Alexander the Great (mid-fourth century B.C.E.), that social order had been remarkably uniform. Its basic unit was the household (*oikos*), consisting of the "father of the family" (*paterfamilias*), his wife, their children, and various others: slaves, clients, retainers, friends. It was an extended rather than a nuclear family. In terms of power, authority ran from the top down, and in terms of dynamics, every lower order showed respect and submission to the upper levels: wife to husband, children to parents, slaves to masters, clients to patrons (see K. R. Bradley, *Discovering the Roman Family* [New York: Oxford University Press, 1991]). The same sort of basic structure also shaped the larger social order. In Paul's day, there were still city-states, but they were no longer the focus of identity the way they had been in classical Greece. Since Alexander, the Mediterranean world was dominated by empire, which in turn was envisaged in terms of a great household (*oikoumenē*), over which the emperor reigned supreme as imperial *paterfamilias*. Like the head of the family, the emperor was patron from whom all goods ultimately derived; like the head of the family, the emperor was owed respect, gratitude, and, above all, submission (see A. Wallace-Hadrill, ed., *Patronage in Ancient Society* [London: Routledge, 1989]).

For those of us on this side of the Enlightenment, it is critical to grasp something about the ancient world that is most strange to us. The very thing that we *most* take for granted, namely, that the social order is *changeable* and should be changed according to the will of its participants (that governments exist by the consent of the governed), is a premise that would have been rejected as outlandish, not only in ancient Rome but also in virtually every nation before the revolutions in the West spawned by the Enlightenment. As children of revolution, in other words, we literally live within a different perception of the social world.

For Paul and his contemporaries, the idea of *changing* the given social order would have been unthinkable. The social order was as stable as nature. Indeed, it was considered "natural." This form of household had been in place for as long as anyone had a record (whether in Greece or ancient Israel). The form of the state (the empire) had existed (in Paul's time) for more than four hundred years—and, let us remember, would survive in the western Mediterranean for hundreds more years, and would carry on virtually unchanged in the eastern Mediterranean for fifteen hundred years. Yes, there were slave revolts; yes, there were wars of national revolt (like that soon to break out in Palestine); but to most these seemed like acts of impiety. Yes, some urban women had, on the basis of a slave population, gained greater freedom of movement and a limited range of options beyond the domestic, but whenever it was felt that the social fabric itself was tearing, there was cause for concern on every side. The social order of household and empire was "according to nature," just as heterosexual relations were. When Paul declares that ruling authority is under God, therefore, he is making—in that time and place—a completely unexceptional statement.

Historical criticism has done a great service by identifying these ancient social realities. Otherwise, present-day readers might think that the New Testament was revealing God's blueprint for the perfect family or the ideal state. We know, of course, that many people *do* read the New Testament just this way, often under the guise of taking the text seriously. In fact, however, to read the text that way is not to take it seriously enough. What New Testament writers such as Paul and Peter were doing in their remarks on households was the same thing a moralist such as Hierocles did in his work *On Duties*—attempting, within a given social order, to define the obligations imposed by that order on the person who wished to be virtuous. Such reflection was necessary because, despite the fact that everyone recognized the social order as natural, it was clear that some of its instruments were not: fathers could be vicious; emperors could be tyrants. Thus, Epictetus could recognize the empire's power to seize his body (and himself lived in exile), but he refused to submit to anyone the judgments of his mind.

Readers today should not, therefore, be shocked at the fundamentally conservative and positive view of the imperial state reflected in 1 Tim 2:1-2; Titus 3:1; 1 Pet 2:13-16, and the present passage. Despite the fact that Jesus was executed under Pontius Pilate, the New Testament is remarkably free of rancor or resentment toward the empire. Early Christians may also have seen the Roman order as a refuge against the vagaries of local resentments and riots. Jews in Egypt turned confidently to the emperor for help when subjected to local abuse (see Philo, *Against Flaccus; Embassy to Gaius*). When Paul was arrested in Jerusalem, only appeal to Caesar enabled him to escape the plots of local Jewish opponents (Acts 25:11).

At the time he wrote Romans, Paul probably saw the empire as the enabler of the Christian mission, and therefore as an instrument of God's will for the salvation of all humans. Rome was in fact remarkably tolerant of religious diversity among its many subject peoples, so long as these did not threaten Roman rule. This explains why Rome would protect Jews against local riots in Alexandria, yet carry out merciless war against Jews in Palestine. It was entirely a matter of imperial control. So long as Christians appeared like diaspora Jews, then, they could enjoy the same sorts of protections as other recognized ethnic cults.

But there were also radical impulses within the Christian movement that potentially had larger social implications. To what extent could the idea of an egalitarian community (neither Jew nor Greek, neither male nor female, neither slave nor free, Gal 3:28), be translated into social expression in the household or city before generating notice and repression? To what extent would Rome tolerate the sort of angry attack on the empire found in Revelation 17–18? Writing to Christians in the imperial city, and knowing as he did Aquila and Priscilla, Paul was aware that Jews had only short years before been expelled from Rome, "at the instigation of Chrestus" (see Introduction), and perhaps wanted to make sure that his own mission (which he hoped would find a sponsor in that city) would not be perceived as one hostile to the imperial order, even though it had to do with Jews and this same "Chrestus."

But why does he take up the question of the empire at this precise place, disconnected from any other "household ethics"? The answer, I think, is to be found in the immediate context. As we have seen so often in this letter, something Paul says leads to the need for a clarification. Already in 1:18, he had spoken of "God's wrath" being revealed against wrongdoers, and he showed how their sins brought grief upon themselves. Then, in 12:19, he had forbidden Christians to take revenge on those who harmed them, telling them to "give place to the wrath," and telling them that God would take care of vengeance on those who hurt them. The question then arises, How is God's wrath to come against those who do the sort of public wrong that cries out for revenge, if Christians are themselves not to retaliate? This question leads Paul to the governing order and the role he sees it playing in God's plans.

Paul's instruction in 13:1 and 13:5 to "be submissive" is not, in light of this analysis, surprising. It is a recommendation that made perfect sense in a world where status and rank were so carefully defined and observed, and in which failure to be "submissive" in the appropriate circumstances could threaten the existence of the community. Nor would many have taken exception to Paul's assertion that "there is no authority except from God and those that exist have been instituted by God." There is some textual disagreement here: some manuscripts have *apo* ("from God"), while others have *hypo* ("by God"), but the basic meaning is the same, namely, God authorizes the given social system. For a comparable Hellenistic Jewish view, see the Wisdom of Solomon 6:1–6, which, despite threatening punishment of rulers for unjust actions, begins with the recognition that: "your dominion was given you by the Lord, and your sovereignty from the Most High" (Wis 6:3). From such a perspective, it also follows that resistance to the order of society is construed as resistance to God, which will incur punishment (Rom 13:2).

Paul, however, goes beyond mere recognition of the social order as derived from God's authority. Like 1 Peter, he expresses a positive evaluation of the way in which the government actually functions. In short, the state rewards the good and punishes the wicked. If one does not want to fear the state, all one need do is be good (13:3). Now any number of people through the ages would have good reason to challenge Paul's assessment. Many governments, however noble in structure, have been tyrannical and unjust in practice; far from rewarding the good and punishing the wicked, they have made a habit of doing the opposite. Paul's statements, in fact, are possible (and tolerable) only in a situation in which the rule of law is in fact basically benevolent. And for all its excesses, the Roman state could be so regarded, particularly at the time Paul was writing. Certainly, Paul could not have made such statements if Christians had been persecuted by the state simply for being Christians. When the state—as already in the case of the Maccabean martyrs—demands ultimate allegiance to itself, then Paul's statements are simply wrong and must be identified as such.

Even more troublesome, however, is the fact that Paul goes a step further. He declares the governing authority to be a "minister of God" (*diakonos tou theou*) who has the job of "executing [God's] wrath on the wrongdoer" (13:4). Paul himself may well have been both innocent and sincere in his assessment. It may have appeared to him that wicked people would also be illegal people and that the state could ferret them out. Thus, the state could do the work of "God's wrath" and allow the Christians not to practice revenge. He could not, I am sure, have envisaged a "Christian empire" that would use the same sword to eliminate its religious dissenters. But his statement does pave the way for a theocratic state (when Christianity becomes the official religion of the empire), and the use of the imperial "sword" (13:4) to punish those "wrongdoers" who in a "Christian empire" are guilty only of having the wrong theology but must be eliminated as heretics for the good of the state.

Paul cannot be held responsible for his practical advice later being taken as divine revelation and as the basis for a Christian theology of the state. That is too much weight for a few words of contingent remarks to bear. The tragedy of Christian history both in the East and the West is that they have been made to bear that weight. Perhaps the most problematic aspect of passage is Paul's advice in 13:5, "therefore one must be subject, not only to avoid God's wrath, but also for the sake of conscience (*syneidēsis*)." As I have noted, even conservative moralists such as Epictetus distinguished between societal obedience and internal consent. The conscience is precisely what no human authority can command. Paul's words, therefore, must be taken in their broadest possible application—"it is a matter of con-science to be a good and responsible citizen of the social order in which you find yourself"—if they are not to be taken as a frightening capitulation to authoritarianism. If he means by "on account of conscience," simply "because it's the right thing to do," that is one thing, but if he means "because one's conscience must submit to the will of the ruling authorities," then he is clearly wrong.

I think it safe to say that Paul does not here advocate submitting one's conscience to the ruling authorities, for that would contradict his insis-tence on the integrity of the individual's conscience in 1 Corinthians 8 and Romans 14. Therefore, the phrase "on account of conscience" must bear the broader sense I have suggested, "because it is the right thing to do." This becomes clearer when Paul specifies as an example the paying of taxes, although once more the religious coloration he gives this is startling to those of us convinced of the desirability of separating religion and the state: "the authorities are ministers of God attending to this very thing" (13:6).

Paul's final statement in this passage is summary in character: "give to everyone who is owed," which is a fair epitome of the approach to social ethics in antiquity. Not the reform of the social order, but "doing what is required" (*ta kathēkonta*) within it. Paul enumerates as examples payment of three kinds: taxes, respect (or "fear"), and honor. In a word, Paul sketches the Christian's relation to the larger world in terms of a basic accommoda-tion to its structures. The passage expresses no reservation as to the limits of such accommodation or where "conscience" might need to choose between what God wills and what the state demands.

What are the hermeneutical implications of Rom 13:1-7 for present-day readers? In many ways, the issues are the same for this passage as for the other "domestic code" passages with which it is cognate.

1. It is a misreading to take Rom 13:1-7 as the revelation of a distinctively Christian view of the state. It is no such thing. Paul is simply responding to a social order that, so far as he can see, is as "natural" as relations between the sexes. The contemporary perception that either one or the other could be changed was unavailable to him.

2. Just as it is important to recognize the time-conditioned and relative character of Paul's perception, so is it equally necessary to recognize that our own post-Enlightenment perspective on the state is also time-conditioned and relative. Our view of society is no more self-evidently "correct" than is Paul's. Just as we now think it is "natural" for people to have a choice of who governs, so did people up to the Enlightenment (and beyond!) think that society is most naturally governed from the top down.

3. The two perspectives can be usefully brought into conversation,

together with all the other voices of the New Testament canon, of tradition, and of experience, as present-day Christians sort through the appropriate way to align their commitment to a crucified and raised messiah with the reality of the larger social order. The value of a variety of voices in the conversation is precisely that they tell us two things simultaneously: that the problem is real and won't go away and that there are a number of legitimate ways of approaching it.

4. Just as Paul's perceptions can be read in a conservative fashion, so can they be read more radically to the opposite effect. If all civil authority is from God and ordered under God, then it equally follows that a civil authority that does not respond to God's will can be considered disqualified as a true authority, and so could be resisted "for conscience's sake." If, for example, a state, such as that in Germany under the Nazis, arrogated to itself ultimate powers *over* conscience or punished those who did no wrong except following their conscience, then, as Christians such as Dietrich Bonhoeffer concluded, "for conscience' sake" such a regime can be actively opposed.

5. Even when all that is said, Rom 13:1–7 has had such a negative history of interpretation and has been put to such wrong use that it remains a passage that must be engaged with considerable delicacy and caution. Simply "reading it off the page" as a directive for life is to misread it and to distort it, for the world in which it made self-evident sense no longer exists and never can again.

The Law of Love (13:8–10)

Paul began his "Christian virtue list" in 12:9 with the exhortation "Let love be sincere," and he concludes his sketch of Christian social obligations with a fuller and richer affirmation of love (*agapē*) as the central Christian moral principle. His statement "owe (*opheilete*) no one anything except to love one another" (13:8) appears to be triggered by his immediately preceding direction to "pay all of them what is owed (*tas opheilas*)" (13:7), but moves in a different direction. In the first case, "what is owed" is formal social obligations: taxes, honor, respect, tolls. The social order can demand these and get them. But the conscience (*syneidēsis*) is not *obliged* by them in the same way it is by the demand for mutual love.

The reason is to be found in the constituting experience of the community. God has shown forth his *agapē* by giving his son while they were yet sinners (5:8); Jesus "loved them" and gave himself for them (8:37); the love of God has been poured out into their hearts through the Holy Spirit (5:5); they are "beloved" (*agapētoi*) of God (1:7, 12; 12:9); nothing can separate them from the *agapē* of Christ (8:35), from the *agapē* of God in Christ Jesus (8:39). If God's *agapē*—his effective and disinterested disposition for their good—has created them as a community, then on the principle of *agens sequitur esse* (acting follows upon being), they must be a community characterized above all by the same quality, are "obliged" to be a community that "walks in *agapē*" (14:15).

There is no need to review the centrality of *agapē* in all the writings of the New Testament (see C. Spicq, *Agapē in the New Testament*, trans. M. A. McNamara and M. A. Richter [New York: Herder, 1963]). The expression "love one another," finds its closest parallel in 1 Pet 1:22 and 1 John 3:11. Although his phrasing is distinctive, Paul is also very much in the mainstream of early Christian tradition by his identifying the love of neighbor as the epitome of Torah. In the Synoptic Gospels (Matt 22:37–39; Mark 12:30–31; Luke 10:27), Jesus responds to a question concerning the central commandment of Torah with the two love commandments: the love of God with the whole mind and heart and soul (Deut 6:6), and the love of neighbor as the self (Lev 19:18). These questions and answers reflect attempts being made in Judaism to find the heart of Torah in a smaller number of commandments (see *b. Makkoth* 24a). In *The Sentences of Pseudo-Phocylides*, the decalogue and Leviticus 19 seem to represent such a summarization. In the Letter of James, likewise, we find together the combination of the decalogue and the command of love from Lev 19:18, which is explicitly called "the law of the kingdom" (Jas 2:8; see L. T. Johnson, "The Use of Leviticus 19 in the Letter of James," *Journal of Biblical Literature* 101 [1982]: 391–401). In Gal 5:13-14, Paul uses language close to our present passage: "for you have been called to freedom, brethren; only don't use your freedom as an opportunity for the flesh, but through love (*agapē*) serve one another. For the whole law (*pas nomos*) is brought to fulfillment (*peplērōtai*) in one word, in 'Love your neighbor as yourself.'"

The present passage in Romans is worth looking at closely if only because its language is so full. Paul has said that nothing should be owed each other except love, "for the one who loves has fulfilled the other law" (13:8). My translation differs dramatically from the RSV, which has, "for he who loves the neighbor has fulfilled the law." Such a translation is possible, but it demands translating the Greek *heteros* ("other") as "neighbor." I prefer the more natural rendering of the grammar of *to heteron nomon peplērōken*, "has fulfilled the other law," by which Paul means Torah. That this is precisely Paul's point is made clear by his recitation of four of the ten commandments: "you shall not commit adultery, you shall not murder, you shall not steal, you shall not covet."

Two points need to be made about this listing of commands from Exod 20:13-17 and Deut 5:17-21. The first is that the order of the commandments follows the sequence given in the LXX rather than in the Hebrew text, thus making Paul's resemblance to Jas 2:11 even more striking. The second is the intriguing fact that Paul has placed in the climactic position the command "you shall not covet," which he had taken in 7:7-10 as the commandment that "the flesh" had taken advantage of to make sin conscious. Certainly, the movement of *agapē* as one that seeks the good of the other by giving of the self is the exact opposite of that *epithymia* which seeks to ground the self by grasping what is another's.

Paul next explains how love of neighbor "fulfills the other law." These diverse commandments ("and any other commandment") are "summarized" by this single one: "You shall love your neighbor as yourself" (Lev 19:18). The Greek term *anakephalaiesthai* means literally "to bring to a head." It can accurately be translated as "summarize," but we see in Eph 1:10 how it can also mean "bring to a fullness." A summary, then, is not always simply an epitome. In this case, Paul means that it is the adequate expression of everything that "the other law" was trying to get at: "love does not do evil to a neighbor; it is therefore the fulfillment (*plērōma*) of law" (13:10). To love therefore is to "fulfill the just requirement of the law (*to dikaiōma tou nomou*," 8:3). Paul's phrasing is particularly striking. In 10:4, he had declared, "Christ is the *telos* of the law," and here, "love is the *plērōma* of the law." The two statements are not contradictory but mutually reinforcing.

By this summary, Paul points the way for the Christian appropriation of Torah. Torah will be regarded as the word of God and as God's revelation. Its authority will be regarded as real but not absolute. Its full significance can be found only with reference to its *telos*, which is God's gift in Christ. Its commandments are obligatory insofar as they express love of neighbor. In this fashion, Christians eventually work out a distinction in Torah between "ritual commandments" that are symbolically meaningful but are not to be observed and "moral commandments" that retain their force as expressions of love.

Eschatological Urgency (13:11–14)

This entire section of moral instruction has been framed on one side by the call to the transformation of consciousness in 12:1-2, and this eschatological reminder in 13:11-14. Both stress a separation from "the frame of this world" and a change into a new identity. What is distinctive to the present passage is its tone of urgency. As in similar passages (see 1 Thess 5:4-11; Eph 6:10-20; 2 Cor 6:2-10), we find certain standard contrasts: day and night (13:12), darkness and light (13:12), sleeping and waking (13:11), drunkenness and sobriety (13:13). We find also the call to take up spiritual warfare (13:12). This is the language of conversion, but also that of moral alertness and growth.

The passage most resembles 2 Cor 6:2 in its emphasis on the urgency of such transformation in view of the "time" or "season." In that place, Paul quotes Isa 49:8, "At the acceptable time, I have listened to you, and helped you on the day of salvation," and applies it: "Behold now is the acceptable time, behold, now is the time of salvation." Such also is his point here: "for now salvation is closer than when we came to have faith" (13:11). But what does Paul mean by salvation being closer? Does Paul here anticipate the end of history, the coming of Jesus to free them from the approaching wrath (1 Thess 1:10; 4:13–16)? Is he suggesting that "the time is very short," and "the frame of this world is passing away" (1 Cor 7:29–31)? Such a reading is possible.

But is this what the passage means within the context of the argument of Romans concerning the good news as "the power for salvation for Jews and Greeks" (1:16)? I have argued that in this letter, Paul thinks of *sōtēria* as the process of forming the people of God out of Jews and Gentiles. Paul's eschatological language in 8:18–23 had exactly that point of reference. He spoke of the birth pangs of all creation awaiting "the revelation of the children of God," an event that appears to take place in a this-worldly context. If Paul's mission is in service of bringing about *this* salvation, that is, the revelation of God's people within creation, then its "being closer than when we first came to faith" is not so much a statement about the end of history as it is an optimistic prognosis concerning the success of God's cause through his ministry.

In this light, the call to the reformation of morals is not a matter of "repent before it is too late," but a matter of "live according to the identity you have been given, for the formation of the entire Israel is closer than you thought, and this people needs to be holy, root and branch." Paul intimated in 11:15 that this social realization of "salvation" would mean "life from the dead," and it is not at all unthinkable that he could also conceive of it as ushering in the age to come and the full triumph of God (see J. Munck, *Paul and the Salvation of Mankind*, trans. F. Clarke [Richmond: John Knox Press, 1959]).

The language of "taking off" and "putting on" clothes as a metaphor for change in identity (13:12–14) may well be connected to the Christian practice of baptism, which in all likelihood involved the putting aside of old garments and being clothed in new ones upon arising from the water, as a symbol of the "new humanity" being adopted (see Gal 3:27; Col 3:8–10; Eph 4:22-25; Jas 1:21;1 Pet 2:1). Certainly the imagery corresponds to that of "dying and rising with Christ" in 6:3–4, also connected to baptism. It has as well the same moral implication. In 6:3-4, Paul told them to "walk in newness of life," and here, "let us walk becomingly as in the day."

The "works of the night" (13:12) that they are to put off—that is, reject—are summarized by another short vice list with only six elements. The first four are apparently fitted to the imagery as the sorts of things one does "at night," that is, vices of drinking and sexual excess. The last two, however, "quarreling and jealousy," remind us that "the darkness" is not literal but a moral metaphor; such vices of hostility thrive in the day as well as in the night. These last two items also provide a transition to Paul's next discussion, which will pick up "disputes and opinions, scorn and judgment" within the context of the community's practical life.

He tells them to "put on the armor of light," reminding us of the military images of 2 Cor 6:7; 10:3-4; Eph 6:11, 13-17. The symbol of light provides the obvious contrast to nighttime vice. It is also probably connected to the ritual of baptism (see Eph 5:8-9, 14; 1 Pet 2:9; 2 Tim 1:10; Heb 6:4). The connection to baptism seems the more likely because Paul immediately resumes the image of "clothing oneself" in 13:14: "But put on the Lord Jesus Christ and make no provision for the flesh to satisfy its desires." By this point in our reading of Romans, I hope it is clear what "the desires of the flesh" are in Paul's lexicon. He does not mean simply the failures of weakness such as come from addiction and craving, but all those malign manifestations of arrogance and self-aggrandizement that are associated with idolatry and sin. Paul's readers are not to "exercise any foresight" for this pattern of life. They are, instead, to adopt wholeheartedly the identity they have been given by faith and baptism into the community." Putting on the Lord Jesus Christ" here exactly matches the command to "be transformed by the renewal of the mind" in 12:2. Paul will spell out in 14:1–15:13 the implications of living "according to the mind of Christ" in community.

RIGHTEOUSNESS IN THE CHRISTIAN COMMUNITY

Romans 14:1–15:13

P aul turns from the general moral principles he laid out in 12:1–13:14 to a specific community situation. What does "putting on the Lord Jesus Christ" (13:14) and "owing nothing to anyone except to love one another" (13:8) mean in practice? This chapter picks up Paul's argument in chapters 9–11 and brings it to a grand conclusion in 15:1–13. The function of chapters 12–13, as we have seen, has been to shape a certain kind of moral consciousness that can, in practical circumstances, "test what is the good, the pleasing, and perfect" (12:2). Now down to cases.

The biggest interpretive issue posed by the present chapter is whether Paul is addressing specific problems in the Roman community, and these problems are of such seriousness as to have motivated the entire composition (see Introduction). It is necessary first, then, to assess the situation as described by Paul, before analyzing his response.

The Situation

Are Paul's comments directed to a real situation or a hypothetical one? Is the condition he describes of a critical sort for this community, or is it chronic in the culturally pluralistic messianic movement? In my reading, I side with those who see Paul's remarks as "hypothetical/typical," and as a reflection on the chronic issues facing the first urban Christians, rather than as a specific response to a crisis in the Roman church or churches.

My support for this position begins with the observation that his description lacks specific detail, compared to the description of crises in Galatia and Corinth. In the Galatian churches, Gentile converts were divided on the issue of circumcision, behind which lay a "judaizing" agenda. The implication was that to be a full-fledged member of the people, full observance of the commandments of Torah was required. Although Paul apparently does not know the identity of the agitators, he is quite clear that the debate concerns Jew and Gentile (Gal 2:14; 4:8), that the specific practice of circumcision was being advocated (5:2; 6:12), and with it the demand to observe Torah (3:12, 24; 4:5, 21; 5:1), together with the observance of "days and months and seasons and years" (4:10). As for the gravity of crisis, Paul places those who upset the Galatians under a curse (1:8-9), hopes that they mutilate themselves (5:12), and implies that they be driven from the community (4:30). This is a Jew–Gentile controversy with a vengeance! How does Paul's language in Romans compare?

1. The Jew–Gentile aspect is muted (see 15:8). Instead, there is an inadequate distinction between those who are "weak in faith" (14:1, 2, 21; 15:1) and those who are "strong" (15:1). The language is similar to that used in 1 Cor 8:7, 9, 10, 11-12 but also picks up from the present composition the "weakness" that was caused by the "flesh" (8:3) and characterized those for whom Christ died (5:6), but was *not* part of Abraham's response in faith (4:19).

2. Circumcision is not an issue.

3. There is nothing said about the necessity of keeping Torah as a condition for salvation.

4. The problem is described as one involving "disputes over opinions," or perhaps, "disputes between opinions," signaling from the start that Paul does not regard the opinions themselves as bearing the weight of fundamental principle.

5. Paul is entirely vague as to the specific differences of opinion. He gives two examples: the main one is differences in diet (some eat everything; the weak eat only vegetables; 14:2, 15, 17, 20); the other is observance of special days (some think one day better; others esteem all days alike, 14:5-6). These differences *can* be correlated to Jew–Gentile differences, with the special day being the sabbath or other Jewish festivals, and the eating of vegetables as an avoidance of meat offered to idols. The point is, however, that Paul's language is so general that, in contrast to Galatians, the connections need to be made by the reader.

6. If there are "parties" (which is not clear), there is no coercive action being taken by one group against another. Instead, Paul points to the kind of "psychological warfare" that is all too recognizable in intentional communities: the strong "despise" the weak and the weak "judge" the strong (14:3).

7. In contrast to the strong action Paul could take in critical cases (see

1 Cor 5:1-5; 2 Thess 3:14), his recommendations here are extremely mild, amounting to a plea for mutual understanding and acceptance (15:7).

The other obvious passage to compare with this one is Paul's discussion of food offered to idols in 1 Corinthians 8-10. Much of what Paul says here corresponds to the positions stated in that letter. But in 1 Corinthians, once more, he is responding to information sent him in a letter from the community (1 Cor 7:1) or reported orally by members of the church (1:11). It is clear from Paul's vigorous directions in 1 Corinthians 5-6 that the church is on the verge of breakup as a consequence of severe disagreement on moral matters, since it has even seen members suing each other in pagan courts over what Paul calls *ta biōtika* ("matters of everyday life"). We know, therefore, that Paul is responding to specific and controverted practices. His discussion is correspondingly "thicker" than in Romans 14. He specifically mentions "eating of food offered to idols" (8:4, 7) such as is sold at a meat market (10:23), and being invited to an unbeliever's table as a guest (10:27), and even "sitting at table in an idol's temple" (8:10). In 1 Corinthians 10, furthermore, he warns against the worship of idols (10:14) and drinking "the cup of demons" at the "table of demons" (10:21). And the entire discussion is explicitly connected to Jew-Gentile differences: "Give no offense to Jews or to Greeks, or to the church of God" (10:32).

In contrast, nothing in Paul's description of the situation or his response to it suggests that here he has been informed of a local crisis and is seeking to remedy it. It appears far more likely that Paul has used his experience of the Galatian and Corinthian controversies as a backdrop for a reflection on the dimensions of "life together" in a culturally pluralistic world.

His missionary effort has been to bring Gentiles "salvation," that is, to bring them within the people of God. His great collection effort is being carried out to reconcile these Gentile communities with the Jewish church in Jerusalem, perhaps in the desire to show what a great "harvest" God had drawn from the Gentiles, so that his fellow Jews might seek to emulate them and be regrafted onto the people God was forming around the messiah Jesus. These experiences and convictions have led him to make the theological argument that God's righteousness can be at once universal in principle (so that all can respond by faith) yet particular in expression (in the historical interplay of Jew and Gentile). Now, in the life of any community made up of Jews and Gentiles, the issue of unity and diversity must be worked out together. In a very real sense, Paul is engaging here the issue that is in the present day referred to as multiculturalism. How can people share a certain unifying community identity without having to lose completely their particular cultural heritage? Which differences divide and disable the community, and which ones should be celebrated as enriching it? How much diversity can a specific community tolerate before it disintegrates? And how can the community discern which practices are essential to its life and which ones are not?

In my view, Paul here uses the examples drawn from his own pastoral experience in Galatia and Corinth to address this problem of unity and diversity, which is the practical expression of the issue of universality and particularity. It probably did exist in the Roman community in some fashion, as it must exist in every community that draws its members from multiple cultural backgrounds. The question, then, is how the transformation of the mind and the putting on of the Lord Jesus Christ and owing each other nothing but love translate into specific attitudes and actions for a community where people do things that are culturally offensive to one another.

Judgment, Scorn, Acceptance (14:1–12)

Paul pays practically no attention to the actual differences in practice, indicating to his readers at once that this is not the real issue. Instead, he focuses on the attitudes accompanying the actions. His psychological grasp of group dynamics is sound. The "weak in faith" (14:1) are those who are "not convinced in their own mind" (14:5) about what they are doing. Such lack of confidence in their own convictions (or in God's acceptance) can lead to the strict observance of rules. One needs boundaries that are external to the self in order to know and control where one is—there is then no need to risk either one's own freedom or trust in acceptance by another. But the self-protection given by strict observance of rules can also generate an attitude of judgment and condemnation of others, particularly those who do not obey the rules (14:3). The opposite attitude is that of the "strong" (15:1), for they are convinced in their own mind, and such knowledge gives them freedom to be flexible and creative, responsive to situations as they arise rather than needing the guidance of precedent. Unfortunately such freedom can also lead to a negative attitude. Those whose knowledge makes them free can often feel and express contempt for those whose fear keeps them confined by conventions (14:3). The attitudes Paul identifies are amazingly contemporary—or perhaps are simply perennial for intentional communities. Who has not lived in a community in which "conservatives" who swear by the law stand in judgment on the "liberals," and the liberals who glory in their freedom hold the conservatives in disdain? For Paul, it is not so much the practice but the attitudes that lead to "quarreling and jealousy" (see 13:13).

Paul's response draws on his entire theological argument to this point. From the start, he has associated the sort of judgment that humans make against each other on the basis of their superior virtue with arrogance and boasting (see 2:1). Humans are not accountable to each other but are answerable to God. Paul affirms again the basic point of 2:16, that God who knows human hearts will judge all people: "We will all stand before the judgment seat of God. For it is written, 'As I live,' says the Lord, 'Every knee shall bow to me and every tongue shall give praise to God'" (14:11). The passage from Isa 45:23 that forms the heart of this citation (with the "as I live" influenced by passages like Isa 49:18) is preceded by the statement that "righteousness shall go out from my mouth." A very high number of Paul's citations in Romans have "righteousness" lurking somewhere in their original context! Paul then adds that "each person will have to give his own account to God" (14:12). Because God alone knows human hearts and judges the dispositions of the heart (including whether they "are convinced in their minds") freedom of conscience must be maintained, and humans are forbidden to judge each other on the basis of appearances.

God is not only a "fair judge" but also a "righteous" judge, who has reached out to reconcile those who had been "weak" and "sinners" to himself (see 5:6). The community should also therefore act on this principle of the strong reaching out to the weak. They should "welcome" (*proslambanein*) the person who is "weak in faith" (14:1), because "God has welcomed him" (14:3). The community, in short, should act with a bias toward acceptance rather than toward rejection, because God has "redeemed" back each member of the community, and each one is now God's "household servant" (14:4) to present his members in obedience to God (see 6:13-19). No one else in the community is privy to this relationship or in a position to judge it: "Who are you to judge someone else's household servant? He stands or falls before his own master, and he will stand, for the master is able to make him stand" (14:4). The principle Paul expounds here is close to that found in Jas 4:11-12: "Do not slander each other my brothers. The one who slanders or judges a brother slanders and judges the law. There is one lawgiver and judge, the one who is able to save and destroy. Who are you to judge your neighbor?"

Paul's language about the master enabling the servant to "stand" must also be read in the light of 5:2: "through him we have obtained access to this gift *in which we stand*. . . ." God's "welcoming" of those who were weak and sinful was through the death and resurrection of Jesus (5:6-10). Those therefore who have "put on the Lord Jesus Christ" (13:14) should live within the awareness of the new relationships this gift has brought about. The best way to decipher Paul's rich thought here is to read 14:7-9 in reverse order. Christ died and came to life, Paul says, for this reason, that he might rule [that is, "be Lord over"] the dead and the living (14:9). Here Paul states clearly the cosmic lordship of Christ that is implicit in 2:16; 5:21; and

8:37-39. It follows, then, that humans belonging to Christ have *their* life and death defined with reference to this Lord: "If we live, we live for the Lord, and if we die, we die for the Lord; if we live therefore or die, we belong to the Lord" (14:8). And if *this* is so, then the principle that Paul enunciates in 14:7 takes on considerable significance: "None of us lives for the self, and none of us dies for the self."

Human existence is from now on defined not in terms of solipsistic self-interest but in terms of relatedness to God, to the Lord Jesus, and to those who belong to this Lord. What has this to do with eating certain foods or observing certain days? For Paul, the essential point is not the doing or not doing but whether either is done "for God" and "in thanksgiving to God" (14:6). But "not living for the self" also changes our understanding of life together. We learn that righteousness is not a matter of "being right" but a matter of "being in right relationship."

Scandal and Edification (14:13–23)

In this next part of Paul's response, the observance of days falls away completely, leaving only the issue of diet under discussion. This makes it even more likely that the discussion as a whole derives from Paul's reflection on his previous experience in Corinth rather than from specific problems in the Roman community. Indeed, Paul's exposition at this point closely resembles that in 1 Corinthians 8-10. Intellectually, Paul agrees with the "strong" position: "I know and am persuaded in Christ Jesus that nothing is profane in itself, but if a person reckons it profane, it is profane for that person" (14:14). Paul does not give any sign that he is aware of the statement in Mark 7:19 that Jesus declared all things clean, but "in Christ Jesus" he has come to the same conclusion.

This is a stunning step forward for Paul the Pharisee. The Pharisaic movement was notable for its strictness with regard to matters of purity, the determination of which things, foods, places, and people were either "clean" (*katharos*) or "profane" (*koinos*). Large portions of the rabbinic law code called the *Mishnah* are taken up by minute discriminations on just such matters (e.g., *Mishnah Tohoroth*). Such distinctions were, with very few exceptions, based on qualities thought to be inherent in the objects— either what it was or what it had come in contact with (see *m. Neg.* 1:1-3:8). The mishnaic system of purity created a *cordon sanitaire* around the Jewish community, ensuring its "otherness" as well as protecting it against infringements against the weightier commandments (see *m. Kel.* 1:6-9).

The statement that everything is by its creation clean ranks among the most radical positions taken by the first Christians over against virtually every form of contemporary Judaism. But Paul goes a step further and declares that the moral character of actions lies in the perception and intention of the actor. This shift to the subject is revolutionary, and because morality lies now in the conscience of the agent rather than simply in the character of a deed considered apart from such intentionality, the demand for clarity and conviction of conscience becomes much greater. Paul notes that indecision or "doubting" with regard to an action already indicates that someone is not acting "out of faith" and is already condemned (14:23)—not because the thing to be done was wrong, but because the person was not convinced in conscience that it was right. The person acted one way while thinking another. The condition is the one James classically designated as "double-mindedness" (Jas 1:8; 4:8). For Paul, there are only the two options of "sin" and "faith" (14:23): one either responds to reality with a genuine openness to God's creation and a trusting obedience to it, or one retreats from the gifts God gives in a fearful and controlling closure.

Paul's focus here, however, is not on the rightness or wrongness of the individual's actions—that is for God to judge—but on the righteousness of community relations. It is in this context that he insists, as in 1 Corinthians 8, that individuals be willing to relativize their "rights" for the sake of others; the issue is not being right but being righteous. They are therefore to stop judging each other (14:13) and are to take more care not to put an obstacle or scandal before each other (14:13). We remember the significance of the "stone of stumbling and scandal" in 9:33: it was what kept Jews from being able to accept Jesus as messiah, because to do so would mean denying their own convictions concerning Torah.

Now Paul does not want that sort of obstacle to be placed needlessly in each other's path. If someone thinks that all food is clean and eating it is acceptable to God, that is fine: "The kingdom of God is not a matter of food and drink" (14:17). The confidence is one that exists between that person and God: "This faith that you have, keep between yourself and God" (14:22). But if such eating "causes a brother to stumble," then it is *not* righteous so to eat: "you are no longer walking in love" (14:15). Remember how Paul defined love as the fulfillment of the law because "love does no evil to a neighbor" (13:10). If someone near me, however, thinks that the food I am eating *is* unclean, even though "everything is clean," it can become a "bad thing for the one who eats through stumbling" (14:20). In other words, if my influence causes another to act contrary to her or his own conscience, then I have placed such a stumbling block before them. I have been willing for the sake of "being right" and eating that bit of food, to "destroy one for whom Christ died" (14:15).

A person must be willing, therefore, to relativize one's own rights for the sake of the other: "it is good not to eat or drink or do anything that makes a brother stumble" (14:21). If the form of love in this community means to "put on the Lord Jesus Christ and make no provision for the desires of the flesh" (13:14), then the pattern of Jesus' faithful death for the sake of others should be followed by each one's willingness to relinquish individual rights for the sake of a brother or sister's salvation (compare 1 Cor 8:11–12). The kingdom of God is not a matter of food and drink, but it *is* a matter of "peace and joy and the Holy Spirit. The person who thus serves Christ is pleasing to God and approved by people (14:17–18; compare 12:2).

To act otherwise is, for the sake of a small private gain, to "destroy the work of God" (14:20), for the work of God is precisely the creation of this community shaped by the ethos of love and self-giving according to the mind of Christ. As in 1 Cor 8:1, Paul places love before knowledge as the essential principle of community life. Knowledge can tell us what is right and knowledge can give us freedom and power. It should not be condemned. But love shows us how to be righteous, for righteousness, as God has shown us in Christ, is the willingness to be foolish in order to make others wise, poor in order to make others rich, weak in order to make others strong, to die in order to give life to others: "Knowledge puffs up, love builds up," was Paul's succinct slogan (1 Cor 8:1). Similarly here, Paul advises the community as a whole, "therefore let us pursue peace and the things that build each other up" (14:19).

The Church and the Mystery of God's Plan (15:1–13)

These verses really represent the climax of Paul's theological argument. He draws together in one place the pattern of edification in the community, the pattern of the messiah Jesus, and the pattern of God's work in the world for Jew and Gentile, so that they appear as one single pattern of self-giving and self-emptying for the benefit of others.

He begins with the process of building the community. It can happen only if those who are *strong* accept those who are weak and help them to grow stronger, not by insisting on the rightness of their own position but by gladly bearing the weight of that weakness themselves. Paul had said in 13:8 that they should "owe no one anything except to love one another." Now he spells that out: "we who are strong (*dynatoi*) are obliged (*opheilomen*) to bear the weaknesses of those who are not strong, and not to please ourselves." And, he continues, "let *each one of us* please the neighbor unto the good, toward building up." Here we find the familiar Pauline emphasis on the growth of the community as a community. The same advice was given in Phil 2:1–4: they are *each* to look to the interests of others rather than just to their own. The idea, of course, is to create an atmosphere of reciprocity and mutuality, which enables everyone to be gifted by otherness and thus to grow. But the heaviest obligation falls on those who are strong enough to let go of their rights and privileges in order to gift others.

Christ, after all, brought about reconciliation by exchanging God's "form" for the "form of a slave" and entering totally into the dark place where sin held sway through the weakness of flesh: the one who did not know sin became sin so that in him we might become God's righteousness (2 Cor 5:21). That pattern of exchange is the fundamental pattern of life together in "the mind of Christ." Jesus was the medium of this exchange: "God was in Christ reconciling the world to himself" (2 Cor 5:19; see Rom 5:6-8). So Jesus becomes the *paradigm* for a life so lived in service to others: "For Christ did not please himself, but, as it is written, 'the reproaches of those who reproached thee fell upon me'" (15:3). The citation is from LXX Ps 68:10. When discussing 11:9, I noted that Paul in that place quoted LXX 68:23-24, and that this psalm was one widely used by the first Christians for interpreting the death of Jesus in the light of Torah. There can be little doubt, then, that Paul has in mind here Jesus' human experience of suffering. The verse immediately preceding this one in the psalm is, "Zeal for your house has consumed me," which in John 2:17 is quoted with reference to Jesus' cleansing of the temple. Paul portrays Jesus as one who suffers the reviling (*oneidismoi*) aimed at another, in this case God. For the sake of God, he bears the reproaches of God's enemies (see R. B. Hays, "Christ Prays the Psalms: Paul's Use of an Early Christian Exegetical Convention," in *The Future of Christology*, ed. W. A. Meeks and A. J. Malherbe [Minneapolis: Fortress, 1993] 122-36).

In order to show how the psalm from the past can speak of the messiah and about themselves, Paul adds in 15:4: "Whatever was written ahead of time was written for our instruction in order that through endurance and through the comfort of the scriptures, we might have hope." The balanced phrase, "through endurance/through the comfort of the scriptures" captures the experiential entry into the texts taken by the first Christians. As they endure the weaknesses of others (and how much of life together demands just that) they understood themselves to be sharing in the pattern of suffering for God that was "promised beforehand in the scriptures" (1:2), and enacted by the death of Jesus, whose identity they have now "put on" (13:14). Paul drives home the point by resuming both terms in his next statement: "May the God of endurance and comfort—[we understand: the God who is with you both in your endurance and in the Scriptures]—give you the ability to think the same way among yourselves according to Christ Jesus" (15:5).

The English cannot quite capture the force of "think the same way" (*to auto phronein*). Paul is using the conventional language of friendship in the ancient Hellenistic world. Friends were those who "thought the same way" (see also Phil 2:2). If they all "think the same way among themselves," then each one will try to be strong and to bear with the weakness of others; this, in turn, will be to think "according to Christ Jesus," just as Paul had stated in Gal 6:2, "Bear one another's burdens, and so you will fulfill the law of Christ." When such reciprocity is active, then they can "harmoniously" (*homothymadon*) "give glory to the God and father through our Lord Jesus Christ" (15:6). The community "gives glory to God"–that is, recognizes and lives by the presence and power of God in the world–"through Jesus Christ"–that is, by living according to the mind of Christ.

Paul now makes the transition back to his argument concerning Jews and Gentiles, connecting the way God has acted toward them with the way the Romans should act in their community: "Therefore welcome one another, just as Christ welcomed you unto the glory of God" (15:7). Paul has now completed the reversal of idolatry's measure of reality on the gauge of the creature (1:19–21). Reality is to be measured not by the creature but by the creator. God is not held to our standards of justice (9:19–21), but we are called to live by God's standard of righteousness. This is what Paul now takes up. "For I say to you" (15:8) offers this statement both as the ground for his previous exhortation and as summary of the argument as a whole: "the messiah became a servant (*diakonos*) of the circumcision for the sake of God's truthfulness, to confirm the promises made to the fathers" (15:8). Jesus is a Jewish messiah, "according to the flesh" (9:5). His being "born of a woman, born under the law" (Gal 4:4) was a demonstration of God's "truthfulness" (*alētheia*) in making the promises to the patriarchs (see 4:13; 9:6–13). By so gifting Israel with Jesus, God showed that his word to them is faithful (9:6).

The next part of Paul's statement is anacoluthic, that is, syntactically disconnected with the previous clause. I think Paul started to say something like, "and Christ became a servant to the Gentiles . . . , etc." But as it stands, that bit needs to be supplied or inferred, for the clause reads, "and the Gentiles for the sake of mercy (*eleos*) to give glory to God." God had made no promises to the Gentiles such as he had to the patriarchs. The gift of the messiah to the Gentiles was therefore the purest gift, an expression of God's mercy (see 9:15, 16, 18, 23; 11:30–32). The goal for which all this was done was that all humans (the "Gentiles" encompass all humanity apart from the Jews) might "recognize and acknowledge the power and presence of God"–as I have consistently tried to give substance to the phrase "glorify God." All the Gentiles, in a word, will do what Paul started by saying they did not do (1:21): live within the explicit recognition of God.

In 15:9–12, Paul cites four passages of Torah that foretell such a praise of

God among the Gentiles. It appears as a "counter-*catena*" to the one in 3:11–18 that showed humans turning away from God under sin. The first three citations all contain some note of praise for God in connection with Gentiles. But each should also be read against the backdrop of its original context. For Paul's first readers, the texts may well have resonated with the associations that Paul clearly intended his selection to carry with it.

The first citation is from LXX Ps 17:50. The psalmist is responding to the way in which the Lord has rescued him from his enemies and says, "on this account I will praise you among the nations, O Lord, and I will sing to your name." And the psalm continues in the next verse, "He [i.e., The Lord] magnifies the salvations (*sōtērias*) of his king, and shows mercy (*eleos*) to his messiah (literally: anointed one, *Christos*), to David and to his seed (*sperma*)." It seems very likely to me that the conjunction of the messiah and the praise of God among the Gentiles helped dictate Paul's choice of this text.

Paul next quotes from LXX Deut 32:43: "Rejoice, O nations, with his people." As such, the text nicely captures Paul's sense of the Gentiles being grafted onto the remnant of Israel to join the people of God. But the passage in Deuteronomy continues beyond that, to the promise of vengeance in behalf of the people Israel and the repayment of its enemies. The opening to the Gentiles, in other words, does not mean the abandonment of Israel.

The third text is from LXX Ps 116:1: "Praise the Lord all you nations, let all the peoples praise him." But the second verse of this shortest psalm says, "for his mercy (*eleos*) has been shown mightily over us, and the truth (*alētheia*) of the Lord remains forever." The same combination of "mercy" and "truth" that Paul used in 15:8–9 is probably not accidental. It is perfectly possible that Paul is deliberately playing on these two terms. We remember that in the LXX, the Greek *alētheia* is often used to translate the Hebrew *ʾĕmet* ("fidelity"), and *eleos* is used to translate the Hebrew *ḥesed* ("loving-kindness"). When the Lord passed by Moses on the mountain (Exod 34:6), Moses cried out, "The Lord, the Lord, a God merciful and gracious, slow to anger and abounding in steadfast love (*polyeleos*) and faithfulness (*alēthinos*)." God's revelation of "truthfulness/fidelity" to the Jews, therefore, and his demonstration of "loving-kindness/mercy" to the Gentiles was, for Paul, the revelation of God's most essential being, according to the testimony of Torah.

The final text in the *catena* demonstrates vividly how Paul expects the reader to "overhear" resonances in the text that he does not quote explicitly. Isaiah 11:10 in the LXX differs considerably from the Hebrew. The MT text reads, "In that day the root of Jesse will stand as an ensign to the peoples; him shall the nations seek, and his dwelling will be glorious." The LXX has: "There will be the root from Jesse, and he who rises will rule over the nations; in him will the nations hope." The element in the passage concerning the "root" fits perfectly the idea of the *remnant* that Paul developed earlier, and a "root from Jesse" can only refer to the descendant of David. Thus, Paul had described Jesus as "from the seed (*sperma*) of David according to the flesh" in Rom 1:3, and, as we have just seen, LXX Ps 17:51 also speaks of "the seed (*sperma*) of David." Most striking in the LXX version is the participle *anistamenos*, which for the LXX translators would have meant one who "rose from the root." For Paul, the "one who rises to rule the nations" is Jesus, who was raised from the dead, and it is in this messiah that the Gentiles have indeed "placed their hope" (see 5:5; 8:24–25).

The Isaiah passage also continues beyond the point of Paul's citation, once more differing in the LXX from the Hebrew: "and in that day, the Lord will put forth his hand to make jealous that remaining portion of the people, which were left from Assyria and Egypt and from Babylon and from Ethiopia . . . and he will lift up a sign to the Gentiles and will gather the remnant of Israel and the kingdom of Judah he will gather from the four corners of the earth" (Isa 11:12). Surely Paul intended these words to "echo" for his readers as well, for they state virtually his entire vision of what the mystery of God holds in store for those who hope: the call of the Gentiles will stimulate the Jews to emulation, so that "the rest of the Jews" will also be restored to the people, "and thus all Israel will be saved" (11:26).

Paul then makes this confident assertion/prayer: "The God of hope will fill [or: may he fill] you with joy and peace in your lives of faith so that you will overflow in the hope and the power of the Holy Spirit" (15:13). This cryptic summary of all that Paul has argued needs no gloss.

PAUL'S PLAN AND APPEAL

Romans 15:14–16:27

As present-day readers move into the last section of Romans, they may understandably carry with them some sense of anticlimax. In terms of this commentary, first of all, much of the substance of this section was dealt with in the introduction. But more tellingly, Paul's concerns here appear to us as all too pedestrian and practical, especially when compared to the great theological argument that ran from 1:16 through 15:13.

It may be well to remember, therefore, that Paul and his first readers would not have come to this section with the same feeling of let-down. The Roman readers must have begun to wonder by this point, what's all this in service of, where is Paul going with this? If he is so pleased with our performance, why is he writing at such length? As for Paul himself, this part of his letter is probably the most demanding, as he tries to work from his theological vision of God's righteousness bringing about salvation for Jews and Greeks to his current plans and future expectations from the Romans. If we read this part of the letter carefully, we shall find ourselves rewarded, for some of Paul's most striking insights come when he is speaking most practically.

Paul's Gentile Mission (15:14–24)

Paul acknowledges that his readers are filled with goodness and knowledge and have the power to instruct each other (15:14), showing the same delicacy about asserting authority over this community that we observed in 1:12. Nevertheless, he confesses to a certain "boldness" in reminding them. The theme of memory is a staple in parenetic literature (see, e.g., 2 Tim 1:3–

14), and expressions such as "we know" and "do you not know" have intentionally been strewn through this composition to that effect (2:2; 3:19; 6:9, 16; 7:14; 8:22, 28; 11:2). Paul does not claim to have been comprehensive; his comments have been *apo merous*, a term that can mean "in part" or "partially" (see 11:25), and is well translated by the RSV's "on some points."

The reason he has been bold enough to touch even on these points is because of his distinctive calling from God, the "gift given to me by God" (15:15). We are reminded of his using this explicitly as a warrant for his moral instructions in 12:3. But what is that special *charis?* In 1:5, Paul had identified it as the gift of apostleship to the Gentiles, and he builds on that now: "to be a minister of Jesus Christ to the Gentiles in the priestly service of the good news, so that the offering of the Gentiles may be acceptable, sanctified by the Holy Spirit" (15:16). This is as full a statement of Paul's apostolic self-understanding as we have.

The strongly cultic language of the self-description matches Paul's earlier plea to the Romans to "offer yourselves as living sacrifices" in 12:1. Paul wants his Gentile churches to be "made holy through the Holy Spirit" (see 1:7), so that they will be "an acceptable offering" to God. This is the first time in Romans that sanctification is explicitly attributed to the Holy Spirit, but one is reminded in this connection of Paul's language elsewhere about the community being a temple of God because of the indwelling of the Holy Spirit (see 1 Cor 3:16; 6:19; Eph 2:18-22). Paul's cultic imagery here can also be associated with his insistence in 11:16 that "if the firstfruit is holy, then also the lump; if the root in holy, then also the branches." Paul's endeavor to shape Gentiles into a "community of holiness" through his moral exhortation is aimed at making them worthy members of God's people. This goal may well also have something to do with Paul's hopes for his collection of money for Jerusalem as a gesture of reconciliation. In 15:31, he will ask the Romans to pray that this collection from Gentile churches may be "acceptable to the saints" in Jerusalem. He uses the same term (*euprosdektos*) as he does here in 15:16. Does he hope that the moral and religious character of the Gentile communities will help recommend them to the "holy *aparchē*, holy *riza*" in Jerusalem?

Even though Paul has not founded the Roman church, therefore, he sees it as part of his responsibility as the apostle for the Gentile mission. It is possible that some of his Pharisaic sense of being a "guide to the blind, light to those in darkness, instructor of the foolish, teacher of children" (2:19-20) has carried over to his apostolic sense of mission as well! Only someone with Paul's impeccable credentials in Torah can adequately "shape up" the Gentile converts into an "acceptable lump" for the Lord—and for Paul's fellow Jews!

In any case, Paul declares that this mission is his "ground for boasting in

Christ Jesus in the things concerning God" (15:17). The RSV translation, "In Christ Jesus I have reason to be proud of my work for God" entirely misses the thematic connections established by Paul's use of *kauchēsis* ("boasting"). Paul has excluded some forms of boasting–those generated by one's own efforts to control reality (see 3:27; 4:2). But by no means does he deny the value of boasting in that which is most real and true. Thus, he declares that "he is not ashamed of the good news," by *litotes* making it the ground of his boasting. Likewise in 5:3, those who have been made righteous by the gift of God in Christ can "boast" in their afflictions. And in 5:11 he declares, "we are boasting in God through our Lord Jesus Christ." We recognize a familiar Pauline distinction. Humans cannot "boast before God" on their own (1 Cor 1:29; 3:21; 2 Cor 5:12; 10:13; Eph 2:9), but they can "boast in what has been given" (1 Cor 3:21), for that is to "boast in the Lord" (1 Cor 1:31; 2 Cor 10:17). As Paul now turns to such a recitation of what he has done, we should understand it (as we do 2 Corinthians 10) as such a "boasting in the Lord," a celebration of what God has brought about through him, rather than an assertion of his own effort or skill. As he says in 15:17, "I will not dare to say anything except what Christ has accomplished through me for the obedience of the Gentiles." This last phrase picks up Paul's statement of purpose in 1:5: he had received the gift of apostleship "for the obedience of faith among all the Gentiles [nations] for the sake of his name."

Paul is not shy about acknowledging the power of his ministry. Some Pauline interpreters have taken Paul's polemic against the "superapostles" in 2 Corinthians 10–13 so seriously that they portray Paul completely in terms of a "theology of the cross" with no emphasis on powerful deeds. An emphasis on visible acts of power, it is supposed, would lead to a "theology of glory," which is supposed to be that of his rivals, and is taken as inimical to the authentic gospel as preached by Paul (see, e.g., E. Käsemann, "The Saving Significance of the Death of Jesus in Paul," in *Perspectives on Paul,* trans. M. Kohl [Philadelphia: Fortress, 1969]). Paul's statement in 1 Cor 1:22 that the Jews failed to accept Jesus because they "sought signs" is connected to "signs of power," but this is not what Paul meant. He was referring there not to "signs of power" but to "signs of being a messiah," such as fitting within Torah or restoring the people. Likewise, in 2 Thess 2:9, Paul's statement about the antichrist working powerful deeds and signs and wonders falsely cannot be taken as a criticism of the working of such deeds authentically.

In fact, Paul is quite comfortable with manifest power being associated with the proclaiming of the good news. In 2 Corinthians 3–5, his insistence that the ministers of the good news are lowly and fragile is necessary precisely because the message itself is so glorious and powerful. And he insists, against those who prefer his rivals to himself, "I was not at all inferior to those superlative apostles, even though I am nothing. The signs of a true apostle were worked among you in all patience, with signs and wonders and mighty works" (2 Cor 12:11–12). Likewise in 1 Corinthians, even though Paul eschews preaching "with lofty words of wisdom" (2:1) and confesses himself to be among the Corinthians "in much weakness and fear and trembling" (2:3), this was so that "your faith might rest not on the wisdom of men but in the power of God" (2:5), and Paul asserts throughout the letter that "the power of God" has been at work among them: the "working of powerful deeds" is in fact one of the gifts given by the Holy Spirit to this community (1 Cor 12:10). Nor is Paul chary of employing such power himself: "I will find out not the talk of these arrogant people but their power. For the kingdom of God does not consist in talk but in power" (1 Cor 4:19–20).

In Gal 3:5, likewise, Paul reminds the "foolish Galatians" who had heard the crucified messiah proclaimed to them and had responded in faith, "Did you experience so many things in vain? Does he who supplies the Spirit to you and works miracles among you do so by works of the law or by hearing with faith?" Finally, in 1 Thess 1:5, Paul tells the Thessalonians, "the good news came to you not only in word but also in the Holy Spirit and with full conviction," and adds in 2:13 that they had received the message "not as the word of men but as what it really is, the word of God, which is at work in you believers." This scattering of references abundantly demonstrates that for Paul the work of God in the world through the ministry of the good news was manifest and powerful.

Here also Paul declares that Christ worked in him "in word and deed" (15:19) among the Gentiles, and he focuses on the *power* that accompanies his preaching. First is the "power of signs and wonders" (15:19). Paul had used the same phrase (*sēmeia kai terata*) as testimony to his authenticity as an apostle in 2 Cor 12:12, and this expression is associated with Paul's ministry also by Acts 14:3 and 15:12. In Acts, of course, all the proclaimers of the good news work such signs and wonders (Acts 2:43; 4:30; 5:12; 6:8; 8:6, 13), as does Jesus himself (Acts 2:22). In the biblical tradition, "signs and wonders" were associated above all with the figure of Moses and the events of the exodus (see Acts 7:36; Deut 29:3; 34:11; LXX Ps 77:43; 134:9). Paul does not say what such signs and wonders might be, but it is not far-fetched to suppose that they would have included the sort of acts of healing and exorcism that are described by the narrative of Acts (e.g., 14:8–10; 16:16–18; 19:11–16). Next Paul speaks of "in the power of the Spirit." Many manuscripts either replace "Spirit" with "God" or add "Holy" to it. In any case, Paul clearly has the Holy Spirit in mind. The experience of the Holy Spirit is intimately associated with the hearing of the good news in Acts 2:38; 10:44; Gal 3:5; 1 Cor 2:12; 1 Thess 1:6.

Having "boasted in the Lord" of the power at work in his preaching that enables him to "fully preach the good news of Christ" (15:19), Paul turns to its geographical reach. His missionary course has described a great circle (*kyklō*) extending from Jerusalem to Illyricum (15:19). Both geographical points deserve some attention. It is noteworthy first that Paul defines Jerusalem as his starting point. Sometimes, in the light of Galatians 2, scholars emphasize Paul's distance from the Jerusalem leadership. At times in the history of scholarship, particularly under the influence of F. C. Baur in the nineteenth century, Paul has actually been portrayed in terms of a sustained animosity toward Jerusalem (see, e.g., P. J. Achtemeier, *The Quest for Unity in the New Testament Church: A Study in Paul and Acts* [Philadelphia: Fortress, 1987]). From this standpoint, the account in the Acts of the Apostles, which shows Paul in a cooperative relationship with Jerusalem, is regarded as a pious gloss. Once more, these sorts of hypotheses need to yield to the actual evidence of the text. Even in Galatians, Paul acknowledges the leadership of the Jerusalem community and finds it important to consult with its leadership concerning his own mission ("lest I should be running or had run in vain," Gal 2:2). The right hand of fellowship he shared with that leadership concerning his mission to the Gentiles was obviously of considerable importance to him (Gal 2:9). Paul also attests that his preaching of the good news is in agreement with those who were witnesses to Christ before him: "whether then it was I or they, so we preach and so you believed" (1 Cor 15:11).

Now, in Rom 15:19, he describes his mission as "from Jerusalem." Such a characterization supports the view that Paul found the Jerusalem church to be of great significance for his mission and confirms rather than contradicts the portrait of Paul in Acts. And if more evidence were required, Paul, as we know, is about to deliver a major collection of money to that community (15:25). When Paul speaks of the good news going to "the Jew first and then the Greek," he does not mean only in the grand scheme of history but also in the recent events of his own life and mission.

Paul's naming Illyricum as the end-point of his mission is also surprising. The term refers to the Roman province of Illyricum, which had been established along the eastern coast of the Adriatic Sea in 35–33 B.C.E. The territory corresponds roughly to present-day Albania and the lands of the former Yugoslavia (Croatia, Bosnia, Serbia). The mention of Illyricum is surprising because none of Paul's letters tells us he worked there, nor does the Acts of the Apostles ever place him there. The only other New Testament writing that puts Paul in contact with this region is 2 Tim 4:10, which mentions among other travel notes, that "Titus has gone to Dalmatia" (another name for the territory). The fact that Paul here claims to have spread the good news as far north and west as present-day Yugoslavia leads to the following conclusions:

1. Scholars do not have all the pieces of the puzzle that makes up the first half-century of the Christian movement.

2. In particular, there are movements of Paul and his associates that are not reported by Acts or by any of his extant letters.

3. Paul's mission is undoubtedly larger than the churches he personally founded, as confirmed also by the Letter to the Colossians, and the sense of responsibility even for the Roman church expressed in the present composition.

4. In this case, one of the Pastoral letters has a piece of historical knowledge about the Pauline mission found nowhere else except here.

Paul turns next (15:20–21) to the motivation that has driven him to such an extensive and impressive effort. He "made it [his] ambition" to preach where no one else had done so. When he says that he did not want to build on another's foundation, he invokes the same "house-building" metaphor that he uses for the apostolic work in 1 Cor 3:10–11: "according to the grace of God given to me, like a skilled master-builder, I laid a foundation, and another man [Apollos] is building upon it . . . no other foundation can any one lay except that which has been laid, which is Christ Jesus." His desire to push beyond the boundaries of other peoples' work to places "where Christ has not been named," tells us something about the urgency expressed in 13:11: "for salvation is nearer to us than when we first came to have faith." In the context of ancient geography, Paul's rapid progress across the Eastern Mediterranean and his success in founding communities wherever he went could readily be regarded as an effort that could bring about the eschatological inclusion of his fellow Jews that he so ardently desired.

As support for his mission to such far-flung territories, Paul quotes Isa 52:15, another indication that this section of the prophet in particular was carefully studied by Paul as a script for God's work in the present: "They shall see who have never been told about him, and those who have not heard shall understand." This verse, we should realize, *immediately* precedes that in 53:1, "Lord who has heard our report" that Paul quoted with reference to his fellow Jews in 10:16. It becomes ever more clear that Paul had pored over the words of the great servant song of Isa 52:13–53:12, finding in it an understanding of how one who had died as a sinner could be the source of righteousness for others, and how despite his rejection by his own people, his name might be carried across the world so that "many nations will be astonished at him" (LXX Isa 52:15).

As we saw in the introduction, Paul offers this mission in the East as the reason he had not yet been able to visit the Roman church (15:22). But now, he declares, "I no longer have any room to work in this region" (15:23). This can be taken either as an expression of completion—he has finished the job—or as an expression of his realization that opposition to him by his fellow Jews will not allow him to keep working in the East. His subsequent arrest in Jerusalem (according to Acts 21:27, at the instigation of a Jew from Asia) suggests that the last reason might have been as compelling as the first. In any case, Paul now wants to work in Spain and, as we have seen, seeks to be "sent on his way" there by the Roman church, after "enjoying their company for a little." As I pointed out in the introduction, the language Paul uses (well camouflaged by the RSV translation) connotes financial support during his stay in Rome and for his expedition to the West. Before undertaking his trip to Rome, however, Paul has one more task to fulfill in the East.

The Collection for Jerusalem (15:25–32)

Paul plans to deliver to the church in Jerusalem a collection of money he (with the help of his delegates) had taken up from the Gentile churches. The effort appears, at this distance, to have been both massive and preoccupying. Its roots appear in Gal 2:10. When Paul consulted in Jerusalem with Cephas, James, and John, they imposed no further obligation on him or his mission to the Gentiles and gave him the right hand of fellowship. But they did ask him to "remember the poor, which very thing I was eager to do." We see from the start, then, that the collection had both a practical and a symbolic dimension. Practically, it was badly needed assistance for a community chronically in need (see Acts 11:27–30). Symbolically, it was a way for Paul to cement the gesture of *koinōnia* (fellowship) with the Jerusalem church that had been signaled by the handshake with its leadership (see G. W. Peterman, "Romans 15:26: Make a Contribution or Establish Fellowship?" *New Testament Studies* 40 [1994]: 457–63).

Paul gave himself energetically to the effort. Despite his chastisement of the Corinthian community, he still expected them to contribute week by week to this effort (1 Cor 16:1–4). This insistence, plus the deepening misunderstandings between Paul and the Corinthians, placed his project in some trouble, and Paul needed to work frantically to keep it afloat. It seemed for a time that the Corinthians would not contribute their share, despite Paul's boast to the Macedonians that they already had (2 Cor 9:3–4). The Corinthians seem to have suspected Paul and his delegate Titus of having defrauded them (2 Cor 11:7-11; 12:16-18). In 2 Corinthians 8-9, then, Paul employs every sort of appeal to persuade them to follow through on their commitment.

The happy announcement that Paul can make to the Romans is that, in fact, the Corinthians did finally pitch in: "for it has pleased Macedonia and Achaia to make a certain fellowship (same word, *koinōnia*) with the poor among the saints in Jerusalem" (15:26). For Paul, however, this is not merely a matter of "good will" (*eudokein*). The Gentile churches, in his view, *owe* the Jerusalem church. In a passage remarkable for what it reveals about the cultural assumptions of Mediterranean culture, Paul asserts, "Indeed, they are in debt to them, for if the Gentiles have come to share in their spiritual blessings, they ought also to minister to them in material things" (15:27). The language of "fellowship" (*koinōnia*) in Paul's world is the language of "friendship" (*philia*). Philosophers had given much thought to the meaning of this sort of human bonding, and cultural perceptions concerning friendship found expression in a number of pithy proverbs, such as "friends are one soul," and "friendship is equality" and "the friend is another self" and "friends hold all things in common" (*tois philois panta koina*), and, most tersely, "friendship is fellowship" (*philia koinōnia*; see Aristotle, *Nicomachean Ethics* VIII-IX).

Such collections of commonplaces worked like systems of association: saying one of them would trigger the memory or awareness of others. This is so much the case that even the use of the term *koinōnia* draws with it the cluster of other associations. This is all the more the case since on the topic of friendship certain values were repeated over and over. Mainly these had to do with *sharing* and *equality*. Friendship was regarded not as a casual acquaintanceship but as the deepest sort of sharing and equality, so that everything one had, the other could also claim. This sharing included— and here we come to Paul's point—both material and spiritual goods. Thus, Paul puts "spiritual blessings" and "material blessings" in a reciprocal exchange.

In 2 Cor 8:12, Paul follows Aristotle in defining "equality" (*isotēs*) not in terms of a mathematical sameness, as Plato had, but in terms of proportionality and reciprocity: one way of sharing responds to another way: "I do not mean that others should be eased and you burdened, but that as a matter of equality your abundance at the present time should supply their want, so that their abundance may supply your want, that there may be equality." So here in Rom 15:27, Paul sees the Gentiles as having received *ta pneumatika* ("spiritual things") from the Jerusalem church—meaning of course, the gospel and the entire heritage of Torah!—and are therefore "obliged" under cultural constraint (*opheilein*, see 1:16; 8:12; 13:8; 15:1) to share *ta sarkina* ("fleshly things"), which in this case means money.

The solemnity of Paul's purpose is underscored by the use of the term "ministering to them" (*leitourgein*), which echoes the cultic language he had employed for his own Gentile mission in 15:16. Paul clearly conceives of his trip to Jerusalem not in terms of a casual errand but as the climax of his work in the East: a solemn "offering of the Gentiles" to the remnant/root of the people in Jerusalem. He therefore must complete this charge before "going on by way of you to Spain" (15:28); he knows that he will have done all that he could do for Jew/Gentile amity in the East and therefore will come to the Romans "in the fullness of the blessing of Christ" (15:29).

That Paul anticipated the danger he faced from "the unbelievers in Judea" is shown by his solemn request for the Roman Christians' prayer. Acts provides a vivid picture of how Paul, from the time of his conversion, was harassed by fellow Jews. At Damascus, he had to escape a plot to kill him by going over the city walls in a basket (Acts 9:23–25; see 2 Cor 11:32–33). In Jerusalem itself he was so intensely opposed by the Hellenist Jews that they sought to kill him (9:29), making it necessary for the Jerusalem church to send him home to Tarsus. Paul confirms such opposition to him on the part of the Jews in Judea, in 1 Thess 2:14–16: "You, brethren, became imitators of the churches of God in Christ Jesus which are in Judea, for you suffered the same things from your countrymen as they did from the Jews, who killed both the Lord Jesus and the prophets, *and drove us out*, and displease God and oppose all men by hindering us from speaking to the Gentiles that they might be saved." Paul obviously knew whereof he spoke, for when he arrived in Jerusalem, he was arrested in the temple precincts and almost killed by a mob (Acts 21:27–36). During the time of his subsequent imprisonment, furthermore, a murderous plot was formed against him (23:12–15), a plot in which even the leaders join (25:2–3). Only Paul's appeal to Caesar (25:11–12) enabled him finally to reach the city of Rome (28:14), not as an apostle ready to go on to Spain but as a prisoner under house arrest (28:30).

With some obvious sense of what awaited him, Paul asks the Romans "to join in prayerful struggle with me in my prayers to God in my behalf" (15:30). He wants two things to happen: that he be delivered from the unbelievers, and that his "service for Jerusalem might be acceptable (*euprosdektos;* see 15:16) to the saints" (15:31). If these things happen, Paul is confident that his future plans will go through, and "by God's will I may come to you with joy and be refreshed in your company" (15:32). In the Introduction, I pointed out that Paul's language here ("being refreshed") again bears financial connotations. Paul will pick up on that in the recommendation of Phoebe that follows. But before doing that, he also exercises "reciprocity," by answering his request for their prayer with a prayer of his own for them: "The God of peace be with you all. Amen" (15:33).

Networking (16:1–23)

I have given some attention to this part of Romans already in the introduction, since it provides information pertinent to establishing Paul's purposes for writing. I argued there that 16:1-2 is a letter of commendation for Phoebe and that the list of greetings in 16:3-17 and 16:21-23 functions as a form of commendation for Paul himself, since he could greet so many people in the Roman church who would, we presume, vouch for him. This time around, I attend more closely to some of the details, especially since these give us some sense of the texture of the Pauline mission (see W. A. Meeks, *The First Urban Christians: The Social World of the Apostle Paul* [New Haven: Yale University Press, 1983] 55–63).

In Paul's designation of Phoebe as "our sister," for example, we observe the practice of using fictive kinship language as a mechanism for group solidarity (Meeks, *First Urban Christians*, 85–89). The designation "brother" is most common (see Rom 1:13; 7:1, 4; 8:12, etc.), whereas the use of *adelphē* ("sister") is much rarer (see 1 Cor 7:15; 9:5; 1 Tim 5:2; Phlm 2). Since the names in this chapter make clear that Paul counted many women as coworkers or as leading members of this church, we are reminded that *adelphos* ("brother") should be taken in a gender-inclusive sense throughout its use in the composition. Such kinship language is not entirely conventional but works within a metaphorical structure. In other letters, Paul can speak of himself as the "father" of the community or of a believer, because he "gave them birth" in Christ (see e.g. 1 Cor 4:15; Gal 4:19; 1 Thess 2:11; Phlm 10). In Romans, Paul can make no such claim since he did not found this church. But the sense of being "brothers and sisters" here connects to Paul's conviction that by the spirit of adoption they can cry out to God, "Abba! Father!" (8:15), and that Christ was intended to be the "firstborn among many brothers" (8:29).

Phoebe holds the position as *diakonos* at Cenchreae, a port to the east of Corinth on the Aegean and considered one of its suburbs (Pausanias, *Description of Greece* 2.2.3). As noted earlier, she is also designated as the *prostatis* of Paul "and many others as well" (16:2). Given the fact that Paul has consistently designated his collection as a *diakonia* (2 Cor 8:4; 9:1, 12, 13; Rom 15:31), and that *prostatis* can bear the meaning of financial patron (appearing as such on inscriptions), we are justified in our evaluation of Phoebe as something like Paul's "financial agent" in his negotiations with the Roman church, as he hopes that it will "help her in whatever way she requires" as she prepares for his trip to Spain (16:1).

In light of Paul's directions for local churches that place restrictions on the activity of women, especially in teaching functions (e.g., 1 Cor 11:2-16; 14:33-36; 1 Tim 2:11-15), and his calling for the submission of women to their husbands in the context of the household (Col 3:18–4:1; Eph 5:21–6:9; Titus 2:4–5), it is important to note that he appeared to find no difficulty with women exercising significant leadership functions in other ways and contexts. Phoebe, of course, is an outstanding example. If her name were not unmistakably feminine, we would be able to detect nothing in Paul's characterization of her that did not match that of the "leading men" in Corinth (1 Cor 16:15–18). Paul also names—before her husband Aquila—Priscilla as a coworker in the Lord (16:3). In the Roman community, Paul singles out (presumably because they hold visible positions of leadership) Mary, "who worked hard among you" (16:6); Tryphaena and Tryphosa, also "workers in the Lord" (16:12); Persis, "who has worked hard in the Lord" (16:12); Rufus's mother (16:13), Julia, and Nereus's sister (16:15).

The characterizations accompanying many of these names suggest that the women are either fellow workers in the missionary field or leaders in the local community. There may be one other woman in the list. In 16:7, Paul greets Andronicus (clearly a male) and another person. The Greek is in the accusative case as *Iounian*, which could be the feminine Junia. The RSV translates it as Junias and clearly opts for the male gender, since it translates the next phrase as "they are men of note." But the matter is not so simple, since the masculine case of the participle would be used inclusively for both genders anyway. In other words, if Andronicus was male and Junia female, the plural form used to include them both would always be grammatically masculine. There is at least the chance, then, that Junia(s) is a woman (see B. Brooten, "Junia . . . Outstanding among the Apostles [Rom 16:7]," in *Women Priests: A Catholic Commentary on the Vatican Declaration*, ed. L. Swidler and A. Swidler [New York: Paulist, 1977] 141–44). If this is so, then she represents a remarkable case, for Paul includes her and Andronicus as "my kinsmen and fellow prisoners, who are notable among the apostles and were in Christ before me" (16:7). The term "kinsmen (*syngeneis*) must, as in 9:3, signify a shared Jewish background. If Junia is a woman, then we would have one female Jew who preceded Paul in the faith and also shared in the work of the apostolate (Paul uses *apostolos* unabashedly). Even if she is a male (!), the verse bears important evidence that the term *apostolos* was used more widely than for the Twelve and Paul (see also Acts 14:14), and that Jews who joined the messianic movement even before Paul were part of the church at Rome. Paul also greets as a "kinsman" (fellow Jew), Herodion (16:11).

The list of names also gives an impression of the mobility of the earliest Christians. If Andronicus and Junia(s) had joined the faith before Paul (16:7), they must have been Jews from outside Rome who traveled and settled there. Although we know of Christians in Rome as early as the year 49, Paul's conversion was ca. 34–37, and it is difficult to conceive of a Roman community that early. So they were probably Jews who had moved to Rome, either from Palestine or some diaspora city such as Damascus or Antioch to which the messianic movement had spread quickly (Acts 9:2; 11:19). In 16:5, Paul makes mention of Epaenetus as "firstfruit from Asia" for Christ. He also uses this expression in 1 Cor 16:15 for Stephanus as the "firstfruit in Achaia," and since in 1 Cor 1:16, Stephanus is mentioned as one of the few Paul had baptized in Corinth, the designation undoubtedly refers to an important early convert of an area who was part of the foundation for a new community. But this *Asian* convert (otherwise nowhere mentioned) is at the time of Paul's writing, resident in Rome.

Even more striking is the case of Priscilla and Aquila. We meet them first in Acts 18:2 as Jewish Christians who had been exiled from Rome under Claudius and who meet Paul in Corinth. Sharing the leather-working trade with him, they become his companions in the gospel as well. When Paul left Corinth eighteen months later, they sailed with him as far as Ephesus and stayed there (Acts 18:18–19), while Paul went on to Jerusalem. In Ephesus, they met Apollos, converted him to Christ, and sent him back to work in Achaia (Corinth; Acts 18:26–27). They are apparently still in Ephesus when Paul writes 1 Corinthians from that city, for he sends greetings to the Corinthians from "Prisca and Aquila my coworkers" (1 Cor 16:19). In 2 Tim 4:19 (if authentic), Paul sends greetings to them, presumably still in Ephesus (see 1 Tim 1:3). But now Paul is able to send them greetings (probably from Corinth, see 16:23) in the church at Rome, as leaders of a house church (see Phlm 2) in that city (16:5). He praises them as "fellow workers in Christ Jesus who risked their necks for my life, to whom not only I, but also all the churches of the Gentiles give thanks" (16:3–4). Priscilla and Aquila give us further evidence for a Jewish Christian presence in Rome at the time Paul is writing, even though, like him, they had worked in the Gentile mission. As befits the capital city of the empire, therefore, the Roman church was made up of a mixture of people from around the world, from different ethnic backgrounds and gender. That Paul knew so many by name in a church he had never visited is testimony to the astonishing mobility and intercommunication of the Pauline mission (see also P. Lampe, "The Roman Christians of Romans 16," in *The Romans Debate,* rev. ed., ed. Karl Donfried [Edinburgh: T & T Clark, 1991] 216–30).

Finally, we take note of those Paul has with him as he writes. Tertius (16:22) is in all likelihood a slave (his name means "third") who is laboring as the scribe taking dictation, but also greets the Christians at Rome "in the Lord." The Quartus mentioned in 16:23 is also probably a slave (his name means "fourth"), probably one of many of the slave class in the Corinthian community (see 1 Cor 1:28; 7:21–24).

Also with Paul is Timothy, his "fellow worker" (16:21). Of mixed parentage (his father a Gentile, his mother a Jew), Timothy was recruited by Paul to replace John Mark as an assistant to himself and Silas after Paul's breakup with Barnabas (Acts 16:1–3). Paul acknowledged his Jewish heritage by having him circumcised (Acts 16:3). Timothy quickly became one of Paul's most trusted associates. He accompanied Paul on his journeys through Phrygia and Galatia into Europe. Separated from Paul for a time in the church at Beroea (Acts 17:14), he rejoined him at Athens (17:16). With Silas, Timothy worked with Paul in Corinth (18:5). He was sent as a delegate with Erastus to Macedonia (19:22) and was one of the group of delegates that accompanied Paul on his journey to Jerusalem (20:4). In addition to the information given by Acts, we find Timothy repeatedly in Paul's own letters. Paul sent him as a delegate to the Thessalonians (1 Thess 3:2, 6), to the Corinthians when Paul was in Ephesus (1 Cor 4:17; 16:10), and to the Philippians when Paul was in prison (Phil 2:19). According to 1 Tim 1:3, he also represented Paul in Ephesus for a period. Timothy's status in the mission is suggested by the fact that he is listed as co-sender of six of Paul's letters (2 Cor 1:1; Phil 1:1; Phlm 1; Col 1:1; 1 Thess 1:1; 2 Thess 1:1) and had two letters written to him by Paul (1 Timothy and 2 Timothy). Timothy's presence here with Paul in Corinth before the trip to Jerusalem fits with the evidence of the other sources.

We notice that Paul also sends greetings to the Romans from "Erastus the city treasurer" (*oikonomos tēs poleōs;* 16:23). There is archaeological evidence for an Erastus serving as a functionary in the city of Corinth in the first century at a rank lower than that of treasurer; the status attributed to him here is by no means impossible (see G. Theissen, *The Social Setting of Pauline Christianity,* trans. J. Schütz [Philadelphia: Fortress, 1982] 73–83). In Acts 19:22, Erastus was sent as a delegate with Timothy to Macedonia. If we put the pieces together, this may well have been in connection with the collection. He is mentioned a final time in 2 Tim 4:20, "Erastus remained at Corinth." Paul also sends greetings from "Gaius who is host to me and to the whole church" (16:23). Gaius is a common name, and the New Testament may contain references to several (see 3 John 1). According to Acts 19:29, a Gaius and Aristobulus were Macedonians who were Paul's traveling companions at the time of the riot in Ephesus. A Gaius from Derbe (in Galatia) is one of Paul's delegates who accompany him in Acts 20:4. Whatever the possible connections to these other texts, the Gaius mentioned here is undoubtedly the one Paul mentions in 1 Cor 1:14, "I did not baptize anyone except Crispus and Gaius." If we put these two texts together, we see another case of a wealthy man (host of Paul and the whole church) who as an early convert has a certain prestige and authority in the church.

Paul sends greetings to the Romans as well from three men who are his "kinsmen," that is, fellow Jews: Lucias, Jason, and Sosipater (16:21). A Jason appears as a leading believer at Thessalonica in Acts 17:5–9. Given the mobility in the messianic movement, it is not impossible for him to have joined Paul in Corinth. Sosipater may be the same person as Sopater of Beroea, who is listed in Acts 20:4 as one of Paul's delegates in connection (probably) with the collection. The last named is *Loukias*, again a common name. There is a "Lucian the Cyrenean" mentioned in Acts 13:1 as one of the "prophets and teachers" who were the leaders of that church who sponsored Paul and Barnabas on their first missionary venture. The Greek *Loukias* might also be taken as the long form of the name *Loukas*, who is mentioned as a Pauline companion in Phlm 24, Col 4:14, and 2 Tim 4:11. Not all of the connections I have made here may be correct, since some of the names involved are common ones, but if any of them work, then the list of those both in Rome and in Corinth at the time of Paul's writing provide a splendid reminder of the demographic and geographic richness of the first Christian movement, as well as the complex character of the Pauline mission.

Final Exhortation and Prayer (16:17–19, 25–27)

There are an unusually large number of textual variants in chapter 16, especially in these last few verses. Some manuscripts, for example, omit 16:25–27 altogether. Others put it after 14:23 or 15:33, or some combination thereof. The reason is not hard to find. There is little obvious coherence in the sequence of verses. 16:17–19 is a warning against false teachers that appears to interrupt the steady flow of greetings in 16:3–16 and 16:21–23. There are also too many apparent "endings": a prayer at 15:33, in some manuscripts another at 16:20, and then the solemn prayer of 16:25–27. It is easy to see how frustrated scribes would seek to "improve" the composition by providing what in their judgment was a more intelligible version. At least one manuscript gave up the task entirely and omitted the chapter as a whole! The fact that in this commentary I have also "re-arranged" the sequence in order to provide a more orderly discussion suggests how real the difficulty is.

But making sense of the present arrangement is not impossible. Even though 16:17–20 appears as something of an afterthought, we notice that it does not so much interrupt the greetings as it separates the greetings *for* the people in Rome and the greetings *from* the people in Corinth. In parenetic and protreptic compositions of that period, moreover, it would not have been unusual to find such a warning against the behavior of others together with a short burst of polemic characterizing them as a kind of negative example the readers are to avoid (see L. T. Johnson, "II Timothy and the Polemic Against False Teachers: A Re-examination," *Journal of Religious*

Studies 6/7 [1978-79]: 1-26). In fact, we find similar elements at the end of some of Paul's other letters (see, e.g., Gal 6:11-17; 2 Thess 3:14-15; 1 Tim 6:20-21).

Paul tells his readers to "watch" some people (see Phil 3:2!) and "stay away from them" (16:17), then describes their behavior in polemical terms (16:18), and then turns to the positive qualities he wants the readers to display. The hardest interpretive decision here is the degree to which the characterization is purely formal—as such polemic frequently was in the ancient world—and how much it might reflect actual behavior in the Roman church (see L. T. Johnson, "The Anti-Jewish Slander of the New Testament and the Conventions of Ancient Polemic," *Journal of Biblical Literature* 103 [1989]: 419-41). In the introduction, I argued that this warning is more formal than specific. In its present position, that conclusion works best. If it *were* placed immediately after 14:33, the language—which even in its present place echoes chapter 14—would take on a much greater vividness.

Note, for example, how the warning against those making "divisions" and "stumbling blocks" (*skandala*) fits into the context of Paul's discussion in 14:1-33, where he tells them to welcome each other but not for "disputes over opinions" (14:1), and where he warns the strong not to put "stumbling blocks" in the way of the weak in faith (14:13). Such behavior would indeed be "against the teaching you have received," a phrase that echoes 6:17, "thanks be to God that you were obedient from the heart to the standard of teaching to which you were committed." And while it is standard polemic to call opponents "slaves of their belly" (see, e.g., Phil 3:18), that charge would take on specific gravity if read against the backdrop of those who chose food over edification of the neighbor. This passage also speaks of those who are "leading the hearts of the innocent astray by sweet talk and flattering words" (16:18). Once more, a standard charge against opponents (see 1 Thess 2:5; 2 Tim 4:3-4). But could it also reflect the failure of the strong to "keep this confidence you have between yourself and God" (14:21) and their effort to persuade others to follow their own practices with regard to food and festivals?

All of these connections work, and Paul may have intended just such back-referencing. The possibility that he might have is what keeps the "Roman Debate" alive and unresolvable. It must be said, however, that these *possible* connections do not, because of the late placement of the passage, leap to consciousness for the present-day reader and may not have for Paul's first readers either. There was, moreover, nothing in Paul's earlier discussion of diet and days to suggest that actual divisions were occurring in the community. Indeed, his entire effort was to encourage a mutual sensitivity for the occasions when they *had* "welcomed each other" (14:1) in their assemblies. The tone of the present passage is to warn against those who don't agree with that approach and follow their own agenda of "being right" rather than being "righteous." It is therefore best viewed as a foil to the positive instruction that follows.

In fact, Paul considers his present readers to be doing well. He had already praised their knowledge and goodness and ability to instruct each other (15:14). Now he emphasizes that *their* obedience has been reported everywhere (16:19; compare 1:8). He rejoices over them. But he wants them to be (in the classic parenetic disjunction) "wise with regard to the good and guileless with regard to evil" (16:19). And he assures them that "the God of peace will quickly trample Satan beneath your feet" (16:20). In Paul's letters, *Satanas* is a force that harasses and threatens the community (see 1 Cor 5:5; 7:5; 2 Cor 2:11; 11:14; 12:7; 1 Thess 2:18; 2 Thess 2:9; 1 Tim 1:20; 5:15). Paul's promise, therefore, is that God will remove such trouble from them and give them the peace that is theirs by virtue of the gift of righteousness given by Christ (see 5:1; compare 1 Cor 14:33).

The final doxology in 16:25–27 is, as I noted above, absent from some manuscripts and variously placed by others. It consists in a single long sentence that magnificently summarizes the argument of Romans in terms of the mystery that is God's purpose. Paul begins with his readers. He prays "to the one who is able to strengthen them according to my gospel and the preaching of Jesus Christ," that is, the one who is powerful enough to enable them to live by this "standard of truth to which they were committed" (6:17). Paul then shifts to the content of that teaching: "a revelation of a mystery that was kept secret through ages but has now been manifested." The contrast between past and present, between secrecy and manifestation, is something of a standard form for revelational discourse (see N. A. Dahl, "Form-Critical Observations on Early Christian Preaching," in *Jesus in the Memory of the Early Church* [Minneapolis: Augsburg, 1976] 30–36).

The language of "mystery" (*mystērion*) recalls 11:25, "I do not want you ignorant, brethren, of this mystery" (see also 1 Cor 2:1, 7; 4:1; 13:2; 14:2; 15:51). The understanding of "mystery" as revealing in particular the way God has worked through the church to reconcile Jew and Gentile, is developed by Paul especially in Colossians (1:26–27; 2:2; 4:3) and Ephesians (1:9; 3:3–4, 9; 6:19). Paul picks up another earlier theme when he states that the mystery has "been made known through the prophetic writings according to the command of the eternal God." From the beginning of the letter (1:2), we have seen how Paul has insisted that Torah is prophetic of the gospel and has "pre-promised the good news." And all of this, as Paul stated already in his greeting to the church (1:6), was "to bring about the obedience of faith to all nations."

Having summarized the argument, Paul brings it to its theologically appropriate conclusion with a final recognition of God's glory. "God alone is wise," and humans, even in such a breathtaking argument as Paul's, can only follow after God's tracings as God moves ahead of them, can only hope that what appears to them as foolish crookedness is in reality the straight lines of a wisdom beyond their own. For himself and for his readers, then, Paul does what idolators refused to do (1:21) and Abraham did not fail to do (4:20), which is to recognize God's presence and power in all of creation: "Glory be to God!" For Paul, his readers, and for present-day readers as well, that presence and power is one that is always "through Jesus Christ." Amen.

LUKE TIMOTHY JOHNSON is the Robert W. Woodruff Professor of New Testament and Christian Origins at Candler School of Theology, Emory University, Atlanta, Georgia. He has taught at Yale Divinity School and Indiana University. His publications include *The Real Jesus: The Misguided Quest for the Historical Jesus and the Truth of the Traditional Gospels*, and *The Letter of James* (Anchor Bible Commentary Series).

BOOKS OF RELATED INTEREST

How to Read the New Testament
Etienne Charpentier
ISBN: 0-8245-0541-7; 128 pp.

How to Read the Old Testament
Etienne Charpentier
ISBN: 0-8245-0540-9; 124 pp.

The Faith of Qumran:
The Theology of the Dead Sea Scrolls
Helmer Ringgren
ISBN: 0-8245-1258-8; 324 pp.

Searching the Scriptures:
Vol. I: *A Feminist Introduction*
Elizabeth Schüssler Fiorenza, Editor
ISBN: 0-8245-1381-9; 416 pp.

Searching the Scriptures:
Vol. II: *A Feminist Commentary*
Elizabeth Schüssler Fiorenza, Editor
ISBN: 0-8245-1424-6; 956 pp.

Im Memory of Her:
A Feminist Theological Reconstruction of Christian Origins
Elizabeth Schüssler Fiorenza
ISBN: 0-8245-1357-6; 396 pp.

The Birth of the New Testament:
The Origin and Development of the First Christian Generation
Raymond F. Collins
ISBN: 0-8245-1276-6; 324 pp.